Words and P
Legally Del

SUPPLEMENT 2008

under the General Editorship of
David Hay MA, LLM
of the Inner Temple, Barrister

Members of the LexisNexis Group worldwide

United Kingdom	LexisNexis Butterworths, a Division of Reed Elsevier (UK) Ltd, Halsbury House, 35 Chancery Lane, **London**, WC2A 1EL, and London House, 20-22 East London Street, **Edinburgh** EH7 4BQ
Australia	LexisNexis Butterworths, **Chatswood**, New South Wales
Austria	LexisNexis Verlag ARD Orac GmbH & Co KG, **Vienna**
Benelux	LexisNexis Benelux, **Amsterdam**
Canada	LexisNexis Canada, **Markham**, Ontario
Chile	LexisNexis Chile Ltda, **Santiago**
China	LexisNexis China, **Beijing and Shanghai**
France	LexisNexis SA, **Paris**
Germany	LexisNexis Deutschland GmbH, **Munster**
Hong Kong	LexisNexis Butterworths, **Hong Kong**
India	LexisNexis India, **New Delhi**
Italy	Giuffrè Editore, **Milan**
Japan	LexisNexis Japan, **Tokyo**
Malaysia	Malayan Law Journal Sdn Bhd, **Kuala Lumpur**
New Zealand	LexisNexis NZ Ltd, **Wellington**
Poland	Wydawnictwo Prawnicze LexisNexis Sp, **Warsaw**
Singapore	LexisNexis Singapore, **Singapore**
South Africa	LexisNexis Butterworths, **Durban**
USA	LexisNexis, **Dayton**, Ohio

© Reed Elsevier (UK) Ltd 2008
Published by LexisNexis
This is a Butterworths title

A CIP Catalogue record for this book is available from the British Library.

ISBN: 978 1 4057 2666 5

Typeset by KerryPress Ltd, Luton, Beds
Printed and bound in Germany by Bercker GmbH

Visit LexisNexis Butterworths at www.lexisnexis.co.uk

Preface

This supplement contains a further selection of definitions from case law and statute.

The law as indicated is that existing at 31 July 2008.

This is the first Supplement to the Fourth Edition to be published. Editorial notes have been revised, particularly reference to Halsbury's Laws of England where volumes have been reissued, or issued for the Fifth Edition.

The style follows that used in the main volumes, which should be consulted first. Notes of statutory repeals or amendments and any other editiorial comments are shown in square brackets.

LexisNexis Butterworths
November 2008

A

AGENT—AGENCY

[For 2(1) Halsbury's Laws of England (4th Edn) (Reissue) para 1 see now 1 Halsbury's Laws (5th Edn) para 1.]

General agent

[For 2(1) Halsbury's Laws of England (4th Edn) (Reissue) para 11 see now 1 Halsbury's Laws (5th Edn) para 11.]

Of necessity

[For 2(1) Halsbury's Laws of England (4th Edn) (Reissue) para 39 see now 1 Halsbury's Laws (5th Edn) para 24.]

Special agent

[For 2(1) Halsbury's Laws of England (4th Edn) (Reissue) para 11 see now 1 Halsbury's Laws (5th Edn) para 11.]

ALLOTMENT

Garden

[For 2(1) Halsbury's Laws of England (4th Edn) (2003 Reissue) para 301 see now 1 Halsbury's Laws (5th Edn) para 510.]

ALLUREMENT

'[63] Both the RTA and Mr Dederer in this court addressed the concept of "allurement" in their submissions. But this is a concept that is more likely to mislead than to assist. Even when the term had determinative legal significance, Barrowclough CJ was able to say in *Napier v Ryan* [[1954] NZLR 1234 at 1240] that the word "has been given a sanctity which I think it scarcely deserves". One can well agree with that sentiment today, especially as the former technical use of that term in occupiers' liability cases has long since been superseded by the decision in *Zaluzna* [*Australian Safeway Stores Pty Ltd v Zaluzna* (1987) 162 CLR 479, 69 ALR 615].

'[64] The continued use of the term "allurement" as a factual epithet tends to conceal more than it reveals. First, "allurement" might be used to indicate no more than that many people have encountered the risk, thus leading to a conclusion one way or another about the probability of that risk eventuating. Secondly, the term might focus attention on the responsibility of the defendant for creating the risk, or for encouraging or enticing people into a dangerous situation. However, in the present case the RTA did not create the risk of shallow water of variable depth, nor did it exhort or encourage young people to dive from the bridge. Thirdly, the term might simply indicate the factual proposition that the particular location or activity was attractive to certain kinds of people. Such an observation is of no legal consequence.' Roads and Traffic Authority of New South Wales v Dederer [2007] HCA 42, (2007) 238 ALR 761 at [63]–[64], per Gummow J

APPOINTMENT

[For 5(3) Halsbury's Laws of England (4th Edn) (Reissue) para 80 see now 5(3) Halsbury's Laws (4th Edn) (2008 Reissue) para 80.]

APPROPRIATE DEVELOPMENT

'[7] The concept of "appropriate development" is well established in the context of Green Belt policy. It reflects a distinction between two stages of the analysis: whether development is "appropriate" in the Green Belt and how much harm to the Green Belt a particular proposal will do (see e g *Kemnal Manor Memorial Gardens Ltd v First Secretary of State* [2005] EWCA Civ 835 at [28], [2005] JPL 1568 at [28], per Keene LJ). Certain categories of development, such as agricultural buildings, recreational facilities, and cemeteries, have traditionally been regarded as acceptable in principle, subject to other planning considerations. "Inappropriate development", which includes most forms of residential or commercial development, is unacceptable in principle, and is permitted only in "very special" circumstances.' R (on the application of the Heath and Hampstead Society) v Vlachos [2008] EWCA Civ 193, [2008] 3 All ER 80 at [7], per Carnwath LJ

ASSESSMENT

Canada [Income Tax Act, RSC, 1985 (5th Supp), c 1, s 165(3). Whether the onus of proof with respect to assumptions of fact first made by the Minister of National Revenue at the confirmation stage of a reassessment pursuant to s 165(3) is on the Crown. The Tax Court held that it was, as the confirmation of an assessment is not part of the assessment process, and that it was inappropriate for the taxpayer to have the onus of disproving assumptions made at the confirmation stage. This view was rejected on appeal.] '[21] [T]he respondent argues that the case law is clear that the taxpayer bears the onus of proof only with respect to the Minister's assumptions of fact made at the time of assessment. The term "assessment" refers to the administrative act of fixing tax liability culminating in the issuance of a notice of assessment. It does not include the administrative appeal process which involves the confirmation of the assessment: see respondent's memorandum of fact and law, at paragraphs 15–17. The respondent relies upon paragraph 49(1)(d) of the *Tax Court of Canada Rules (General Procedure)* requiring every reply to state "the findings or assumptions of fact made by the Minister when making the assessment".

...

'[32] [W]hile it is true that assessment, reassessment and confirmation refer to three specific actions by the Minister under the Act in the process of determining the tax liability of a taxpayer, the word "assessment" also refers to

the product of that process. Hugessen JA nicely described the two meanings of the word in *Canada v Consumers' Gas Co* [1987] 2 FC 60 (CA). At page 67 he wrote:

> What is put in issue on an appeal to the courts under the *Income Tax Act* is the Minister's assessment. While the word "assessment" can bear two constructions, as being either the process by which tax is assessed or the product of that assessment, it seems to me clear, from a reading of sections 152 to 177 of the *Income Tax Act*, that the word is there employed in the second sense only. This conclusion flows in particular from subsection 165(1) and from the well established principle that a taxpayer can neither object to nor appeal from a nil assessment.

'[33] I agree with the motions Judge that the appeal is not from the confirmation of the assessment. The appeal is, to use the words of Hugessen JA, from the product of that assessment: see also *Parsons*, at page 814, where Cattanach J held that the "assessment by the Minister, which fixes the quantum and tax liability, is that which is the subject of the appeal." That product refers to the amount of the tax owing as initially assessed or determined, and subsequently confirmed. From the perspective of the process itself, the assessment pursuant to sections 152 to 165 is not completed by the Minister until, within the time allotted by the Act, the amount of the tax owing is finally determined, whether by way of reconsideration, variation, vacation or confirmation of the initial assessment: see *Parsons*, at page 814.' Canada v Anchor Pointe Energy Ltd [2008] 1 FCR 839, 283 DLR (4th) 434, [2007] FCJ No 687, 2007 FCA 188 at [21], [32]–[33], per Letourneau JA

B

BENEFIT

Benefit of the law

Canada [Canadian Charter of Rights and Freedoms, s 15(1); appeal from a Federal Court decision dismissing the appellant's judicial review application of the Minister of Foreign Affairs' refusal to inscribe 'Jerusalem, Israel' on the appellant's Canadian passport as his place of birth in accordance with special Passport Canada policy prohibiting Canadian citizens born in Jerusalem after 14 May 1948 from indicating country of birth on passport.] '[41] Before addressing whether the three elements required to establish discrimination are present in this case, it is necessary to consider a preliminary issue: does the Passport Canada policy in issue generally confer a "benefit of the law" within the meaning of subsection 15(1) of the Charter? The issue here is not whether the Passport Canada policy is a "law," as it is well established that laws for the purpose of section 15 include government policies (see *McKinney v University of Guelph* [1990] 3 SCR 229, at page 276). Rather, the issue is whether the Passport Canada policy confers a "benefit" on others, which it denies to Mr Veffer. In our view, it does not. We will explain.

'[42] The meaning of the word "benefit" has not been the subject of judicial scrutiny, in so far as it is used in section 15 of the Charter. In fact, the guarantee of "equal benefit of the law" is a relatively new creation. Before the enactment of the Charter in 1982, paragraph 1(*b*) of the *Canadian Bill of Rights* [RSC, 1985, Appendix III] only guaranteed "the right of the individual to equality before the law and the protection of the law". It was thought, as a result of the Supreme Court decision in *Bliss v Attorney General (Can)* [1979] 1 SCR 183, that the equality guarantee was intended to address burdens imposed by legislation, and not benefits conferred. With the insertion of "equal benefit of the law" in subsection 15(1) of the Charter, Parliament has ostensibly created a broader, more comprehensive, equality guarantee. The guarantee of "equal benefit of the law" has since been used to successfully challenge substantial things like the denial of pension benefits and employment insurance schemes, the provision of medical treatment, and other legislative benefits schemes.

'[43] In recent cases, such as *Auton* [*Auton (Guardian ad litem of) v British Columbia (Attorney General)* [2004] 3 SCR 657, (2004) 245 DLR (4th) 1] and *Gosselin* [*Gosselin v Quebec (Attorney General)* [2002] 4 SCR 429, (2002) 221 DLR (4th) 257], the Supreme Court has indicated somewhat imprecisely that subsection 15(1) guarantees "equal treatment", which might imply that a claimant need only show a differentiation to engage the equality guarantee. However, it is not just any differential treatment which is sufficient to invoke subsection 15(1). What is significant is treatment which denies "equal protection" or "equal benefit of the law". These words must have a discernible meaning in our Charter, and it is imperative that a claimant who intends to make a serious allegation of discrimination demonstrate that the so-called treatment complained of falls within the language of the equality guarantee, that is, that equal benefit or equal protection has been denied.

'[44] What, then, constitutes a "benefit" for the purposes of subsection 15(1) of the Charter? It is helpful, in deciding this threshold requirement, to review how some other fundamental freedoms of the Charter are understood. As already discussed, the freedom of religion and conscience right in paragraph 2(*a*) of the Charter protects only government conduct which interferes with the practice or observance of religious beliefs that are substantial.

'[45] Consistent with that, the jurisprudence has established that section 7 of the Charter is engaged only where an applicant can demonstrate that government conduct seriously interferes with an individual's "life, liberty and security of the person." To explain, it is not every deprivation of an individual's liberty or security of the person which engages section 7 of the Charter, for almost every piece of government legislation could be said to restrain individuals in one way or another. "Liberty" has been defined, for the purpose of section 7, as freedom from physical restraint, and freedom from state compulsions or prohibitions which affect important and fundamental choices (see *Blencoe v British Columbia (Human Rights Commission)* [2000] 2 SCR 307, at paragraph 49). Similarly, "security of the person" has been defined as freedom from state interference with bodily integrity and serious state-imposed psychological stress (*Blencoe*, at paragraph 55). While the right to "life" has not been extensively discussed, it surely includes the right to be free from a risk of death and free from excessive waiting times for medical treatment in a public health care system (see *Chaoulli v Quebec (Attorney General)* [2005] 1 SCR 791).

'[46] In keeping with this theme, the guarantee of "equal benefit of the law" in subsection 15(1) of the Charter must be understood to refer to benefits which objectively have some meaningful consequence to the individuals affected. In our view, this threshold requirement has not been met in this case.

'[47] Mr Veffer argues that the "benefit" conferred on others, which is not available to him, is the ability to express an important aspect of his religious identity in a government identity document. While Mr Veffer may sincerely believe that this amounts to a denial of a "benefit" that is conferred on others, we are not persuaded that

this is the case. The purpose of a passport is, as already discussed, to identify an individual as a Canadian citizen and to facilitate travel to other countries. Here, Mr Veffer was issued a passport, the passport identifies him as a Canadian citizen, and there is no evidence that the absence of a country name beside "Jerusalem" hinders his ability to travel in any way. Nor is there any suggestion that the addition of a country name will improve his ability to travel or be identified as a Canadian citizen.

'[48] We emphasize that the equality guarantee is one of the most fundamental values protected in the Charter, and an allegation that the government has discriminated against someone must not be taken lightly. By the same token, subsection 15(1) should not be used simply because an individual is displeased with some differential treatment under a government policy. In our view, it would trivialize the equality guarantee if it were used to attack every situation where an individual subjectively feels annoyed or offended by legislation that affects him differently than others. To engage section 15 of the Charter, an applicant must, therefore, demonstrate that a meaningful "benefit of the law" has been denied. This Mr Veffer has not done.' Veffer v Canada (Minister of Foreign Affairs) [2008] 1 FCR 641, 283 DLR (4th) 671, [2007] FCJ No 908, 2007 FCA 247 at [41]–[48], per Richard CJ, Linden and Ryer JJ A

C

CERTIFIED PRACTISING ACCOUNTANT

Australia '[5] In addition, the applicant is specifically recognised in reference works such as the *Penguin Macquarie Dictionary of Economics & Finance*. The term "certified practising accountant" or "CPA" is defined as:

> A member of the AUSTRALIAN SOCIETY OF ACCOUNTANTS who has completed a minimum number of hours additional study above the Society's entry requirements and intends to continue to keep abreast of new accounting practices and developments. This new, higher class of accountants was introduced in 1983.

...

'[30] I will deal first with the applicant's case based upon Mr Dunn's stated refusal to undertake not to use the term "certified practising accountant" in his letterhead. I am satisfied, on the evidence, that those of the applicant's members who have been accorded the qualification of "certified practising accountant" have acquired a reputation through that designation. I accept the applicant's submission that the combination of those three words have a secondary meaning, namely that a person who has that designation has obtained "membership of [the applicant] which, by its tests and examinations and by its rules and requirements as to qualification, confer[s] on its members a status different from that of other members of the profession" who do not have the same qualification: *Society of Accountants & Auditors v Goodway & London Association of Accountants Ltd* [1907] 1 Ch 489 at 500.

'[31] In *Aust Society of Accountants* [*Australian Society of Accountants v Federation of Australian Accountants Inc* (1987) 9 IPR 282], Woodward J reached precisely the same conclusion regarding the words "certified practising accountant". His Honour's decision was upheld by a Full Court. Of course, that decision turned on a question of fact in a case involving only one of the two parties before me. However, it is fair to say that his Honour reached that view on the basis of only 3 years of promotion of the designation "certified practising accountant". The evidence before me is much stronger. The term has now been used for more than 23 years, and as previously indicated has found its way into both state and Commonwealth legislation.

'[32] For these reasons, Mr Dunn's argument that the word "certified" means nothing more than "qualified", and that as he has a degree in accounting, and practises as an accountant, he is entitled with impunity to describe himself as a "certified practising accountant", must fail. The term has a distinct secondary meaning, and as a consequence Mr Dunn's use of it would be likely to mislead or deceive.

'[33] Mr Dunn's argument fails at other points as well. Though he has a degree, one would not normally describe the University that granted it to him as having "certified" him as a practising accountant. The reason is plain. Many graduates in accounting do not go on to practise in that field.

'[34] In my view, Mr Dunn's use of the designation "certified practising accountant" would be likely to induce at least some members of the public, including his own clients, to believe that some professional body or organisation has conferred that status upon him. The reality is that no such body or organisation has done so. His certification is self awarded. He has never been given that certification by the applicant, or by any other body capable of conferring it upon him.' *CPA Australia Ltd v Dunn* [2007] FCA 1966, (2007) 74 IPR 495, BC200710880 at [5], [30]–[34], per Weinberg J

CERTIFIED PUBLIC ACCOUNTANT

Australia '[36] Much the same can be said about Mr Dunn's use of the phrase "certified public accountant". That term closely resembles the designation "certified practising accountant". The visual and aural similarities are real. It is clearly established that the use of different but similar words and phrases can constitute misleading or deceptive conduct. For example, in *Mobileworld Communications Pty Ltd v Q & Q Global Enterprise* (2003) 61 IPR 98, [2003] FCA 1404 the court was concerned with the use by one business of the name "Crazy Ron's". Allsop J held that that name was misleading or deceptive because of its similarity to the pre-established trade name "Crazy John's". His Honour further concluded that disclaimers would not be sufficient, and that injunctive relief was appropriate.

'[37] Finally, the use of the term "certified public accountant" would be likely to mislead because it suggests that there is some organisation that awards that qualification, and that Mr Dunn has satisfied the requirements of that organisation in order to acquire that status. In fact, the evidence reveals that there is no such organisation. Mr Dunn has not undertaken any continuing education of the kind that the applicant requires in order to grant certification, and he has not undertaken any examinations which are a prerequisite to the designation in question. He may be a public accountant holding tertiary qualifications. However, he is not a "certified public accountant" because no professional body or organisation has conferred that title upon him.' CPA Australia Ltd v Dunn [2007] FCA 1966, (2007) 74 IPR 495, BC200710880 at [36]–[37], per Weinberg J

CHANGE

Canada '[106] On this item in the Quebec application, therefore, the Court must determine whether the legislative amendment made to the RSTA [Retail Sales Tax Act] to include the GST [Goods and Services Tax] in the QST [Quebec Sales Tax] base is a "change … in the rates or in the structures of provincial taxes or other modes of raising the revenue" of Quebec within the meaning of paragraphs 6(1)(*b*) of the Act and 12(1)(*b*) of the Regulations [Federal-Provincial Fiscal Arrangements Regulations 1987] which the Minister should take into account in his calculation of Quebec's revenue subject to stabilization from that source for the 1991–1992 fiscal year.

...

'[118] Paragraph 12(1)(*b*) of the Regulations indicates that the amount to be deducted from revenue subject to stabilization for the current fiscal year corresponds to the amount of the increase of the revenues in the fiscal year that results from changes either in the rates or in the structures of provincial taxes or other modes of raising revenue.

'[119] Two points are essential in considering this first point at issue. First, it must be a change made by the province. Secondly, the change must be to the rates or structures either of provincial taxes or of other modes of raising provincial revenue.

'[120] The ordinary meaning of the word "change" is [TRANSLATION] "alteration" (*Le Nouveau Petit Robert*); [TRANSLATION] "making more or less different, altering" (*Trésor de la langue française*).

'[121] "*Structure*" means [TRANSLATION] "organization of the parts of a whole" (*Trésor de la langue française*); [TRANSLATION] "complex and extensive organization, considered in its essentials" (*Le Nouveau Petit Robert*).

'[122] In English "change" means "alteration, variation" and "structure" means "The organization of the elements or parts" (*Black's Law Dictionary*, 8th ed).

'[123] In the implementing Regulations the legislature gave a non-exhaustive list of what may be regarded as changes in the rates or structure either of provincial taxes or other modes of raising revenue …:

'[124] In the case at bar, faced with the termination of the FST and introduction of the GST, a new direct tax, by Canada, Quebec amended the RSTA to specifically include the GST in its definition of selling price or purchase price. This amendment authorized Quebec to tax the GST through the QST.

'[125] Canada acknowledges that Quebec made a change which Canada describes as a legislative, not a fiscal change, because before the GST, Quebec taxed the FST, the federal tax, through the QST: nothing has in fact changed as Quebec still taxes a federal sales tax.

'[126] The problem is one of construction of legislation. According to *Rizzo & Rizzo Shoes* [at paragraph 21], above, the analysis is to "[read] the words of an Act … in their context and in their grammatical and ordinary sense harmoniously with the scheme of the Act, the object of the Act, and the intention of Parliament."

'[127] To begin with, I have no difficulty concluding that by its ordinary and grammatical sense, seen in the context of the examples which the legislature itself set out in its Regulations, the amendment of the RSTA to allow application of the QST to the GST represents a change (amendment to the RSTA) in the structure (a significant part) of one of its modes of raising revenue (the retail sales tax). I find in Quebec's favour on this point.

'[128] Before the GST, Quebec, through the QST, did not directly tax the FST: it taxed the purchase price paid by the consumer at retail, which itself included the FST imposed at the point of production. The amendment allowed Quebec to tax the GST directly. In practice, in the case of the SAQ, the GST could tax the latter's mark-up, which was not the case with the FST, as it was included in the base price of its products sold to the public.

'[129] In Canada's submission, the judgment in *Rizzo & Rizzo Shoes*, above, held that the Act and Regulations should be interpreted in a general context taking into account the spirit of the Act, the scheme of the Act and the intention of Parliament.

'[130] As mentioned in the Canada-Alberta arbitration, the purpose of the Act is to facilitate transfer of revenue collected by the federal government to the provinces to finance the public services which each province provides within its legislative powers. In particular, the purpose of Part II of the Act is to stabilize revenue in the provinces to compensate for a decline in revenue in one year compared with that of the previous year.

'[131] As the Canada-Alberta arbitration also indicated, the Minister must add the provincial revenue for the year of the application to offset provincial fiscal changes so as to accurately measure the revenue subject to stabilization in the two years, notwithstanding the changes desired in a province's fiscal policy. In other words, the purpose of the Minister's adjustments is to ensure that provincial revenue in both years in question is comparable on an equivalent fiscal basis, otherwise the comparison would be distorted. The comparison exercise is a question of substance, not form.

'[132] Canada is right in saying that in 1990 the QST taxed a federal sales tax (the FST) and that with the legislative amendment the QST in 1991 continued to tax a federal sales tax (the GST). Ms Daigneault was right in saying that the methodology used by Quebec (the VDTAX exercise) did not permit an appropriate comparison between 1991–1992 and the previous year. The financial impact of this change is not what is alleged by Quebec.

'[133] I feel that these two factors cannot serve to deny the fact that, by amending the RSTA, Quebec made a change in the fiscal structure of the QST.' Quebec (Attorney General) v Canada [2008] 2 FCR 230, [2007] FCJ No 1086, 2007 FC 826 at [106], [118]–[133], per Lemieux J

CHILD—CHILDREN

[For 5(3) Halsbury's Laws of England (4th Edn) (Reissue) para 125 see now 5(3) Halsbury's Laws (4th Edn) (2008 Reissue) para 125.]

COMPENSATED

Canada [Canadian International Trade Tribunal Act, RSC, 1985 (4th Supp), c 47, s 30.15.] '[45] With respect, I do not agree with Evans JA when he states that the term "compensated," as used in relation to paragraph 30.15(2)(e), is a generic word. In my view, compensated means given compensation and compensation is a term with an established legal meaning. The principles of compensation are well understood in the law relating to damages for breach of contract. In my view, it is appropriate to have general reliance on those principles, since, after all, the procurement process that underlies the complaint in issue is essentially contractual in nature and the complaint at issue relates to "designated contracts." ' Canada (Attorney General) v Envoy Relocation Services [2008] 1 FCR 291, 283 DLR (4th) 465, [2007] FCJ No 626, 2007 FCA 176 at [45], per Ryer JA (dissenting)

COMPILATION

Australia '[30] Mr Golvan SC for the appellant sought leave to amend its statement of claim to raise an allegation that its label was a "literary work". The definition of that term in s 10(1) [of the Copyright Act 1968 (Cth)] includes.

    (a) a table, or compilation, expressed in words, figures or symbols.

The appellant says its label is a "compilation".

...

'[32] The application to amend should be refused, primarily for the reason that the proposed amendment lacks arguable merit. The notion of compilation involves a collecting and putting together or arranging or organising of disparate data. That is not the case with the appellant's label. It is simply a photograph and a description of an object. It conveys the one message.' Woodtree Pty Ltd v Zheng [2007] FCA 1922, (2007) 74 IPR 484, BC200710705 at [30], [32], per Heerey J

CONSUMER

(2) 'Consumer' means—

    (a) a person who purchases, uses or receives, in Great Britain, goods or services which are supplied in the course of a business carried on by the person supplying or seeking to supply them, or

(b) a person who purchases, uses or receives relevant postal services in Northern Ireland.

(3) 'Consumer' includes both an existing consumer and a future consumer.

(4) For the purposes of subsection (2)—

(a) a person who uses services includes, in relation to relevant postal services, an addressee;

(b) 'goods' includes land or an interest in land;

(c) 'business' includes a profession and the activities of any government department, local or public authority or other public body.

Consumers, Estate Agents and Redress Act 2007, s 3

CONSUMER MATTERS

(5) 'Consumer matters means—

(a) the interests of consumers, and

(b) any matter connected with those interests.

Consumers, Estate Agents and Redress Act 2007, s 3

CONTROL

[Under the Sexual Offences Act 2003, s 53(1) a person commits an offence if he intentionally controls any of the activities of another person relating to that person's prostitution and he does so for or in the expectation of gain.] '[1] The main point in this appeal concerns the meaning of the word "control" in s 53(1) of the Sexual Offences Act 2003, which created a new offence of controlling the activities of a prostitute for gain in place of the previous statutory offence of living on the earnings of prostitution.

...

'[20] In our judgment, "control" includes but is not limited to one who forces another to carry out the relevant activity. "Control" may be exercised in a variety of ways. It is not necessary or appropriate for us to seek to lay down a comprehensive definition of an ordinary English word. It is certainly enough if a defendant instructs or directs the other person to carry out the relevant activity or do it in a particular way. There may be a variety of reasons why the other person does as instructed. It may be because of

physical violence or threats of violence. It may be because of emotional blackmail, for example, being told that "if you really loved me, you would do this for me". It may be because the defendant has a dominating personality and the woman who acts under his direction is psychologically damaged and fragile. It may be because the defendant is an older person, and the other person is emotionally immature. It may be because the defendant holds out the lure of gain, or the hope of a better life. Or there may be other reasons.

'[21] Sex workers are often vulnerable young women with disturbed backgrounds, who have never known a stable relationship or respect from others and are therefore prey to pimps. It is all too easy for such a person to fall under the influence of a dominant male, who exploits that vulnerability for financial gain. Exploitation of prostitution for financial gain is the broad mischief against which s 53 is aimed, whether or not it involves intimidation of the prostitute or prostitutes concerned. At one stage it was submitted by Mr Gerasimidis that some degree of absence of free will on the part of the prostitute is an essential ingredient of control. But on reflection he withdrew that submission and, in our judgment, he was right to do so. If, for example, a group recruits young women from overseas and puts them to work in organised prostitution in the United Kingdom, we do not see any ground for saying that the prosecution would have to prove absence of free will in order to be able to show that the organisers were controlling the activities of the women for gain.

'[22] Although, as we have stressed, we do not seek to substitute alternative words for the word "control" which Parliament has used, our approach to the interpretation of the word in its statutory content is consistent also with its ordinary English usage. The Concise Oxford Dictionary defines "in control of" as "directing an activity". It defines the noun "control" as "power of directing, command". By contrast, it does not includes the words "compel, force or coerce", although they would doubtless be forms of control.' R v Massey [2007] EWCA Crim 2664, [2008] 2 All ER 969 at [1], [20]–[22], per Toulson LJ

Effective control

New Zealand [Under the Proceeds of Crime Act 1991, s 43(3)(b), one of the criteria for the grtant of a restraining order is that there are reasonable grounds for believing that the property is subject to the 'effective control' of the respondent.] '[24] With respect to the concept of effective control, the legislative intent expressed in s 43(3) and (4) and s 29 of the Act suggests that the court is not to be limited in its inquiries by legal or equitable rights of ownership. This proposition derives support from the commentary on s 29 of the Act in *Adams on Criminal Law – Sentencing* (looseleaf ed), which states at para PC29.01 that:

> "This section is intended to enable the Court to go behind any corporate structure, trust, family relationship, or the like disguising the true and effective control of property by a particular person. In such situations, the Court is to determine whether particular property is to be treated as the property of offenders not by reference to their legal or equitable rights, but by reference to the degree to which they are able to treat the property as their own: *DPP v Walsh* [1990] WAR 25 (1990) 43 Crim R 266. In other words, as expressed in *Connell v Lavender* (1991) 7 WAR 9, the question is whether the defendant in fact has the power to regulate possession, use, or disposition of the property in question (that is, the de facto power to give or refuse consent to a proposed course of action in relation to it)."

'[25] *Director of Public Prosecutions v Walsh* [1990] WAR 25 involved a doctor who fraudulently forged his patients' signatures to vouchers that he then billed to, inter alios, the Australian Health Insurance Commission. As part of his sentence, the Judge ordered that he pay $303,423.78 in reparation to the Commonwealth. He did not make this reparation and, as a result, the Director of Public Prosecutions applied under the Proceeds of Crime Act 1987 (Cth) to obtain a declaration that properties owned by the defendant be made available to satisfy that order. That Act required under s 28(3) that the properties be under the effective control of the defendant for such an order to be made. Seaman J, giving the judgment of the Supreme Court of Western Australia, accepted at p 34 the submission that effective control:

> "... means that degree of control which results in Walsh being able to treat these properties as his own at the date on which an order under s 28(3) might be made."

'[26] In *Connell v Lavender* (1991) 7 WAR 9 the Supreme Court of Western Australia again considered the issue of effective control. That case involved a search warrant pursuant to the Crimes (Confiscation of Profits) Act 1988 (WA), seeking to gather information with a view to an application for a confiscation order or a restraining order. A specific definition of effective control was provided in that Act. However, the Court first considered the general meaning of effective control, Rowland J finding at p 22:

> "In my opinion, the ordinary meaning of 'control' is de facto control or control in fact. The question then is: what effect does the adjective 'effective' have upon the meaning? ... In my opinion, 'effective control' in the context of the statute means de facto control. The expression contemplates control that is practically effective, in the sense that the person concerned has in fact the capacity to control the possession, use, or disposition of the property."

The definition of effective control contained in the relevant legislation in *Connell v Lavender* was wider than that expressed at p 22.

'[27] These cases support the proposition that, when considering the issue of tracing the proceeds of crime, the court is entitled to consider the real, de facto position of the respondent in relation to the property. The intent is that the respondent should not profit from his crime purely because of the legal structure by which he chooses to organise his assets. In order to determine whether the respondent had effective control of the property, the court must ask whether in fact the respondent had the capacity to control, use, dispose of or otherwise treat the property as his own.' Solicitor-General v Bartlett [2008] 1 NZLR 87 at [24]–[27], per Stevens J

Under the control of a government institution

Canada [Appeal from a Federal Court decision dismissing an application for judicial review of a decision by the Canadian Human Rights Commission to disclose a final audit report containing findings about compliance with the Employment Equity Act 1995 by the Canadian Imperial Bank of Commerce (the appellant CIBC). The CIBC argued that since the Employment Equity Act 1995, s 34 prohibits the release of the information which it provided to the Commission without its consent, it had the power to decide if the information was to be released. This argument turned on the meaning of the phrase 'under the control of a government institution' found in the Access to Information

Act 1985 ('ATIA'), s 4.] '[23] The CIBC's argument on this issue turns on the meaning of "under the control of a government institution," a phrase which is found in section 6 of the ATIA ... and section 4 [as am by SC 1992, c 1, s 144, Sch VII, item 1(F); 2001, c 27, s 202], reproduced below:

4.

(1) Subject to this Act, but notwithstanding any other Act of Parliament, every person who is

   (*a*) a Canadian citizen, or

   (*b*) a permanent resident within the meaning of subsection 2(1) of the *Immigration and Refugee Protection Act,*

    has a right to and shall, on request, be given access to any record under the control of a government institution.

'[24] The CIBC's argument, briefly stated, is that since section 34 prohibits the release of the information which it provided to the Commission without its consent, it has the power to decide if the information is to be released. As a result, the information is not within the control of the government institution.

'[25] The CIBC relies upon *Andersen Consulting v Canada* [2001] 2 FC 324 (TD) (*Andersen Consulting*) for the proposition that where material in the Crown's hands is subject to a limitation as to the use to which it may be put, that material is not within the control of a government institution. In *Andersen Consulting*, the limitation was the implied undertaking which, it will be recalled, is the rule which precludes the use of information obtained in the course of the discovery process in civil litigation for any purpose other than the litigation itself.

'[26] As there is no statutory definition of control, the Commission relies upon *Canada Post Corp v Canada* (*Minister of Public Works*) [1993] 3 FC 320 (TD) for the proposition that records which are in the possession of the government are within its control.

'[27] The application Judge noted the introductory words of section 4, "notwithstanding any other Act of Parliament," and interpreted them to mean that the "provisions of the ATIA take precedence over other statutory provisions restricting disclosure, except for those provisions included in Schedule II of the ATIA": see reasons for decision, at paragraph 47. The broad exemption of the statutory provisions listed in Schedule II arises from section 24 of the ATIA:

   24. (1) The head of a government institution shall refuse to disclose any record requested under this Act that contains information the disclosure of which is restricted by or pursuant to any provision set out in Schedule II.

'[28] Section 34 of the EEA does not appear in Schedule II of the Act. The application Judge concluded from this that Parliament intended the ATIA to apply to information in the Commission's hands, notwithstanding the privilege created by section 34.

'[29] Finally, the application Judge distinguished *Andersen Consulting* on the basis that while the implied undertaking kept the control over the documents in question out of the Crown's hands, in the present case, the legal obligations created by the EEA and the ATIA put the control over the final report into the Commission's hands. No legal restriction such as section 34 of the EEA operated to remove control of the final report from the Commission.

'[30] The application Judge concluded that exempting the information protected by section 34 of the EEA from the operation of the ATIA would deprive the broad language of section 4 ("notwithstanding any other Act of Parliament") of any practical significance.

'[31] The CIBC attacked the application Judge's conclusion by pointing to the *Treasury Board Manual: Access to Information Policy and Guidelines* [Chapter 2–00 "Guidelines – General"] which define "under the control" as follows:

   Under the control (*relever de*) — A record is under the control of a government institution when that institution is authorized to grant or deny access to the record, to govern its use and, subject to the approval of the National Archivist, to dispose of it.

'[32] In addition, the CIBC pointed to other statutory dispositions which limit the use to which information gathered under the EEA may be put. ...

...

'[34] The CIBC also revisited the *Andersen Consulting* case and pointed out that the key to the reasoning in that case was the distinction between, on the one hand, a unilateral limitation imposed by one party or a mere contractual limitation on the use which may be made of information and, on the other hand, a condition imposed by the law itself on the government institution which receives a document. In this case, the CIBC argued that the Commission received the CIBC information subject to the limits imposed by section 34 so that the case fell squarely within the principle set out in *Andersen Consulting*.

'[35] In addition, the CIBC challenged the application Judge's reasoning with respect to section 4 of the ATIA by pointing out that the latter only applies if the information in question is under the control of the government institution. As a result, the question of whether a record is under the control of the government institution must be answered without regard to section 4. The application Judge erred to the extent that he reasoned that the final report was under government control because section 4 applied "notwithstanding any other Act of Parliament".

'[36] As a preliminary matter, I am satisfied, on the basis of the colour coded material filed by the CIBC that the bulk of the information contained in the final report was information provided to the Commission in the course of the EEA audit, and was not drawn from public sources. To that extent, there is a factual foundation for the argument that the final report is caught by the privilege created by section 34 of the EEA. In my view, the application Judge erred when he concluded that it was sufficient that the information in the final report be of the same sort as information in the public record. As will be seen later, the test is whether the information itself can be found in the public record.

'[37] The question as to whether records are under the control of a government institution has arisen on a few occasions. The jurisprudence was summarized by Hugessen J in *Andersen Consulting*, as follows at paragraph 14:

> While there appears to be virtually no juris-
> prudence under the *National Archives of
> Canada Act*, the cases under the *Access to
> Information Act* have taken a generous view
> of the sense to be given to the concept of
> control. In particular, it has been held that
> an obligation of confidentiality imposed by
> the originator of the document (*Baldasaro,
> Blacklock and Tucker v Canada* (1986) 4
> FTR 120 (FCTD)), by the governmental
> recipient (*Canada (Information Commis-
> sioner) v Canada (Immigration and Refu-
> gee Board)* (1997) 4 Admin LR (3d) 96
> (FCTD)), or by a party entering into con-
> tractual relations with the government
> (*Canada Post Corp v Canada (Minister of
> Public Works)* [1995] 2 FC 110 (CA)), do
> not operate to remove such documents from

being in the "control" of a government department within the meaning of that statute.

'[38] In short, an expectation of confidentiality arising from the dealings between the source of the record and the government institution is not sufficient to withdraw a record from the control of the government institution.

'[39] *Andersen Consulting* is not an ATIA case. *Andersen Consulting* deals with section 5 of the *National Archives of Canada Act*, RSC, 1985 (3rd Supp), c 1, which prohibits the destruction or disposition of records "under the control of a government institution." It is the use of this phrase in both the *National Archives of Canada Act* and ATIA which invites the application of the reasoning in that case to the facts of the present dispute.

'[40] The difficulty with the CIBC's argument is that it confounds control of the record and control of the information. If one were to draw an analogy, one might think of the difference between ownership of a book and ownership of the copyright in the content of the book. The owner of a book has the control of the physical volume, even though he or she may not be authorized to reproduce the work contained in that book.

'[41] In the same way, the Commission has control of the final report, considered as a record, even if there may be limits on the use which it may make of the information contained in the report. The fact that section 34 imposes certain limits on the Commission's ability to disseminate the information contained in the record is not a reason for concluding that the record itself is not under the control of the Commission. While the application Judge did not employ this reasoning, he came to the same conclusion and so, there is no reason to interfere with his conclusion on this issue.' Canadian Imperial Bank of Commerce v Canada *(Chief Commissioner, Human Rights Commission)* [2008] 2 FCR 509, 283 DLR (4th) 513, [2007] FCJ No 1113, 2007 FCA 272 at [23]–[32], [34]–[41], per Pelletier JA

CORPORATE MANSLAUGHTER/ CORPORATE HOMICIDE

(1) An organisation to which this section applies is guilty of an offence if the way in which its activities are managed or organised—
    (a) causes a person's death, and
    (b) amounts to a gross breach of a relevant duty of care owed by the organisation to the deceased.

(2) The organisations to which this section applies are—
  (a) a corporation;
  (h) a department or other body listed in Schedule 1;
  (c) a police force;
  (d) a partnership, or a trade union or employers' association, that is an employer.

(3) An organisation is guilty of an offence under this section only if the way in which its activities are managed or organised by its senior management is a substantial element in the breach referred to in subsection (1).

(4) For the purposes of this Act—
  (a) 'relevant duty of care' has the meaning given by section 2, read with sections 3 to 7;
  (b) a breach of a duty of care by an organisation is a 'gross' breach if the conduct alleged to amount to a breach of that duty falls far below what can reasonably be expected of the organisation in the circumstances;
  (c) 'senior management', in relation to an organisation, means the persons who play significant roles in—
    (i) the making of decisions about how the whole or a substantial part of its activities are to be managed or organised, or
    (ii) the actual managing or organising of the whole or a substantial part of those activities.

(5) The offence under this section is called—
  (a) corporate manslaughter, in so far as it is an offence under the law of England and Wales or Northern Ireland;
  (b) corporate homicide, in so far as it is an offence under the law of Scotland.

(6) An organisation that is guilty of corporate manslaughter or corporate homicide is liable on conviction on indictment to a fine.

(7) The offence of corporate homicide is indictable only in the High Court of Justiciary.

(Corporate Manslaughter and Corporate Homicide Act 2007, s 1)

CRIMINAL CONDUCT

[Proceeds of Crime Act 2002, s 340.] '[5] In order to bring home any or all of these offences the Crown had to prove that the funds involved constituted "criminal property" within the meaning of s 340 of the POCA [Proceeds of Crime Act 2002], which also defines "criminal conduct" for the purpose of these statutory offences. Section 340 provides in part as follows:

> "(2) Criminal conduct is conduct which—(a) constitutes an offence in any part of the United Kingdom, or (b) would constitute an offence in any part of the United Kingdom if it occurred there.
>
> (3) Property is criminal property if—(a) it constitutes a person's benefit from criminal conduct or it represents such a benefit (in whole or in part and whether directly or indirectly), and (b) the alleged offender knows or suspects that it constitutes such a benefit.
>
> (4) It is immaterial—(a) who carried out the conduct; (b) who benefited from it ...
>
> (5) A person benefits from conduct if he obtains property as a result of or in connection with the conduct."

...

'[6] The essence of the issue in this appeal may be put shortly. To establish guilt under s 327 or s 328, must the Crown prove what particular criminal conduct, or at least what type of criminal conduct, has generated the benefit which the alleged criminal property represents? Or is it enough if they can show, no doubt by reference to the large sums involved and the defendants' want of any apparent means of substance (as well as any other relevant evidence), that the money in question can have had no lawful origin—even if they have no evidence of the crime or class of crime involved? The Crown say the latter suffices. In his terminating ruling the learned trial judge held that it did not. ...

...

'[22] As Mr Bartlett submitted, what has to be proved in order to establish guilt under s 327 or s 328 of the POCA is that the defendant had dealt with what he knew or suspected was criminal property, that is (see s 340(3)) property which constitutes or represents a person's benefit from conduct which constitutes an offence in any part of the United Kingdom. Does that import a requirement to prove the particular offence, or class of offence, said to have been committed? The force of Mr Bartlett's negative answer to this question rests, we consider, in the fact that the statutory words appear to contain no reference, certainly no express reference, to any need to *particularise* the crime or class of crime in question. However the respondents submit that authority, including learning in the Court of Appeal, rules out the Crown's position or at least creates very considerable obstacles in its way; and in fact demonstrates that at least the class or type of crime must be identified and proved.

...

'[32] It is convenient first to measure the impact of *R v Gabriel* [[2006] EWCA Crim 229, [2007] 1 WLR 2272] and *R v K* [[2007] EWCA Crim 491, [2007] 2 Cr App Rep 128]. Neither was in terms concerned with the question we must answer, whether in a money laundering case the class of crime said to constitute "criminal conduct" has to be proved. However such a requirement might be thought to be implicit in, or at least consistent with, Gage LJ's reasoning in [26] of *R v Gabriel*; and in *R v K* the "necessary inference" referred to in [34] is in context surely an inference as to the class of crime in question. In our view neither of these authorities offers material support for the Crown's position in the present case, and both at least sit with (even if they do not march with) the contention the other way.

'[33] The cases on the civil enforcement provisions, *Green*'s case [2005] All ER (D) 261 (Dec) and *Szepietowski*'s case [2007] All ER (D) 364 (Jul), with respect have more to tell us. In that context it is clear that the class of offence in question has to be proved. It is true, however, that the language of the material sections in Pt 5 of the POCA is different from that of s 340. In *Green*'s case Sullivan J specifically relied on particular features of those provisions, notably ss 241(3) and 242(2)(b) (see [18]–[21] of his judgment), in support of his conclusion that in seeking relief under Pt 5 the Director must identify at least in general terms the type of conduct relied on as constituting criminal conduct. Moore-Bick LJ in *Szepietowski*'s case (at [106]) placed some reliance on s 304. Part 7, and in particular s 340, contains no analogue to those provisions, and to that extent *Green*'s case and *Szepietowski*'s case are distinguishable from the present case.

'[34] But there is more to be said about this learning. Neither Sullivan J nor the Civil Division of this court limited their reasoning to narrow considerations of language. Sullivan J expressed himself in more strategic terms in [25] of *Green*'s case, and his approach was taken up by Moore-Bick LJ at [102] of *Szepietowski*'s case. For convenience we repeat this extract from the latter passage:

> "He [sc Sullivan J] concluded that Parliament had deliberately steered a careful course between requiring the director to prove the commission of a specific criminal offence or offences by a particular individual or individuals and allowing her to make wholly unparticularised allegations of 'unlawful conduct' of the kind that would require a respondent to justify his lifestyle. I agree."

'[35] In earlier passages in his judgment Sullivan J (at [3]) had dwelt in some detail on materials placed before him 'in order to identify the particular legislative purposes of the Act and the mischief to which Pt 5 of the Act is addressed'. We need not go into the details of the documents. He acknowledged (at [5]) that—

> "there is no real dispute as to the legislative purpose of the Act, the mischief to which Pt 5 was directed, or the context in which it was enacted. Although the terminology varies, all four documents recognise that 'a careful balance has to be struck between the civil rights of the individual and the need to ensure that the State has the tools to protect society by tackling crime effectively'."

'[36] This "careful balance" is plainly reflected in Sullivan J's conclusions as to the construction of Pt 5, in his more general remarks at [25], and in Moore-Bick LJ's indorsement of that view at [102] of *Szepietowski*'s case. We have to decide whether a like approach should be adopted to the criminal provisions of Pt 7.

'[37] We have already referred to the linguistic differences between Pt 5 and s 340. In our judgment they are not so pressing as to yield a conclusion that the legislature in enacting Pt 7 intended, in the context of *criminal* measures, to strike the balance between civil rights and the protection of the public at a markedly different place from where, as authority shows, it lies in relation to Pt 5. Indeed it would be anomalous, not to say bizarre, if the Crown were not required to identify the class of crime in question in a criminal prosecution while the Director is so required in a civil enforcement suit. Sullivan J's description of the legislative purpose of the POCA, adopted by Moore-Bick LJ, is surely no less apt as a guide for the application of Pt 7 as it is for that of Pt 5.

'[38] In short, we do not consider that Parliament can have intended a state of affairs in which, in any given instance, no particulars whatever need be given or proved of a cardinal element in the case, namely the criminal conduct relied on. It is a requirement, to use Sullivan J's expression, of elementary fairness.' Prosecution Appeal (No 11 of 2007); R v W [2008] EWCA Crim 2, [2008] 3 All ER 533 at [5], [6], [22], [32]–[38], per Laws LJ

CRIMINAL PROPERTY

[Proceeds of Crime Act 2002, ss 329, 340. The question was whether stolen goods acquired by a thief or handler were 'criminal property' for the purposes of the offence of acquiring criminal property contrary to s 329(1)(a).]] '[4] At the conclusion of the prosecution evidence the recorder rejected a submission of no case to answer, advanced on the basis that no evidence had been adduced by the prosecution that the motorcycle [a child's motorcycle stolen in the course of a burglary] was "criminal property" for the purposes of the 2002 Act. The applicant then gave evidence in support of his defence that he had bought the motorcycle for £20 and that at no stage did he suspect that it was criminal property. In his summing up, the recorder directed the jury that there was no dispute that the motorcycle was criminal property but the prosecution had to make them sure that the applicant knew or suspected that it was criminal property.

'[5] The basis of the application to this court was that the recorder was wrong to reject the submission of no case.

'[6] Section 329 of the 2002 Act reads: "(1) A person commits an offence if he—(a) acquires criminal property; (b) uses criminal property; (c) has possession of criminal property."

'[7] Relevant definitions are to be found in s 340:

> "(3) Property is criminal property if—(a) it constitutes a person's benefit from criminal conduct or it represents such a benefit (in whole or part and whether directly or indirectly); and (b) the alleged offender knows or suspects that it constitutes or represents such a benefit …
>
> (5) A person benefits from conduct if he obtains property as a result of or in connection with the conduct …
>
> (8) If a person benefits from conduct his benefit is the property obtained as a result of or in connection with the conduct …
>
> (10) The following rules apply in relation to property— (a) property is obtained

by a person if he obtains an interest in it … (d) references to an interest, in relation to property other than land, include references to a right (including a right to possession)."

'[8] The essential submissions made in the skeleton argument for the applicant were that the person who stole the motorcycle in the course of the burglary did not obtain an "interest" in it within the meaning of s 340(10)(a), since "interest" must mean a lawful interest, and did not therefore obtain property within the meaning of that provision; by working through the earlier provisions of s 340, it followed that the motorcycle in this case was not "criminal property"; and the applicant could not therefore have been guilty of acquiring criminal property even if he was the thief or a handler of the motorcycle.

'[9] Those arguments were met by written submissions from Mr Perry QC, for the Crown, contending that a thief does obtain an "interest", within the meaning of s 340(10), in the property he steals, because he obtains a right to possession of that property. Mr Perry relied on *Costello v Chief Constable of Derbyshire Constabulary* [2001] EWCA Civ 381, [2001] 3 All ER 150, [2001] 1 WLR 1437. In that case the claimant was found to be in possession of a motor car which was to his knowledge stolen. The police seized the car from him pursuant to s 19 of the Police and Criminal Evidence Act 1984 and retained it pursuant to s 22 of the 1984 Act since the owner was unknown. The claimant brought an action against the chief constable for delivery up and damages. The Court of Appeal held that the statutory provisions vested in the police no title to the property seized but only a temporary right to retain it for specified purposes; and that when that right expired, the police were obliged to return the car to the claimant since he had a possessory title in it even though it was stolen. Lightman J, with whom the other members of the court agreed, expressed his conclusion on that issue as follows (at [31]):

"In my view on a review of the authorities, (save so far as legislation otherwise provides) as a matter of principle and authority possession means the same thing and is entitled to the same legal protection whether or not it has been obtained lawfully or by theft or by other unlawful means. It vests in the possessor a possessory title which is good against the world save as against anyone setting up or claiming under a better title. In the case of a theft the title is frail, and of likely limited value (see e g *Rowland v Divall* [1923] 2 KB 500, [1923] All ER Rep 270), but none the less remains a title to which the law affords protection ... This conclusion is in accord with that long ago reached by the courts that even a thief is entitled to the protection of the criminal law against the theft from him of that which he has himself stolen (see e g Smith and Hogan *Criminal Law* (9th edn, 1999) p 522."

'[10] Mr Perry submitted that, applying that principle to the facts of the present case, the applicant clearly acquired criminal property and was properly convicted of an offence contrary to s 329 of the 2002 Act. The motorcycle was stolen in the course of a burglary. The thief obtained an interest in it, namely a right to possession. It followed that the motorcycle was property obtained by him as a result of criminal conduct and constituted his benefit from such conduct. It was therefore criminal property.

...

'[12] ... In our judgment there is no answer to Mr Perry's submissions. The stolen motorcycle was property obtained by the thief, within the meaning of s 340(10)(a), since the thief obtained a right to possession of it and, by s 340(10)(d), an interest includes a right to possession; and it was self-evidently obtained as a result of or in connection with criminal conduct. It therefore constituted the thief's benefit from criminal conduct. It follows that the first part of the definition of criminal property, in s 340(3)(a), was satisfied. The second part, in s 340(3)(b), depended on whether the applicant knew or suspected that it constituted or represented such a benefit. That was an issue that the recorder properly left to the jury and that the jury decided against the applicant. The recorder, who did not have the benefit of Mr Perry's argument, based his rejection of the submission of no case on a construction of s 340(10) that Mr Perry has not sought to uphold; but his instincts were sound and his conclusion was correct. His directions to the jury captured the substance of the matter accurately and no complaint has been made about them.' R v Rose; R v Whitwam [2008] EWCA Crim 239, [2008] 3 All ER 315 at [4]–[10], [12], per Richards LJ

CUSTODY

Legal custody

'[9] In *E v DPP* [2002] EWHC 433 (Admin), [2002] Crim LR 737 the appellant was a 14-year-old boy who had been remanded by the youth court into secure local authority accommodation to attend a hearing in four days' time. He was not in fact detained by the local authority because secure accommodation could not be found. He was nevertheless brought to the court on the date to which he had been remanded by a member of the local authority's youth offending team. He left court before his case was called on. He was subsequently re-arrested and in due course convicted in the youth court of escape from lawful custody. He appealed on the ground that he had not at the material time been in custody. The Divisional Court dismissed his appeal. Forbes J, delivering the leading judgment, said this:

"[19] I agree with Mr Spackman's submission that whether a person can be said to be in custody at any particular time is a question of fact to be decided by reference to the circumstances of each individual case. 'Custody' is an ordinary English word, which should be given its ordinary and natural meaning, subject, of course, to any special meaning given to it by statute. In the Shorter Oxford English Dictionary the word 'custody' is defined in the following terms, amongst others: 'Confinement, imprisonment, durance'.
[20] As it seems to me, for a person to be in custody, his liberty must be subject to such constraint or restriction that he can be said to be confined by another in the sense that the person's immediate freedom of movement is under the direct control of another. Whether that is so in any particular case will depend on the facts of that case."

...

'[12] Those appear to us to be the only relevant authorities. It seems to us that the definition of "custody" adopted by Forbes J in *E v DPP* [2002] Crim LR 737 is plainly authoritative and helpful.

'[13] We should however also refer to s 13(2) of the Prison Act 1952, which reads as follows:

"A prisoner shall be deemed to be in legal custody while he is confined in, or is being taken to or from, any prison and while he is working, or is for any other reason, outside the prison in the custody or under the control of an officer of the prison and while he is being taken to any place to which he is required or authorised by or under this Act ... to be taken, or is kept in custody in pursuance of any such requirement ..."

That provision is not formally definitive of the meaning of the phrase "lawful custody" for the purpose of the offence of escape from lawful custody. Nevertheless it is a useful pointer to the general understanding of the concept of custody, and it seems to us wholly consistent with the formulation adopted by Forbes J in *E v DPP*.

'[14] In our view the conception underlying the decisions in the cases to which we have referred,

and also s 13(2) of the 1952 Act, is that a person may be in custody, notwithstanding that he is not physically confined, provided that he is nevertheless under the direct control of—that is in the charge of—a representative of authority. ...' R v Montgomery [2007] EWCA Crim 2157, [2008] 2 All ER 924 at [9], [12]–[14], per Underhill J

D

DATE

Australia '[6] The critical issue of construction of s 49(4) [of the of the Criminal Law Consolidation Act 1935 (SA)] concerns the import of the phrase "was on the date on which the offence is alleged to have been committed". The phrase is placed in a subsection stating that what follows shall be a defence to a charge under s 49(3) [of sexual intercourse with a person aged between 12 and 17 years]. The phrase appears twice, in paras (a) and (b)(i), and thus has an impact upon each of the two defences just described.

'[7] An accused does not make allegations, particularly as to the date on which the alleged offence was committed. The passive voice is used in the expression "is alleged", but the better construction attaches the phrase to the elements of the charge against which s 49(4) provides for defences.

'[8] What then is conveyed in s 49(4) by the term "the date"? In answering that question it would be inappropriate to begin with what might follow from the general proposition that in reckoning time by days ordinarily the law takes no account of fractions of a day. A solar day of 24 hours is a division of time. Here, what is to be construed is the statutory expression "the date". It is true that in popular usage "date" may identify a particular day on the calendar. But the term "the date" encompasses more than that, including both a particular point in time at which, and a period of time within which an event or transaction occurs.

'[9] In *Hackwill v Kay* [[1960] VR 632 at 634], O'Bryan, Dean and Monahan JJ considered the authorities supporting the general proposition that an allegation in an indictment or information of a date as that of the commission of the offence is immaterial unless it be an essential element of the offence. Upon the proper construction of the statutory provision before them, their Honours concluded that the date was such an essential element.

...

'[11] In the present case, the particulars of the offences identified the date alleged as "between the 31st day of January 1986 and the 28th day of February 1986 at Renmark or another place". This would have been sufficient to identify "the date" within the meaning of s 49(4) of the Act. The submission by the respondent is that no particular date was essential to its case other than that in 1989 when the complainant would have no longer been under the age of 17 as indicated by s 49(3). This should not be accepted. The above words in the particulars were an element of the offences charged.

'[12] Between the periods 31 January and 28 February 1986, the complainant undoubtedly was not above the age of 16 years and under the age of 17 years. There was no possibility of a defence based upon s 49(4). But if, as the appellant contended at trial, he had had sexual intercourse with the complainant only at a later date (in 1989), he had an immediate answer to the charges.

'[13] The appellant submits as the first ground of appeal to this court that (a) the only offences with which the appellant was charged were offences which could not engage a defence under s 49(4); and (b) hence the date of the offences as alleged in the particulars had to be proved. That submission should be accepted.

'[14] The trial miscarried in a serious respect because there was never any charge against the appellant alleging a date in 1989 as the date of the offences. To a charge in that form, there properly could have been propounded a defence based upon paras (a) and (b)(ii) of s 49(4), namely upon the age of the complainant as 16 years or above and the belief of the appellant on reasonable grounds that the complainant was of or above 17 years of age.

...

'[16] The appellant correctly submits that "the date" spoken of in s 49(4) is that alleged in the information upon which the trial (and any pre-trial proceedings) are conducted. The date might have been amended by the court pursuant to s 281(2) of the Act but the prosecutor did not seek such an amendment, nor the provision of alternative counts.' W v R [2007] HCA 58,

(2007) 241 ALR 199, BC200710770 at [6]–[9], [11]–[14], [16], per Gummow J

DEBT

Provable debt

Australia '[7] In this court, Mr Foots argues that the costs order made against him was a provable debt within the meaning of s 82 of the Bankruptcy Act as it was a debt or liability arising out of an obligation incurred before his bankruptcy. That "obligation" was said to arise from the judgment against him for the money sum awarded on 1 September 2005. Alternatively, Mr Foots submitted that the phrase "all debts and liabilities" in s 82 is broad enough to encompass an obligation that is incidental to a provable debt, even if the incidental obligation was not a necessary concomitant in law of the provable debt. However, Mr Foots did not submit that the costs order itself was a relevant "obligation" or that it was a "contingent" liability within the meaning of s 82.

...

'[10] Section 82 limits provable debts both by subject-matter, in that they must answer the statutory descriptions, and temporally, in that they must arise before (not after) bankruptcy. At first glance, neither criterion is fulfilled in the present case: this particular costs order was incurred after bankruptcy, and the appellant was under no obligation to pay those costs beforehand.

'[11] A second aspect of s 82 flows from the first. Contrary to the appellant's submissions, there is no express or implied textual support for the notion of a debt being provable if it is incidental to, or consequent upon, a debt which is itself provable. Those debts which are provable are spelled out by the section: matters falling outside those categories are not provable.

...

'[24] As already remarked, in this court, the appellant contended, first, that his exposure to an adverse costs order was, in the terms of s 82(1) of the Bankruptcy Act, a debt or liability arising from an "obligation" incurred prior to his bankruptcy, and, secondly, that it was a liability "incidental" to a provable debt.

...

Obligation incurred prior to bankruptcy?

'[35] What, then of the appellant's first submission? This is, that his exposure to an adverse costs order arose from an "obligation" incurred prior to his bankruptcy. The submission should be rejected: no such obligation arose

until the costs order was made. This conclusion is consistent both with the Australian authorities upon which Chesterman J had relied and the twentieth century English authorities regarding the proof of costs in bankruptcy, particularly *Re A Debtor* [[1911] 2 KB 652], *Re Pitchford* [[1924] 2 Ch 260] and *Glenister* [[2000] Ch 76, [1999] 3 All ER 452]. Each of these authorities emphasises the distinct nature of the proof of a costs order and the proof of an underlying debt.

'[36] The most that can be said, as Mummery LJ observed in *Glenister* [at Ch 84, All ER 458], is that "[o]nce legal proceedings have been commenced there is always a possibility or a risk that an order for costs may be made against a party". But that risk is not a contingent liability within the sense of s 82(1). The order for costs itself is the source of the legal liability and there is no certainty that the court in question will decide to make an order. It should be remarked that in support of his reasoning in *Glenister* [at Ch 83;All ER 457], Mummery LJ referred to what had been said by Kitto J in *Community Development Pty Ltd v Engwirda Construction* Co [(1969) 120 CLR 455 at 459, [1970] ALR 173 at 174–175] and by Tadgell J in *Federal Commissioner of Taxation v Gosstray* [[1986] VR 876 at 878]. The first submission by the appellant should be rejected.

Incidental?

'[37] Upon like considerations, and again contrary to the appellant's submissions, it cannot be said that exposure to an adverse costs order is "incidental" to liability for the underlying judgment debt. For reasons that will be explored later in these reasons, it is highly doubtful that the text of s 82 supports the notion of "incidental" liabilities that are not themselves provable debts. However, it is sufficient for present purposes to observe that, as a factual and legal matter, costs are no longer an "incident" of either verdict or judgment. As explained above, the making of an adverse costs order turns upon discretionary considerations that arise independently of the entry of judgment against the debtor.

...

'[65] If the distraction of *British Gold Fields* [*Re British Gold Fields of West Africa* [1899] 2 Ch 7] is resisted when construing the text of the Bankruptcy Act, and the nature of a costs order is appreciated, several difficulties lie in the path of the admission to proof of the costs order made against Mr Foots. First, the order made falls outside s 82(1) because it was made after bankruptcy, and was thus not a liability "to which a bankrupt was subject *at the date of the bankruptcy*, or to which he or she may become subject before his or her discharge by reason of an obligation incurred *before the date of the bankruptcy*" (emphasis added). Secondly, as explained earlier in these reasons, Mr Foots was under no antecedent obligation to pay costs until the order was made against him. Thirdly, there is no scope in the text or structure of the Bankruptcy Act for the notion of an obligation or liability "incidental" to a provable debt. The necessary corollary of the appellant's argument is the admission that such an obligation is not itself a provable debt, but is only "incidental" to one. If such an obligation is not a provable debt, when then should it be admitted to proof? Dressing the notion in the language of "incidence" does not alter matters: rather, it is apt to disguise the text of the Bankruptcy Act.

...

'[67] Had the costs order made by Chesterman J on 3 February 2006 been made and taxed before the appellant's bankruptcy ensued, it would have been a provable debt. Even if the order had not been taxed before bankruptcy, it would nonetheless have been provable as a debt incurred "by reason of an obligation incurred before the date of the bankruptcy"; namely the antecedent making of the costs order. However, the order was made only after bankruptcy had already intervened, and the appellant's liability to meet that order did not arise from an obligation incurred before bankruptcy. Thus, it was not a provable debt, and the stay contained in s 58(3) of the Bankruptcy Act was not engaged. His Honour was therefore entitled to make the costs order against Mr Foots.' Foots v Southern Cross Mine Management Pty Ltd [2007] HCA 56, (2007) 241 ALR 32, BC200710620 at [7], [10]–[11], [24], [35]–[37], [65], [67], per Gleeson CJ, Gummow, Hayne and Crennan JJ

Australia '[11] The issue is whether a cross-claim by a director against a co-director for equitable contribution to the former's exposure to liability under ss 588G and 588M of the Corporations Act, is a debt or liability which falls within the ambit of s 82(1) of the Bankruptcy Act, and therefore a provable debt under s 58(3)(b).

'[12] In order to be such a debt or liability the bankrupt must have been subject to it at the date of the bankruptcy or it must be one to which he may become subject before his discharge by reason of an obligation incurred before the date of bankruptcy.

'[13] It is not necessary to set out in full ss 588G and 588M of the Corporations Act.

'[14] Those sections provide that if a person is a director of a company which incurs a debt when it is insolvent, or becomes insolvent by incurring that debt, and at the time there are reasonable grounds for suspecting the company is, or would become, insolvent, and that director is aware that there are grounds for suspecting insolvency, or if a reasonable person in a like position would be so aware, the liquidator of the company may recover from that director "as a debt due to the company" the amount of the loss or damage suffered by the creditor in relation to the debt.

'[15] Ordinarily, the damage suffered by the creditor represents the amount of the debt owed by the company to him or her which remains unsatisfied because of the company's inability to pay it.

...

'[30] The distinguishing feature between an insolvent trading claim directly against a director and this claim is the interposition of what is required for an obligation to make equitable contribution.

'[31] The real question, it seems to me, is whether the engrafting onto the insolvent trading claim of the requirements for an equitable contribution liability of a coordinate obligor takes the claim outside the ambit of s 82(1) of the Bankruptcy Act.

'[32] This involves a consideration of the nature and requirements for equitable contribution liability, in particular whether it truly is a discretionary remedy and, if so, what the nature is of that discretion.

[33] The doctrine of equitable contribution was considered by the High Court in *Burke v LFOT Pty Ltd* (2002) 209 CLR 282, 187 ALR 612, [2002] HCA 17. Gaudron A-CJ and Hayne J, at [14], held that in general terms the principle of equitable contribution requires that those who are jointly or severally liable in respect of the same loss or damage should contribute to the compensation payable in respect of that loss or damage either equally where they are liable in the same amount or proportionately where the amount of their liability differs. The doctrine of equitable contribution applies both at common law and at equity and is usually expressed in terms requiring contribution between parties who share coordinate liabilities or a common obligation to make good the one loss. Their Honours referred to *Dering v Earl of Winchelsea* (1787) 1 Cox 318 at 322 29 ER 1184 at 1186 as

support for the notion that coordinate liability is one that depends on common interest and common burden.

'[34] The circumstances in which a court will order contribution are not closed: *Burke v LFOT* at [48]–[51] per McHugh J.

'[35] The doctrine stems from the equitable precept that equality is equity. However, this maxim is not to be interpreted literally and it is not necessary to demonstrate that each of the co-obligors owes exactly the same duty founded on exactly the same legal source in precisely the same amount to the identical obligee: *Burke v LFOT* at [92]–[95] per Kirby J.

'[36] It seems to me that directors of the same company who are liable to the liquidator in respect of the insolvent trading of that entity where the liquidator could recover from each of them as a debt due to the company the amount of the loss or damage suffered by a creditor, have coordinate liability attracting the doctrine of equitable contribution.

'[37] Indeed, the cross-claim depends for its existence on such a coordinate liability. If such a liability did not exist, on the facts pleaded, the cross-claim would be liable to be struck out on that basis alone.

'[38] It may be accepted that a claim for equitable contribution could be met by defences generally available to meet equitable claims, such as unclean hands, laches and acquiescence. Culpability on the part of the claimant is a factor bearing on the right to equitable contribution. Also, contribution cannot be obtained from a person who is entitled to indemnity from the claimant: *Burke v LFOT* at [15]–[18] per Gaudron A-CJ and Heydon J.

'[39] It does not seem to me that it can properly be said, however, that the right to contribution in equity depends on the exercise by the court of a discretion at large. A right to such contribution exists in equity if there is coordinate liability. The nature and extent of contribution may depend on relative culpability and the availability of any equitable defence. However, that is the same in the case of almost any equitable claim. Liability for contribution arises from objective circumstances not from the exercise of discretion.

'[40] Neither the fact that there must be initial direct liability on the claimant, nor the fact that the circumstances which pertained at the relevant time may affect the extent of the liability of the respondent to the claim (which circumstances must be examined by the court if they are raised), makes the liability to contribute

any less a liability which has arisen by reason of obligations incurred before the bankruptcy.

'[41] There is nothing in the language of s 82(1) of the Bankruptcy Act that restricts the term "debts and liabilities" to debts due only in law and not in equity: *Wilson v Official Trustee in Bankruptcy* (2000) 97 FCR 196, 170 ALR 430, [2000] FCA 282 at [34]–[38] per Emmett J.

'[42] The coordinate liability asserted existed as much as the director's several liability as at the date of the bankruptcy. As pleaded, there was an existing obligation upon each of the directors as at the date of the bankruptcy to pay as a debt due to the company the loss suffered by the relevant creditors as a consequence of the insolvent trading and an obligation on each of those directors inter se to bear their equitable contribution to it which obligation would arise in a future event namely, that one of them became liable to pay more than his just share: compare *Lofthouse v Cmr of Taxation* (2001) 164 FLR 106, [2001] VSC 326 at [42]–[48] per Warren J; *Lyford v Carey* (1985) 3 ACLC 515.

'[43] There does not seem to be any good reason in principle or logic why a claim by the liquidator of Buzzle against the bankrupt would be met by s 82(1) of the Bankruptcy Act because the necessary circumstances arose before the sequestration, but a claim for contribution by another director arising from the same circumstances against the bankrupt would not.

'[44] The entirety of the acts and omissions of both Apple and the bankrupt which gives rise to their respective liability occurred before the bankruptcy.

'[45] The broad policy of the bankruptcy law was referred to by James LJ in *In re Hide; ex parte Llynvi Coal & Iron Co* (1871) LR 7 Ch App 28 at 31–2 as follows:

> Every possible demand, every possible claim, every possible liability, except for personal torts, is to be the subject of proof in bankruptcy ... The broad purview of this Act is, that the bankrupt is to be a freed man.

'[46] It seems to me that an outcome that a direct claim against the bankrupt would be provable, but a claim for contribution against him by a co-director in respect of a coordinate liability arising out of the same circumstances would not be provable would be contrary to that broad policy.

'[47] In my view, the claims sought to be promoted in the cross-claim fall within the ambit of s 82(1) of the Bankruptcy Act and require leave of the court to be proceeded with and, in the absence of that leave, must be stayed.' *Buzzle Operations Pty Ltd (in liq) v Apple Computer Australia Pty Ltd* [2007] NSWSC 930, (2007) 214 FLR 48, (2007) 64 ACSR 300, BC200707396 at [11]–[15], [30]–[47], per Hammerschlag J

DECISION

Canada [Proceeds of Crime (Money Laundering) and Terrorist Financing Act, SC 2000, c 17, s 30.] '[10] Section 30 of the Act, however, provides as follows:

30.

(1) A person <u>who requests a decision of the Minister under section 25</u> may, within 90 days <u>after being notified</u> of the decision, appeal the decision by way of an action in the Federal Court in which the person is the plaintiff and the Minister is the defendant.

(2) The *Federal Courts Act* and the rules made under that Act that apply to ordinary actions apply to actions instituted under subsection (1) except as varied by special rules made in respect of such actions.

(3) The Minister of Public Works and Government Services shall give effect to the decision of the Court on being informed of it. [Emphasis added.]

'[11] That section allows anyone who has made a request under section 25 to appeal by way of an action before the Federal Court in which the person is the plaintiff, within 90 days "after being notified of the decision". The Act does not specify which decision. Subsection 30(1), however, refers to a request under section 25, which provides as follows:

25.

A person from whom currency or monetary instruments were seized under section 18, or the lawful owner of the currency or monetary instruments, may within 90 days after the date of the seizure request a deci-sion of the Minister as to whether subsec-tion 12(1) was contravened, by giving no-tice in writing to the officer who seized the currency or monetary instruments or to an officer at the customs office closest to the place where the seizure took place. [Em-phasis added.]

'[12] Section 25 refers to the decision of the Minister as to whether subsection 12(1) of the Act was contravened. It is therefore that decision that is at issue in subsection 30(1). The Minister makes that decision under section 27 of the Act, which provides:

27.

(1) Within 90 days after the expiry of the period referred to in subsection 26(2), the Minister shall decide whether subsection 12(1) was contravened.

(2) If charges are laid with respect to a money laundering offence or a terrorist activity financing offence in respect of the currency or monetary instruments seized, the Minister may defer making a decision but shall make it in any case no later than 30 days after the conclusion of all court proceedings in respect of those charges.

(3) The Minister <u>shall</u>, without delay after making a decision, <u>serve</u> on the person who requested it a <u>written notice of the decision together with the reasons</u> for it. [Emphasis added.]

'[13] There is no doubt that the action that may be brought relates to the decision made by the Minister under section 27.' *Tourki v Canada (Minister of Public Safety and Emergency Preparedness)* [2008] 1 FCR 331, 2007 FC 186, 284 DLR (4th) 356, [2007] FCJ No 685 at [10]–[13], per Desjardins JA

New Zealand [Social Security Act 1964, ss 10A, 12I, 12J; appeal to Appeal Authority against 'decision' or 'determination' of the Chief Executive of the Department of Work and Income.] '[22] It was the argument of Mr McKenzie QC that because Mr Arbuthnot was seeking to appeal to the Authority against only the BRC's ruling concerning the change of address, it was not open to the Chief Executive to raise any issue about conjugal status. That, counsel said, was the "same matter" in terms of s 12I(2) in respect of which the Authority was given all the powers, duties, functions and discretions of the Chief Executive in order to hear and determine the appeal. The limits of the appeal had been circumscribed in that way. He supported his argument by pointing out that the appeal provisions refer to both determinations and decisions which, he said, had different meanings. He said that his client's appeal to the Authority had been limited to the determination by the BRC concerning the change of address. It was not against the whole of the decision of the BRC. Essentially this was the same argument that the Court of Appeal rejected, and we think it was right to do so.

'[23] There is no pattern in the use of the two expressions in the relevant statutory provisions lending any support to this argument; nor, it is to be observed, could Baragwanath J find one in *Wharerimu v Chief Executive of Department of*

Work & Income [[2000] NZAR 467]. The words seem to have been used interchangeably, probably as a product of numerous amendments over the years to a statute enacted over 40 years ago which is starting to show its age.' Arbuthnot v Chief Executive of the Department of Work and Income [2007] NZSC 55, [2008] 1 NZLR 13 at [22]–[23], per Blanchard J

DESIGNED OR ADAPTED FOR LIVING IN

[Leasehold Reform Act 1967, s 2(1). Claim for enfranchisement of a building built as a private residence in 18th century, subsequetly used partly for business.] '[5] My Lords, the short issue in this appeal is whether a property at 21 Upper Grosvenor Street, London W1 is a "house" within the meaning of s 2(1) of the Leasehold Reform Act 1967 as amended.

...

'[7] Section 2 of the 1967 Act defined "house" and "house and premises"; sub-s (1) is the only provision of relevance for present purposes, and it was in these terms:

"… 'house' includes any building designed or adapted for living in and reasonably so called, notwithstanding that the building is not structurally detached, or was or is not solely designed or adapted for living in, or is divided horizontally into flats or maisonettes; and—(a) where a building is divided horizontally, the flats or other units into which it is so divided are not separate 'houses' although the building as a whole may be; and (b) where a building is divided vertically the building as a whole is not a 'house' though any of the units into which it is divided may be."

'[8] Over the past 40 years, significant amendments were made from time to time to the 1967 Act, with a view to extending its reach. Thus, the low rent and rateable value limits in s 1(1) were substantially amended by the Housing Act 1974, then again by the Leasehold Reform, Housing and Urban Development Act 1993, and most recently by the Commonhold and Leasehold Reform Act 2002. More importantly for present purposes, any requirement that the tenant should occupy or should have occupied the house as his residence in s 1(1) was removed by the 2002 Act, in all but a few cases. However, despite the significant amendments that have been made from time to time to s 2(1) of the 1967 Act, the primarily relevant provision for the purpose of this appeal, has remained unchanged.

...

'[15] It is clear that to be a "house" for the purposes of s 2(1) of the 1967 Act, a property must satisfy two requirements, namely: (a) it must be "designed or adapted for living in", and (b) it must be "reasonably so called", ie it must reasonably be called a house. The judge concluded the property was not a house within the meaning of s 2(1), because it was not, as at October 2003, "designed or adapted for living in". Had he not reached that conclusion, he said that he would have accepted that it could "reasonably [be] called" a house. The Court of Appeal agreed. Before turning to the question of whether the property was designed or adapted for living in, it is right to record that, in the light of the reasoning of this House in *Tandon v Trustees of Spurgeons Homes* [1982] 1 All ER 1086, [1982] AC 755, the judge was plainly correct to conclude that the property could reasonably be called a house.

'[16] Grosvenor's case is that the property was not, as at October 2003, "designed or adapted for living in", because it was not physically fit for immediate residential occupation. That was accepted by both courts below. The judge said, in para 29 of his judgment, that the words "designed or adapted for living in" carried with them a notion of premises with "somewhere to sleep, to cook, to wash and simply to be when not out at work or out otherwise, and, depending on the size of the place, that is commonly provided by a bedroom, kitchen, a bathroom and WC and maybe a living room of some kind". In his judgment in the Court of Appeal ([2006] 1 WLR 2848), Laws LJ (with whom Tuckey and Carnwath LJJ agreed) described (at [6]) the three upper floors as: "unoccupied and very dilapidated … incapable of being occupied as residences", and in [19] he said that "because of the grave dilapidation apparent from the photographs the upper floors of the [property] were not at the [relevant time] designed or adapted for anything."

'[17] While I accept that for present purposes one is largely concerned with the physical state of the property, I disagree with these conclusions. It seems to me that, as a matter of ordinary language, reinforced by considering other provisions of the subsection, and supported by the original terms of s 1(1), as well as by considerations of practicality and policy, the property was, as at October 2003, "designed or adapted for living in" within s 2(1). The fact that the property had become internally dilapidated and incapable of beneficial occupation (without the installation of floor boards, plastering, re-wiring, re-plumbing and the like) does not detract from the fact that the property was "designed … for living in", when it was first built, and nothing that has happened subsequently has changed that. While internal structural works will no doubt have been carried out to the property from time to time over the past 275 years, it seems very likely from the floor plans that its layout, in terms of internal walls, partitions and staircases, has not changed much since the property was built. In any event, the upper three floors have always been laid out for residential use.

'[18] In my judgment, the words "designed or adapted for living in", as a matter of ordinary English, require one first to consider the property as it was initially built: for what purpose was it originally designed? That is the natural meaning of the word "designed", which is a past participle. One then goes on to consider whether work has subsequently been done to the property so that the original "design" has been changed: has it been adapted for another purpose, and if so what purpose? When asking either question, one is ultimately concerned to decide whether the purpose for which the property has been designed or adapted, was "for living in".

'[19] The notion that the word "designed" in s 2(1) is concerned with the past is reinforced by the later words in the same section "was or is solely designed or adapted …" The use of the past tense is striking in a section which contains a number of verbs only in the present tense. In my judgment, the expression is to be construed distributively: thus, the word "was" governs "designed", and the word "is" governs "adapted". The present tense is appropriate for "adapted" because, as my noble and learned friend Lord Scott of Foscote pointed out in argument, there could have been several successive adaptations, and it is only the most recent which is relevant. The word "was" is in any event difficult to reconcile with Grosvenor's case (as accepted by the judge and the Court of Appeal), as it would be irrelevant whether the property could have been fit for residential occupation at any time in the past.

'[20] Furthermore, the notion that s 2(1) is concerned with whether a property could be physically lived in sits rather ill with the fact that s 1(1), as originally enacted, required, in every case of enfranchisement, the tenant to have occupied the house as his only or main residence. The requirement that a property be in such a physical state that it can be lived in seems

somewhat arid and valueless if there is a requirement that it is, and has been, actually lived in.

'[21] I also find it hard to see what policy considerations would have driven a requirement that a property be fit to live in before a tenant could enfranchise, especially if, as mentioned, there was an actual residence requirement anyway. I can, however, discern a reason for having a requirement that a property must either have been originally designed for living in, or must subsequently have been physically adapted for that purpose. The legislature may well have thought it inappropriate to deprive a person of his freehold under the 1967 Act unless he (or his predecessor) (a) had built it, or permitted a tenant to build it, for living in, or (b) had subsequently permitted it to be adapted for living in.

'[22] Furthermore, the issue of whether a property is fit for immediate residential occupation, the test adopted by the courts below, could easily lead to arguments and uncertainty. As the words I have quoted from the first instance judgment reveal, it may be a matter of debate whether a particular property is so fit if it has no bathroom or no kitchen, or if there is no sitting room. The resolution of such an issue would inevitably be a matter of subjective opinion in many cases. Also, it appears that a tenant's notice would be invalidated if it happened to have been served on a day when he was having his only bathroom refitted: the property would not have been fit for immediate occupation on that day, as it had no usable washing and toilet facilities. Of course, the answer to this may well be that one does not treat the property as physically "frozen" on the relevant day. However, once one departs from the strict test of fitness for immediate residential occupation, the uncertainties multiply. No such difficulties, as I see it, are likely to arise if the words in question are given their natural meaning.

…

'[25] There are two further points concerning the words "designed or adapted for living in" I should mention. The first relates to the facts of this case, and the second is more general. On the facts of this case, I have concentrated on how the property was originally "designed", but it is arguable that it was "adapted" in the 1940s. It is unnecessary to resolve the point, because, if it was so adapted, it was an adaptation for mixed business and residential purposes. In other words, the property would have been adapted for business use on the lower three floors and "adapted for living in" on the upper three floors. It is clear from s 2(1) that, in order to be a "house", the property need not be "solely" adapted for living in, so it would make no difference to the outcome of this appeal if that were the correct analysis. The issue was, unsurprisingly, not much debated, but I incline to the view that the original design of the property is what matters in this case. Its original internal layout as a single residence appears to have survived substantially unchanged throughout, the three upper floors have always been envisaged as being for "living in", and (perhaps less importantly) the internal fitting out of the lower three floors has a residential character, and the external appearance has not been altered since well before the property ceased being used as a residence in single occupation.

'[26] The second further point concerning the words "designed or adapted for living in" is whether a property would be a "house" if it had been designed for living in, but had subsequently been adapted to another use. As a matter of literal language, such a property would be a house, because "designed" and "adapted" appear to be alternative qualifying requirements. At least at first sight, such a conclusion seems surprising, so there is obvious attraction in implying a qualification that, if a property has been, and remains adapted for a purpose other than living in, the tenant cannot rely upon the fact that it was originally designed for living in. However, a term is not easily implied into a statute, and further reflection suggests that the literal meaning of the words is not as surprising as it may first appear, particularly bearing in mind the existence of the residence requirement in s 1(1) of the original Act. It is unnecessary to decide this point, and, particularly as it was only touched on in argument, I do not think we ought to do so.' Boss Holdings Ltd v Grosvenor West End Properties [2008] UKHL 5, [2008] 2 All ER 759 at [5], [7]–[8], [15]–[22], [25]–[26], per Lord Neuberger of Abbotsbury

DETERMINATION

See DECISION

DIRECTLY CHOSEN BY THE PEOPLE

Australia [Commonwealth Constitution ss 7, 24.] '[112] … [T]he words "directly chosen by the people" are to be understood as an expression of generality, not as an expression of universality. Because the power to delineate the franchise

was given to the parliament, the ambit of exceptions to or disqualifications from the franchise was a matter for the parliament itself, so long always as the generality of "directly chosen by the people" was preserved.

'[113] The scope, or content, of that "generality" cannot be charted by precise metes and bounds. The nature of its content, however, is indicated by the range of provisions made by the several state laws that were "picked up", at federation, by [the Commonwealth Constitution] s 30. All of those laws disqualified some prisoners from voting. Excepting prisoners from the franchise did not and does not deny the generality required by "directly chosen by the people".' Roach v Electoral Commissioner [2007] HCA 43, (2007) 239 ALR 1, BC200708182 at [112]–[113], per Hayne J

DISHONESTLY

New Zealand

'[33] The question under s 228 [of the Crimes Act 1961] is similarly confined. That section requires the Crown to prove that, with intent to obtain any of the things mentioned, the accused "dishonestly" and "without claim of right" took, obtained, used or attempted to use any document.

'[34] "Dishonestly" is defined by s 217 in these terms:

> dishonestly, in relation to an act or omission, means done or omitted without a belief that there was express or implied consent to, or authority for, the act or omission from a person entitled to give such consent or authority.

Two things have present significance about this statutory definition. The first is that the word "belief" is not accompanied by the word "honest". The second is that there is no suggestion that the belief has to be reasonable or based on reasonable grounds. It is the existence of the belief which matters, not its reasonableness. Of course the word "honest", in the phrase "honest belief", was designed to signify that the belief must actually be held. Despite the tautology, its usage in that sense is unobjectionable. It is preferable, however, to follow the drafting of the definitions of dishonestly and claim of right by not qualifying the word "belief" at all. The potential difficulty with the word "honest" in the phrase "honest belief" is its capacity to be understood as signifying an ability for the accused person to frame their own moral code (the so-called "Robin Hood" defence). That, of course, is not its purpose, but juries can be confused as to the sense in which the word is used. It is best to avoid the issue when summing up by using language such as "did the accused believe?" rather than "did the accused have an honest belief?" The verb in this context is easier than the noun.

'[35] The expression "claim of right" has replaced the older and more familiar expression "colour of right". It is defined in s 2 of the Crimes Act as follows:

> **claim of right**, in relation to any act, means a belief that the act is lawful, although that belief may be based on ignorance or mistake of fact or of any matter of law other than the enactment against which the offence is alleged to have been committed.

The same two points can be made about the word "belief" in this definition. A qualifying belief does not have to be reasonable or based on reasonable grounds nor have those responsible for the drafting thought it necessary to qualify the word "belief" by reference to honesty. A belief is a belief.

...

'[43] The objective facts of a particular case may be such that the jury can properly infer that the accused had a dishonest mind unless he or she can raise a reasonable doubt on the basis of a relevant but mistaken belief. In this respect the international jurisprudence is consistent with New Zealand's view that, provided the accused's belief is actually held, it does not have to be reasonable. This approach recognises the common law principle that mens rea is, in most cases, a subjective concept. Hence a mistaken belief in facts or circumstances that would, if correct, exculpate the accused does not have to be reasonable or based on reasonable grounds.

...

'[51] It is ... clear that New Zealand is not out of line and, in any event, we now have statutory definitions of "dishonestly" and "claim of right". They are both directed to the accused's belief. Section 228 does not require the use of a document to be "objectively" dishonest. It is the user's state of mind which will determine whether his use was dishonest. All elements of the crime are now covered by the statutory language and definitions. There is no call for any common law overlay.

'[52] The Solicitor-General submitted that the introduction of the definition of "dishonestly" in s 217 of the Crimes Act provided this Court with the opportunity to assess whether it was appropriate for New Zealand to continue to assess dishonesty solely on the basis of what he called subjective considerations. The definition in s 217 has already been set out. It does not, in itself, suggest or encourage a movement away from the traditional approach, which is to consider whether the accused actually held the asserted belief. From the evidentiary point of view, the more reasonable the belief, the more likely it was held, and vice versa; but it is not necessary that the belief itself be reasonable.

'[53] It is clear that ordinarily when Parliament wishes a question of belief to have some objective control it makes express provision to that effect. A good example is sexual violation. A belief in consent must be based on reasonable grounds. The absence of any reference in s 217 to the relevant belief having to be reasonable or based on reasonable grounds is significant.

'[54] The legislative history of s 217 also supports the view that the definition it enacts was designed to allow a defence of belief in lawfulness even if that belief is unreasonable. The section began life as cl 178 of the Crimes Bill 1989. In that form it was longer and much more complicated than s 217. There was no defence of "colour of right" or "claim of right". Rather, cl 178 stated that an act or omission requiring the authority of another person would be dishonest if the accused did not believe that any such authority had been given and had "no reasonable grounds for believing" that the other person would have given that authority had he or she been asked. The intention of the drafters, as demonstrated by the following statement in the Explanatory Note, was to remove the capacity of an accused to argue a "Robin Hood" type defence:

> "[Clause 178] restricts the present law to the extent that it will no longer allow by way of defence a subjective view of what is morally right or wrong."[Explanatory Note, p xxii]

'[55] The Bill was revised by the Crimes Consultative Committee under the chairmanship of Sir Maurice Casey. The revised Bill, which accompanied the Committee's report in 1991, contained a new and simpler definition of "dishonestly" in cl 176. This definition was ultimately enacted in 2003 as s 217. It is not necessary to trace the intervening parliamentary history, as it has no relevance to the point under consideration. The revised Bill adopted, for offences of dishonesty generally, the formula "dishonestly and without claim of right", adapted from the then existing legislative definition of theft, which used the formula "fraudulently and without colour of right".

'[56] There are two aspects of the Committee's revision that are significant for the purposes of this case. The first is the deliberate removal of the reference to the accused having "no reasonable grounds for believing" that authority would have been given if sought. The Committee's report contains the following passage under the heading "Matters of Interpretation":[47]

> "The revised definition of 'dishonestly' … deletes the objective test of 'reasonable grounds' for belief that an act or omission is authorised." [Report of the Crimes Consultative Committee on the Crimes Bill 1989 (1991), p 64]

'[57] The new formula also introduced to the Bill a defence of "claim of right"; distinguishable from the earlier legislative term "colour of right". Colour of right, subject to certain qualifications, had meant "an honest belief that an act is justifiable". As we have seen, claim of right refers to a "belief that an act is lawful". The change from "justifiable" to "lawful" and the dropping of the word "honest" as a qualifier of the word "belief" confirmed the intention behind the 1989 Bill that a "Robin Hood" defence should not be available. The Committee explained [at p 65]:

> "The term 'dishonestly' remains but is confined by our proposed definition to conduct which is known or believed to be without proper authority. While the Committee does not support the use of an objective standard to assess the defendant's belief that the act in question was authorised, at the same time the bill should remove any doubt that an idiosyncratic moral view about what actually constitutes dishonest behaviour will excuse the defendant from liability."

'[58] The significance for present purposes of this history is that it is clear those who framed the new definitions did not seek to introduce any reasonableness qualification of the relevant beliefs. The beliefs contained in the definitions of "dishonestly" and "claim of right" were not meant to be subject to a reasonableness control, albeit their reasonableness will obviously have evidential relevance to the question whether they were actually held. It would in these circumstances be wrong for this Court to read in a requirement that the beliefs referred to in the statutory definitions must be reasonable.' R v Hayes [2008] NZSC 3, [2008] 2 NZLR 321 at [33]–[35], [43], [51]–[58], per Tipping J

DISQUALIFIED

[For 40(2) Halsbury's Laws of England (4th Edn) (Reissue) para 755 et seq see now 40(2) Halsbury's Laws (4th Edn) (2007 Reissue) para 1057 et seq.]

DRAWING

Australia '[19] The appellant asserts that its label is an "artistic work" within the meaning of the definition in s 10(1) of the Copyright Act 1968 (Cth). The relevant part of that definition reads:

> *artistic work* means:
> (a) a painting, sculpture, drawing, engraving or photograph, whether the work is of artistic quality or not;

'[20] "Drawing" is defined to include "a diagram, map, chart or plan".

'[21] The appellant's case is that its label is a drawing. It is submitted that the words and the placement of the photograph were part of an overall design which constituted a "drawing". As already mentioned, no copyright is asserted in the photograph itself. However, it is said that the "drawing" consists of a number of visual elements selected and arranged by the appellant. These elements are the digitised photograph of the box and a series of words in specific fonts, colours and sizes. These elements, so the argument goes, have been carefully arranged in a spatial sense, with each element assuming a specific position that gives the overall arrangement a particular visual effect.

'[22] In dealing with this issue the learned magistrate discussed *Lott v JBW & Friends Pty Ltd* (2000) 76 SASR 105, [2000] SASC 3. The work there in question was a graphic bar with the words "Opera in the Outback". The report does not contain a reproduction. Mullighan J held that it was a "drawing". His Honour said (at [14]):

> [14] The graphic designer had to create a design and make choices about the layout, font, colour and dimensions of each part of the design. Having perused the graphic … I do not regard it as so simple as to deny copyright … The selection of the font from a computer program is no less creative than manual drawing …

'[23] In the present case her Honour, correctly in my view, pointed out at [29] that *Lott* is not authority for the proposition that anything a graphic designer prepares is a drawing.

'[24] The same point was made by Mr Minahan, counsel for the respondents, in his written submissions. The submissions, he said, involved the use of a computer and selection of typeface and decisions about layout and presentation including headings and indentation. The same could be said for a newspaper. However neither the submissions nor a newspaper would be regarded as a drawing.

'[25] Her Honour adopted the statement in S Ricketson, *The Law of Intellectual Property, Copyright Designs and Confidential Information*, at para 7.365:

> Essentially, a drawing is a two-dimensional work in which shapes and images are depicted by lines, often without colouring.

'[26] I would agree that this is the ordinary meaning of the term "drawing". The *Macquarie Dictionary* gives us several definitions of the noun "drawing":

2. representation by lines; delineation of form without reference to colour.
3. a sketch, plan, or design, esp one made with pen, pencil, or crayon.

'[27] In the context of the visual arts, the traditional distinction has been between paintings, which are coloured, and drawings, which are monotone, usually, but not always, black upon white. The statutory definition, particularly by its inclusion of maps, makes it clear that for the purposes of the Act something may be a drawing notwithstanding that it is coloured. However, the essence of a drawing remains the concept of a representation of some object by a pictorial line.

'[28] In the present case the work in question consists substantially of a photograph, which is not in ordinary speech a drawing and which the statute specifically treats as something distinct from a drawing. The only other visual item is the text. Text is not a drawing. I do not think that by adding a non-drawing to a non-drawing one can end up with a drawing, however much skill goes into the placement and arrangement.

'[29] Certainly for something to be a "drawing" for copyright purposes no great complexity or (as the statute tells us) artistic quality is required. In *Millar & Lang Ltd v Polak* [1908] 1 Ch 433 the works held to be drawings included words such as "Greetings", "Friends ever". "Good luck", "Lest we forget", and "For old times sake" in a distinctive form within an ornamental oval or circular scroll. In *Roland Corporation v Lorenzo & Sons Pty Ltd* (1991) 33 FCR 111, 105 ALR 623, 22 IPR 245 the devices held by Pincus J to be drawings were

based on the letters "R" and "B" but, as is apparent from the report at CLR 112; ALR 624; IPR 246, were quite stylised. As his Honour said at CLR 114; ALR 626; IPR 248, they were "by no means random and were plainly drawn with care, to obtain an effect". Clearly a letter or letters of the alphabet can provide the subject matter for a drawing. One thinks of the illuminated manuscripts of medieval works such as the Book of Kells. However, in the present case the text is fulfilling a semiotic function. It is communicating to the reader the message that within the cardboard box will be found a wooden photo box with six albums which hold 120 10 × 15 cm photos. The pictorial image of that box is conveyed by a photograph, which is not a drawing.' Woodtree Pty Ltd v Zheng [2007] FCA 1922, (2007) 164 FCR 369, (2007) 74 IPR 484, BC200710705 at [19]–[29], per Heerey J

DUE

As they fall due

[Insolvency Act 1986, s 123.] '[36] In the 1985 Act [Insolvency Act 1985], repeated in s 123 of the 1986 Act, commercial and balance sheet insolvency are for the first time split apart. In place of the mandatory requirement to take account of contingent and prospective liabilities there has been added in s 123(1)(e) the phrase "as they fall due" after "debts". The mandatory requirement to consider contingent and prospective liabilities now only appears in s 123(2). There is no English authority on the question whether, as Mr Trower submitted, those changes prevent reference to prospective, ie future, debts under s 123(1)(e).

'[37] To the limited extent that academic writers have addressed this point, they are divided. ...

...

'[41] There is a wealth of Australian authority on the question of whether a cash flow or commercial insolvency test permits references to debts which will fall due in the future, ie in English terminology "prospective debts", rather than "prospective or contingent liabilities". The reason why this question has, unlike in England, been analysed in such detail in Australia is probably that neither the Australian courts nor legislature have developed a balance sheet test of the type found in s 123(2).

...

'[51] It is clear from that brief review of the Australian decisions that in an environment shorn of any balance sheet test for insolvency, cash flow or commercial insolvency is not to be ascertained by a slavish focus only on debts due as at the relevant date. Such a blinkered review will, in some cases, fail to see that a momentary inability to pay is only the result of a temporary lack of liquidity soon to be remedied, and in other cases fail to see that due to an endemic shortage of working capital a company is on any commercial view insolvent, even though it may continue to pay its debts for the next few days, weeks or even months before an inevitable failure.

'[52] Furthermore, the common sense requirement not to ignore the relevant future was found to be implicit in the Australian cases in the simple phrase "as they become due".

'[53] Returning to the English legislation, it is, in my view, critical to note that when separating out balance sheet insolvency from commercial insolvency in 1985 the legislature did not merely remove the requirement to include contingent and prospective liabilities in framing s 123(1)(e) out of its predecessor, but added what in Australia have always been regarded as the key words of futurity, namely the phrase "as

they fall due". In that context "fall due" is, in my judgment, synonymous with "become due".

...

'[56] In my judgment, the effect of the alterations to the insolvency test made in 1985 and now found in s 123 of the 1986 Act was to replace in the commercial solvency test now in s 123(1)(e), one futurity requirement, namely to include contingent and prospective liabilities, with another more flexible and fact sensitive requirement encapsulated in the new phrase "as they fall due".

'[57] In the case of a company which is still trading, and where there is therefore a high degree of uncertainty as to the profile of its future cash flow, an appreciation that s 123(1)(e) permits a review of the future will often make little difference. In many, if not most, cases the alternative balance sheet test will afford a petitioner for winding up a convenient alternative means of proof of a deemed insolvency.' Re Cheyne Finance plc [2007] EWHC 2402 (Ch), [2008] 2 All ER 987 at [36]–[37], [41], [51]–[53], [56]–[57], per Briggs J

E

ENDOWMENT

New Zealand [The Local Government (Rating) Act 2002, Sch 1 Pt 1 cl 5(e) exempted from rates land 'owned or used by, and for the purposes of The Royal New Zealand Foundation of the Blind, except as an endowment'. A question arose whether the exemption from rates applied to the land of the foundation which it did not occupy itself but held for the purpose of deriving investment income.] '[10] There is dictionary and case authority as to the meaning and connotations of the term "endowment". They are of limited assistance in the present case. *Black's Law Dictionary* defines endowment as:

> "A gift of money or property to an institution (such as a university) for a specific purpose, esp. one in which the principal is kept intact indefinitely and only the interest income is used."

A similar concept is indicated by the *Oxford English Dictionary* for "endow":

> "... to provide (by bequest or gift) a permanent income for (a person society, or institution)."

"Endowment" is defined as:

> "The property or fund with which a society, institution etc. is endowed."

'[11] But the term has not always been used to connote a particular provenance or the specific purpose of the provision of income. So, in the Charitable Trusts Act 1863 (UK), endowment meant, in effect, all property of every description belonging to or held in trust for a charity, for any purpose. The origin of the property was irrelevant. '[12] The Auckland City Empowering Act 1913 required the Auckland City Council to hold land "as and for an endowment for the benefit of the inhabitants of the City of Auckland, and not for any special purpose". In dealing with that provision in *Auckland City Corporation v R* [[1941] NZLR 659 at 667], Fair J determined that the land was "held for the specific purpose of ensuring that income be derived from it". He

cited Lord Cranworth LC in *Edwards v Hall* [(1856) 25 LJ Ch (NS) 82 at 83]:

> "By the endowment of a school, an hospital or a chapel, is commonly understood, not the building, or providing a site for a school, or hospital, or chapel, but the providing of a fixed revenue for the support of those by whom the institutions are conducted."

'[13] The term under consideration does not, of course, stand alone in the Act but in a context. That context is concerned with purpose, not origin. The meaning and effect of Part 1 of Schedule 1, cl 5(e), is that land will be exempt if it is owned or used by the Foundation for its purposes, unless it is owned or used as an endowment. And, as the authorities we have mentioned indicate, in common usage the term "endowment" connotes, essentially, land held in order to produce income, even though it may also connote a gifted provenance. That this type of land holding or use is envisaged by the exception is indicated by the statutory history of the term in a rating context.

...

'[23] Thus, the catalogue of exempted land which has been accumulated over a period of about 130 years indicates a policy of not excluding from rates land which, although held for or by an organisation with a generally charitable or public service objective, is nevertheless used to produce revenue. '[24] It would be difficult to understand why the various Acts which, over many years, have excluded land owned or used or held as an endowment would be concerned with the provenance of the land. Indeed, s 40(1) of the Finance Act (No 4) 1931 and s 35(1) of the New Zealand Foundation of the Blind Act 1955, referring as they do to "land ... otherwise in any manner acquired", suggest that the legislature specifically regarded provenance as irrelevant. On the other hand, it is not at all difficult to understand why the legislature would be unwilling to exempt from rates land being used to produce revenue. Rates are a normal expense of the use of land for commercial purposes.

'[25] Having regard to the commonly accepted view that the essential quality of an endowment is to provide a source of income, and to the case law, and to the legislative history and context of the expression "endowment", we are satisfied that the Court of Appeal correctly determined that the land in question was not exempted from rates because it is land owned or used as an endowment. ...' Royal New Zealand Foundation of the Blind v Auckland City Council [2007] NZSC 61, [2008] 1 NZLR 141 at [10]–[13], [23]–[25], per Anderson J

ENGINE

['Other engine calculated to destroy human life or inflict grievous bodily harm' in Offences against the Person Act, 1861, s 31.] '[2] The statement of offence in count three alleged setting a mantrap with intent, contrary to s 31 of the Offences Against the Person Act 1861. The particulars were that between 1 January 2006 and 11 July 2006, the appellant set or placed, or caused to be set or placed, a mantrap or other engine calculated to destroy human life or inflict grievous bodily harm, with intent that the same or whereby the same may destroy or inflict grievous bodily harm on a trespasser or other person coming into contact therewith.

'[3] This offence is rarely charged. The question in this appeal was whether, having heard evidence from a defence expert, the recorder was right to reject the submission that, as a matter of statutory construction, an undoubtedly dangerous contraption positioned by the appellant on top of some farm equipment in a shed on his land was capable or not of falling within the ambit of s 31. The recorder decided that it was so capable. He directed the jury accordingly. The jury concluded that the contraption was indeed an engine for the purposes of s 31 and that the necessary intent had been proved: hence this appeal.

...

'[6] The contraption set by the appellant was neither a spring gun nor a mantrap. The conviction could only have been sustained if it was an "other engine calculated to destroy human life or inflict grievous bodily harm". It was exhibit 5 at the trial. We have examined it. Briefly, it is a spiked metal object made from two pieces of heavy steel plate into which some 20 four-inch long nails, protruding at different angles, are welded. It was connected by a metal rod or wire to the roof frame of a shed on the appellant's land. Another wire connected it to the shed door. When the shed door was opened it was activated and the force of gravity caused it to swing downwards and catch the person entering through the door.

'[7] On 11 July 2006, in the course of a lawful investigation of the appellant's property, an army officer pushed open the shed door. As he did so, with good sense, he took the precaution of holding his arm across his face. The spiked object struck his forearm rather than his face. Two nails entered into his clothing, and a third punctured his forearm. His injuries could well have been very much more serious than they were.

'[8] It was submitted on behalf of the appellant that this object was not and could not be treated as an engine. The power needed to work it was applied exclusively by nature, gravity. No other form of stored energy or force was involved. This therefore was not a mechanical contrivance at all, and the decision of this court in *R v Munks* [1963] 3 All ER 757, [1964] 1 QB 304 provides clear authority for the proposition that if the object was not such a contrivance it could not be an "other engine" for the purposes of s 31.

...

'[10] The 1861 Act brought the statutory offences against the person then in force into a single statute. The precursor to s 31 of the 1861 Act was the Spring Gun Act 1827. It was enacted in the period after the Napoleonic Wars which were followed by poverty and hunger throughout the country and when resort to trespass to find food became commonplace. Landowners responded by setting traps and spring guns and other devices, to catch and discourage trespassers and poachers. These were not purely defensive measures (for example, broken glass on walls or spiked fences) but aggressive, dangerous objects intended to cause really serious harm or death. The preamble to the 1827 Act reads: "Whereas it is expedient to prohibit the setting of spring guns and man traps, and other engines calculated to destroy human life, or inflict grievous bodily harm". This provides an ample indication of the legislative purpose of this statute, which was re-enacted in s 31 of the 1861 Act and therefore, since 1827, spring guns and other engines calculated to kill or inflict grievous bodily harm have been illegal in England unless kept in a dwelling house at night as a protection against burglars.

'[11] A spring gun can be described as a gun, often a shotgun, rigged up so as to fire when a string or other triggering device is tripped by contact of sufficient force to "spring" the trigger. Someone stumbling over or treading on the string or triggering device causes it to be discharged and in consequence is wounded. Mantraps take many forms, although the most common is something like a large bear trap, with steel springs armed with teeth which meet on the victim's leg and trap him. Both spring guns and mantraps appear to involve the deployment of stored energy, and this consideration led Mr Magarian to reject the suggestion in argument that a disguised deep hole dug in the ground with a vicious spike or spikes fixed at the bottom would constitute a mantrap. While we are inclined to agree that a shallow hole, on its own, might not do so, probably because it would not be calculated to inflict grievous bodily harm, as a matter of statutory construction, notwithstanding the concession by the Crown in *R v Munks* [1963] 3 All ER 757, [1964] 1 QB 304, we entertain no doubt that a deep hole containing potentially lethal spikes would fall within the description "mantrap". The legislation is not confined to objects which operate through "stored energy".

'[12] On the face of it any engine calculated to kill or inflict grievous bodily harm falls within the ambit of s 31. The Oxford English Dictionary, among other descriptions, describes an engine as a "mechanical contrivance, machine, implement, tool". Something of the breadth of its meaning at the time when the 1827 Act came into force is identified in the dictionary itself where, among other references, we find a pair of scissors described as a "little engine" in the *Rape of the Lock* (1712–1714) and a description of "engines of restraint and pain" at the victim's feet in *Death Slavery* (1866). Indeed at much the same time, in *Barnard v Ford* (1869) 4 Ch App 247, the court rejected a proposition which would turn it "into an engine of fraud". None of these references dilutes or could dilute the authority of *R v Munks*, although they suggest that the Crown's argument in that case was more constrained than it perhaps should have been.

'[13] In these circumstances, there is no reason for giving (and every reason, given the evident purpose behind the legislation, for not giving) the words "spring gun" or "mantrap" or "other engine" an unduly narrow meaning. In *R v Munks*, it is true that a very wide definition of the word "engine" was rejected, and in the context of the electrical device with which it was concerned the word "engine" was said to connote a mechanical contrivance. However we reject the argument implicit in Mr Magarian"s

submissions that *R v Munks* was intended to or could redefine the statutory language of s 31 by replacing the words "other engine" with "other mechanical contrivance". The court cannot re-write statutory language which has been unamended for nearly 200 years. In any event the words "mechanical contrivance", as used in *R v Munks*, are not to be applied restrictively so as to lead to the exclusion of a contraption which falls within the ambit of the statute. On the rare occasions when this question arises for decision, the object itself as well as the manner, if any, in which it may be activated should be examined pragmatically to see whether, looked at overall, it falls within the statutory language. In *R v Munks*, the placing of cables on or by a door through which an electric current could pass was held not to be sufficient of a mechanical contrivance to be an "engine". In the present case, using ordinary language, the contraption was certainly a contrivance. It was mechanical, since as a mechanism, it was triggered into dangerous movement by inadvertent pressure on a wire or string. In short therefore it is properly described as a mechanical contrivance or machine, and it unquestionably is an "other engine" for the purposes of s 31 of the 1861 Act. For these reasons the main ground of appeal failed.' R v Cockburn [2008] EWCA Crim 316, [2008] 2 All ER 1153 at [2]–[3], [6]–[8], [10]–[13], per Sir Igor Judge P

ESCAPE

See also Custody

From lawful custody

[Whether a prisoner on temporary release who failed to return to prison at the expiry of the period of release under the Prison Rules 1999, SI 1999/728, r 9 could be guilty of the common law offence of escape from lawful custody.] '[3] … Rule 9 of the Prison Rules 1999, SI 1999/728, headed "Temporary release", by para (1) provides for the Secretary of State to "release temporarily a prisoner to whom this rule applies" in various circumstances specified in para (3) of the rule.

'[4] The appellant was granted temporary release under r 9. We do not have very much information about the nature of the release arrangement, but apparently he was released each morning to go to some form of employment, being one of the circumstances identified under para (3). We are told in a letter from the governor of the prison that he was "not under any form of supervision", but we were told by counsel that he was obliged to return to the prison at a specified time each evening.

'[5] On the evening of 2 April 2006 the appellant did not return to prison at the appointed time. He remained at large until 19 May, when he was observed by chance by a police officer and arrested. He was charged with escape from lawful custody. On the advice of counsel he pleaded guilty, and he was sentenced at Woolwich Crown Court to a term of eight months' imprisonment, to run consecutively to the term which he was already serving. He has since received advice that the admitted facts did not disclose the offence charged. If that advice is correct, the original advice which he received at the time that he entered his plea was wrong and the Crown properly accepts that this would be one of those exceptional cases where the court should entertain an appeal notwithstanding the appellant's plea of guilty.

'[6] The issue for us is thus simply whether a prisoner on temporary release in the circumstance set out above who fails to return to prison at the expiry of the period of release is guilty of the offence of escape from lawful custody.

'[7] The ingredients of the offence of escape from lawful custody were authoritatively established by this court in *R v Dhillon* [2005] EWCA Crim 2996, [2006] 1 WLR 1535. ... David Steel J, delivering the judgment of this court, conducted a thorough review of the authorities and summarised their effect at para [21] of his judgment in the following terms:

"In our judgment, these authorities demonstrate that the prosecution must in a case concerning escape prove four things: i) that the defendant was in custody; ii) that the defendant knew that he was in custody (or at least was reckless as to whether he was or not); iii) that the custody was lawful; and iv) that the defendant intentionally escaped from that lawful custody."

...

'[8] It will be seen that although the summary of the ingredients of the offence provides an invaluable starting point the specific problem which arose in *R v Dhillon* was different from the issue in the instant case, which is essentially whether, on the undisputed facts, the appellant is to be regarded as having been "in custody" in the period immediately prior to, or at the moment of, his non-return; in other words, whether the first ingredient identified by David Steel J is present. As to that, there is very little guidance in the cases. With commendable diligence Mr Levy has unearthed and discussed in his advice in support of the appeal a number of authorities in which various issues in relation to the applicability of the offence were dealt with, in particular *R v Allan* (1841) Car & M 295; *R v Hinds* (1957) 41 Cr App Rep 143; *R v Timmis* [1976] Crim LR 129, *R v Frascati* (1981) 73 Cr App Rep 28; *Nicoll v Catron* (1985) 81 Cr App Rep 339; *R v Moss and Harte* (1985) 82 Cr App Rep 116 and *R v Reader* (1986) 84 Cr App Rep 294. He has also referred us to the definition of "escape" set out in the 1795 edition of Hawkins' *Pleas of the Crown* (7th edn) vol III, Ch 18, p 242, namely that the offence is committed—

"if the party were lawfully in prison for any cause whatsoever, whether criminal or civil, and whether he were actually in the walls of a prison ... or in the custody of any person who had lawfully arrested him."

None of these authorities, however, concern the position of a prisoner on temporary release or in any close analogous situation. Nor do they contain any relevant discussion of principle. There are only three cases which it seems to us do offer some assistance, which we will consider in turn.

...

'[14] In our view the conception underlying the decisions in the cases to which we have referred, and also s 13(2) of the [Prison Act 1952], is that a person may be in custody, notwithstanding that he is not physically confined, provided that he is nevertheless under the direct control of—that is in the charge of—a representative of authority. ...

'[15] On that basis, we do not believe that a person who fails to return to prison at the end of a period of temporary release under r 9 can be said to have escaped from custody. He is not during his period of temporary release in custody, because not only is he not in prison but he is not under the direct or immediate control of any representative of authority. As we have already noted, the governor of the prison has confirmed in the present case that the appellant was under no form of supervision during his release. It is indeed of the essence of "temporary release" from custody that while it lasts the appellant is not in custody. That is what release involves. Of course it is true that the moment of the alleged escape does not occur during the currency of release but only at the point that it comes to an end and the appellant fails to return to custody. From that moment on he should no doubt have been in custody. But we do not think that it can be said that the reason he is not in custody is that he has "escaped" from it. As a matter of common sense and ordinary language what has happened is not that he has escaped from custody but that he has failed to return to it.' R v Montgomery [2007] EWCA Crim 2157, [2008] 2 All ER 924 at [3]–[8], [14]–[15], per Underhill J

ESSENTIAL (TERM OF CONTRACT)

Australia '[99] ... I am prepared to accept that it is useful to maintain the rule that some contractual terms, limited in number, are so critical to particular contracts that their breach will give rise to an automatic right to terminate. I accept that such terms can be identified and characterised a priori as "essential". I would not disagree that whether or not a term is to be so characterised is a question to be determined with reference to the actual content of the contract, viewed in the context of the entire commercial relationship between the parties.' Koompahtoo Local Aboriginal Land Council v Sanpine Pty Ltd [2007] HCA 61, (2007) 241 ALR 88, BC200710839 at [99], per Kirby J

EXCUSE (NOUN)

Just excuse

New Zealand '[8] There is no authoritative decision providing a definition of what constitutes "just excuse" in terms of s 352 [of the Crimes Act 1961: for a witness not to give evidence].

'[9] Counsel for the witness relied primarily on the approach taken by Williamson J in *R v C T B (No 2)* (High Court, Dunedin, T 16/91, 18 February 1992). In that case the witness was living with the accused and was also the victim of the crime with which he had been charged. She sought to be excused from giving evidence on the basis that it would adversely affect her family's future. By family she included herself, the accused, their two-year-old son, and the child that she was expecting in three months' time. The witness was just 20 years of age at the time. Moreover, her evidence was to the effect that the accused had benefited from counselling and treatment during the lengthy period that had elapsed since the alleged offending.

'[10] Williamson J noted that the Act did not give any guidance to what is meant by just excuse. In concluding that a just excuse had in fact been offered he said at p 2:

"Viewed in the context of overall justice or fairness, from her personal viewpoint I do not consider that the Court can exclude her excuse as being other than a just one. Such a determination must be made, however, not only on the basis of the person offering the excuse but also in the context of an objective assessment. It could well be argued that the task of the law is to consider the circumstances of the community as a whole and that persons who commit offences of the nature alleged in this case are dangerous and consequently that an excuse not to give evidence in relation to such activities could hardly ever be a just one. The decision though must be made in the context of the particular allegations, the overall circumstances, the relationship between the persons and the circumstances of the witness at the time when the refusal to give evidence is made."

'[11] The issue of "just excuse" was considered again, albeit in a different context, by the Court of Appeal in *Controller and Auditor-General v Sir Ronald Davison* [1996] 2 NZLR 278. In that case the Court was considering sections in the Commissions of Inquiry Amendment Act 1995 that empowered a commissioner to impose sanctions, including detention, on witnesses who, without offering any just excuse, refused to answer questions or produce documents. The "just excuse" offered by the applicants in that case was based on several grounds including reliance on the doctrine of sovereign immunity and exposure to the risks of prosecution in another jurisdiction (the Cook Islands) for failure to comply with the secrecy laws of that jurisdiction. In other words, they claimed protection against self-incrimination.

'[12] Richardson J considered at p 330 that the commissioner needed to take into account several considerations. These included:

  (a) an assessment by the commission of the vital national interests of New Zealand in the inquiry, including New Zealand's international relationships with the Cook Islands and other states;

  (b) the importance to the commission's inquiry of the information sought;

  (c) any alternative means of accessing that information from other sources;

  (d) the nationality and ordinary residence of the prospective witnesses and the location of the document;

(e) the nature and extent of the witnesses' commercial and personal connections with the Cook Islands; and

(f) the nature and extent of the risk to the witnesses and any other immediately affected that requiring testimony would impose and personal consequences for them.

'[13] The Court of Appeal therefore took into account a range of competing considerations relating to the adverse affects on the applicants in the event that they were required to give evidence, and the adverse affect on the commission if that evidence was not given.

'[14] The decision in the *Controller and Auditor-General* case was affirmed by the Privy Council in *Brannigan v Sir Ronald Davison* [1997] 1 NZLR 140. Their Lordships considered that the statutory exceptions of "sufficient cause" and "just excuse" provided ample scope for all the circumstances to be taken into account. The Bench said at pp 147–148:

> "Inherent in these two expressions, which are synonymous in this context, is the concept of weighing all the consequences of the refusal to give evidence: the adverse consequences to the enquiry if the questions are not answered, and the adverse consequences to the witness if he is compelled to answer."

'[15] In the present case I consider that I must undertake a similar exercise in which I weigh the adverse consequences to the witness if she is compelled to give evidence against the adverse consequences for the administration of justice if she is not required to do so. ...' R v Lologa [2007] 3 NZLR 844 at [8]–[15], per Lang J

F

FORECAST

Australia '[75] Last, Village argued that the draft ANEF [Australian noise exposure forecast under the Air Services Act 1975 (Cth)] was not a forecast at all. This is because, it argued, a projection as to when Canberra Airport's maximum capacity would be reached is not "based on present indications". For this, Village relied on one definition of "forecast" in the *Oxford English Dictionary* (2nd ed, vol VI) to support its argument, namely:

> … a forecasting or anticipation; a conjectural estimate or account, *based on present indications*, of the course of events or state of things in the future. [Emphasis added.]

'[76] But the same dictionary gives a definition of the verb "forecast" as "to estimate, conjecture, or imagine beforehand (the course of events or future condition of things)". Conjecture involves the formation of an opinion or supposition as to facts on grounds which themselves are insufficient and includes guessing and surmising: see the definition in the *Oxford English Dictionary* (2nd ed). In my opinion, the ordinary and natural meaning of the word "forecast" as used in the term "ANEF" must connote conjecture, at least to some degree. This is so whether the ANEF is made under the Air Services Act, the Airports Act or the standard. So, a forecast can involve a number of inputs, some more certain or capable of proof than others. The formula from which an ANEF is derived is complex. It involves both technical calculations about the particular noise that will be produced in certain circumstances and assumptions as to what might produce those circumstances. There is no necessity that every element of a forecast in an ANEF be founded in fact or be based on a prediction with which all reasonable people will agree. Businesses, entrepreneurs and governments all make budgets or forecasts of their projected economic performance. It is unsurprising that a good many do not come true and there is informed debate about whether the assumptions underlying them are appropriate.' The Village Building Co Ltd *(ACN 056 509 025)* v Airservices Australia [2007] FCA 1242, (2007) 241 ALR 685, BC200706932 at [75]–[76], per Rares J

FORFEITURE

Canada '[9] The word "forfeiture" (*confiscation*) means, in law, "a divestiture of specific property without compensation" (*Black's Law Dictionary*, 8th ed, 2004, at page 667). That definition was cited by the Supreme Court of Canada in *R v Ulybel Enterprises Ltd* [2001] 2 SCR 867, at paragraph 44, which dealt with the word "forfeiture" (*confiscation*) in subsection 72(1) [as am. by SC 1991, c 1, s 21] of the *Fisheries Act*, RSC, 1985, c F-14.' Tourki v Canada *(*Minister of Public Safety and Emergency Preparedness*)* [2008] 1 FCR 331, 284 DLR (4th) 356, 2007 FC 186, [2007] FCJ No 685 at [9], per Desjardins JA

FRIENDLY SOCIETY

[For 19(1) Halsbury's Laws of England (4th Edn) (Reissue) para 103 see now 50 Halsbury's Laws (5th Edn) para 2083.]

G

GAME OF CHANCE

'[1] In 1960, Parliament by enacting the Betting and Gaming Act 1960 made significant changes to many centuries of legislation in respect of betting and gaming. The Act repealed many old Acts of Parliament, gave a new definition to "gaming" and established a licensing regime for those who provided premises for gaming. Those and other provisions were consolidated into the Gaming Act 1968. Section 52(1) of that Act (substantially re-enacting s 28 of the 1960 Act) defined "gaming", subject to provisions that are immaterial, as "the playing of a game of chance for winnings in money or money's worth" and a "game of chance" as:

> "'game of chance' does not include any athletic game or sport, but, with that exception, and subject to subsection (6) of this section, includes a game of chance and skill combined and a pretended game of chance or of chance and skill combined."

Subsection (6) provided:

> "In determining for the purposes of this Act whether a game, which is played otherwise than against one or more other players, is a game of chance and skill combined, the possibility of superlative skill eliminating the element of chance shall be disregarded."

'[2] Sections 3 and 4 of the 1968 Act prohibited levying a charge in respect of gaming or a charge on stakes or winnings, unless the premises were licensed; s 8 provided that if gaming took place contrary to the prohibitions, an offence was committed. The issue on this appeal is whether the judge correctly directed the jury in respect of the statutory definitions of a game of chance in circumstances where the appellant organised a specific type of poker game at unlicensed premises.

'[3] There has been no decision which can be found on the meaning of the provision defining a game of chance since the change in the law over 40 years ago. It is not clear why this is the position. It has proved very difficult to ascertain whether there have been many prosecutions, as no records were kept where there was an acquittal and convictions were deleted after a given period of time. We are grateful to counsel for the Crown for ascertaining in these difficult circumstances that since the change in the law in 1960, it can now only be established that the first recorded conviction was in 1998 and thereafter there have been a few convictions each year. The report of a Joint Committee of the Lords and Commons published in April 2004 (HL Paper 63-I, HC Paper 139-I) recorded that the Gaming Board and the police acknowledged difficulties in tackling illegal gaming due to a lack of police expertise and police time.

'[4] In 2005 Parliament amended the provisions again by the Gambling Act 2005; a game of chance in s 6 of that Act is defined:

> "(2) In this Act 'game of chance'—(a) includes—(i) a game that involves both an element of chance and an element of skill, (ii) a game that involves an element of chance that can be eliminated by superlative skill, and (iii) a game that is presented as involving an element of chance, but (b) does not include a sport."

Subsection (6) gives the Secretary of State a power by regulation to provide that a specified activity carried on in specified circumstances is or is not to be treated as a game, a game of chance or a sport. It is not necessary to refer to these provisions any further as no contention was advanced that the provisions are relevant to the construction of the 1968 Act.

'[5] … The appellant contended (on the basis which we will set out) that the test as to whether TH poker was a game of chance depended on whether skill predominated over chance; as TH poker was predominantly a game of skill, it was not a game of chance within the meaning of s 52(1). The judge in a short ruling rejected that submission and held that no gloss was required on the definition in the 1968 Act, though he accepted the prosecution submission that the prosecution had to prove that there must be a significant element of chance, though not necessarily a predominant one, as most games contained some elements of chance even to an infinitesimal extent.

...

'[6] The contention elegantly and succinctly advanced by Mr Luba QC on behalf of the appellant was that Parliament had radically altered the law in 1960, that it was no longer relevant to examine the old cases and that on the true construction of the 1968 Act, the judge should have directed the jury that a game where skill predominated over chance was not a game of chance within s 52(1) of the 1968 Act.

...

'[8] Mr Luba submitted that the change in the law effected by the 1960 Act had the consequence that it was no longer appropriate to rely on the older cases to which he had referred us. The 1960 Act effected a fundamental change, as the short summary which we have set out demonstrates; the Act rendered gaming lawful on the conditions set out in the Act and repealed the old statutes. The complexity of the old law with different tests applicable to cards and automatic machines was no longer relevant. The test as to gaming and a game of chance was set out in the Act and it was for the jury to determine whether on the facts the game was a game of chance as defined in the Act.

'[9] We agree with that submission. As Parliament had made a significant change of the applicable law and provided a statutory definition of a game of chance, it is, in our view, no longer necessary or helpful to refer to the old cases. In the present case, reference was made to *R v Tompson* [[1943] 2 All ER 130, [1943] 1 KB 650] before the judge; we can quite understand why, in the absence of any authority on the post-1960 regime, it was done. However, Mr Luba QC was correct in saying that it was wrong to do so.

'[10] In relation to the definition in the 1968 Act to which the judge should have sole regard, Mr Luba QC submitted that it was clear that the definition in the Act could not be applied literally; construed properly, he contended that it was clear that a game which was predominantly a game of skill was not a game of chance within the statutory definition ...

'[11] Although, for the reasons we have given we agree with Mr Luba that it was not appropriate to have regard to the old law and that the issue is one of construction of the provisions of the 1968 Act, we consider that the judge directed the jury correctly on the 1968 Act.

(i) The meaning of a game of chance set out in s 52(1) of the 1968 Act is not by its terms an exhaustive definition, as the word "include" is used. However, it does not seem to us that this was intended by Parliament to enable a more restrictive definition to be given. It is clear that Parliament could have adopted a test of preponderance; it did not and we see no reason to write into the Act a further restriction or qualification which Parliament could easily have included but which it did not.

(ii) In our view, the definition in the Act is in simple terms and needed little elaboration; it was a question of fact for the jury to determine whether on the statutory definition TH poker was a game of chance.

(iii) It may be in some cases the definition would need some elaboration. If a prosecution was brought where the element of chance was insignificant or de minimis, then it would be necessary to spell out that that element of chance should be ignored in determining whether the game is a game of chance. For example, if chance was to be used to determine which player had the right to start a game, but the game was otherwise a game of skill, then that element should be regarded as insignificant or de minimis and therefore should be ignored.

(iv) In his direction to the jury the judge may have gone further than this in favour of the appellant. He directed the jury that there must be a significant or meaningful element of chance as opposed to an element which was simply token, notional or a scintilla. In our view, as Parliament has provided that games of combined skill and chance are to be treated as games of chance without any qualification, then the only circumstance where chance should not be taken to make a game of skill and chance a game of chance is where the element of chance is such that it should on ordinary principles be ignored—that is to say where it is so insignificant as not to matter. Parliament did not provide that in a game of mixed skill and chance that the element of chance had to be significant for the game to be a game of chance; there is no reason for the courts to do so.

(v) It seems to us that the element of absurdity to which so much weight was attached on behalf of the appellant is properly catered for by ignoring chance where the element of chance is so insignificant as not to matter.

(vi) We have reached this conclusion on the basis of our interpretation of s 52(1) of the 1968 Act. It was common ground that s 52(6) was directed at the operation of games played against "the bank" such as in casinos or where gaming machines are used, as it refers to games "played otherwise than against one or more other players". It was argued on behalf of the appellant that, as Parliament had considered it necessary to refer to "superlative skill eliminating the element of chance" in relation to games played against "the bank", Parliament had envisaged courts would, in determining whether a game of combined skill and chance was a game of chance, have regard to the predominance of the elements of skill and chance. We do not consider that this in any way follows; on the contrary, on the definition of a game of chance as set out in the 1968 Act, if there was no element of chance (as that had been eliminated by superlative skill), it would not be a game of chance and skill combined. The subsection was therefore directed at bringing within the definition games against the bank where (if such exist) skill had eliminated any element of chance.

(vii) Argument was also directed to the question of whether assistance as to the statutory definition of a game of chance could be derived from s 40(2) which provided an exemption from s 3 in certain circumstances in respect of miners' welfare institutes or clubs. It was contended by the Crown that the exemption was directed in part at bridge clubs and, if the test was one of predominance of chance over skill, then that provision would have been unnecessary. We do not think that this subsection really assists either way.

(viii) We were grateful to Mr Luba for referring us to the United States and Canadian authorities. We do not think that any real help can be derived from the United States authorities where the concept of predominance has become embedded. Although the definition of game in the Canadian statute under consideration was exhaustive, the approach of the majority of the Supreme Court of Canada in *Ross v R* [(1968) 70 DLR (2d) 606, Can SC] to the construction of the Canadian legislation is very much the approach we have adopted in relation to the United Kingdom legislation; for the reasons that are evident from this judgment, we were not persuaded by the views of Spence J.' R v Kelly [2008] EWCA Crim 137, [2008] 2 All ER 840 at [1]–[6], [8]–[11], per Thomas LJ

GOODYEAR INDICATION

'[8] In *Goodyear* [*R v Goodyear* [2005] EWCA Crim 888, [2005] 3 All ER 117, [2005] 1 WLR 2532] this court introduced a procedure by which defendants can make a written application to a Crown Court for an indication of the level of sentence which the court will be minded to pass in the event of a guilty plea. The court, if minded to accede to this application, will indicate in open court the maximum sentence which it is minded to impose if a guilty plea is entered within a reasonable time. If a guilty plea is entered the court is bound to comply with this indication.' R v Transco plc [2006] EWCA Crim 838 at [8], per Lord Phillips of Worth Matravers CJ

GUIDELINE

Canada '[2] This appeal concerns the validity of Guideline 7 *Guidelines Issued by the Chairperson Pursuant to Section 159(1)(h) of the Immigration and Refugee Protection Act: Guideline 7: Concerning Preparation and Conduct of a Hearing in the Refugee Protection Division*, issued in 2003 by the Chairperson of the Board pursuant to the statutory power to "issue guidelines … to assist members in carrying out their duties": *Immigration and Refugee Protection Act*, SC 2001, c 27 (IRPA), paragraph 159(1)(h). The key paragraphs of Guideline 7 provide as follows: "In a claim for refugee protection, the standard practice will be for the R[efugee] P[rotection] O[fficer] to start questioning the claimant" (paragraph 19), although the member of the Refugee Protection Division (RPD) hearing the claim "may vary the order of questioning in exceptional circumstances" (paragraph 23).

…

'[65] An initial question is whether guidelines issued under IRPA, paragraph 159(1)(h) constitute delegated legislation, having the full force of law "hard law". If they do, Guideline 7 can no more be characterized as an unlawful fetter on members' exercise of discretion with respect to the order of questioning than could a rule of procedure to the same effect issued under IRPA, paragraph 161(1))(a): *Bell Canada v Canadian Employees Association* [2003] 1 SCR 884, at paragraph 35 (*Bell Canada*).

'[66] In my view, despite the express statutory authority of the Chairperson to issue guidelines, they do not have the same legal effects that statutory rules can have. In particular, guidelines cannot lay down a mandatory rule from which members have no meaningful degree of discretion to deviate, regardless of the facts of the particular case before them. The word "guideline" itself normally suggests some operating principle or general norm, which does not necessarily determine the result of every dispute.

'[67] However, the meaning of "guideline" in a statute may depend on context. For example, in *Friends of the Oldman River Society v Canada (Minister of Transport)* [1992] 1 SCR 3, at pages 33–37, La Forest J upheld the validity of mandatory environmental assessment guidelines issued under section 6 of the *Department of the Environment Act*, RSC, 1985, c E-10, which, he held, constituted delegated legislation and, as such, were legally binding.

'[68] In my view, *Oldman River* is distinguishable from the case before us. Section 6 of the *Department of the Environment Act* provided that guidelines were to be issued by an "order" "*arrêté*" of the Minister and approved by the Cabinet. In contrast, only rules issued by the Chairperson require Cabinet approval, guidelines "*directives*" do not. It would make little sense for IRPA to have conferred powers on the Chairperson to issue two types of legislative instrument, guidelines and rules, specified that rules must have Cabinet approval, and yet given both the same legal effect.

'[69] Guidelines issued by the Human Rights Commission pursuant to subsection 27(2) [as am. by SC 1998, c 9, s 20] of the *Canadian Human Rights Act*, RSC, 1985, c H-6, have also been treated as capable of having the full force of law, even though they are made by an independent administrative agency and are not subject to Cabinet approval: *Canada (Attorney General) v Public Service Alliance of Canada* [2000] 1 FC 146 (TD), at paragraphs 136–141; *Bell Canada*, at paragraphs 35–38.

'[70] In *Bell Canada*, LeBel J held (at paragraph 37), "[a] functional and purposive approach to the nature" of the Commission's guidelines, that they were "akin to regulations." a conclusion supported by the use of the word "*ordonnance*" in the French text of subsection 27(2) of the *Canadian Human Rights Act*. In addition, subsection 27(3) [as am. by SC 1998, c 9, s 20] expressly provides that guidelines issued under subsection 27(2) are binding on the Commission and on the person or panel assigned to inquire into a complaint of discrimination referred by the Commission under subsection 49(2) [as am. *idem*, s 27] of the Act.

'[71] In my opinion, the scheme of IRPA is different, particularly the inclusion of a potentially overlapping rule-making power and the absence of a provision that guidelines are binding on adjudicators. In addition, the word "*directives*" in the French text of paragraph 159(1)(*h*) suggests a less legally authoritative instrument than "*ordonnance*."

'[72] I conclude, therefore, that, even though issued under an express statutory grant of power, guidelines issued under IRPA, paragraph 159(1)(*h*) cannot have the same legally binding effect on members as statutory rules may.' Thamotharem v Canada *(Minister of Citizenship and Immigration)* [2008] 1 FCR 385, [2007] FCJ No 734, 2007 FCA 198 at [2], [66]–[72], per Evans JA

H

HARDSHIP

New Zealand '[64] A question arises as to the meaning of "any hardship" in s 48(d)(i) [of the Proceeds of Crime Act 1991]. *Adams* [*Adams on Criminal Law – Sentencing* (looseleaf ed)], para PC48.03 suggests that a comparison with the meaning of undue hardship in s 15(2)(b) of the Act is relevant. That section deals with the grounds for issuing a forfeiture order, stating that in making such an order the court must consider, inter alia, any undue hardship that might be caused to any person as a result of making a forfeiture order. At para PC15.05(2), the learned authors of *Adams* discuss the rationale for the undue hardship criterion:

> "Of course, when a forfeiture order is made there will always be hardship to an offender and sometimes to a third party. The word 'undue' indicates that something more than the ordinary hardship arising in consequence of the execution of the forfeiture order is intended: *Lyall v Solicitor-General* [1997] 2 NZLR 641; (1997) 15 CRNZ 1 (CA); *Solicitor-General v Sanders* (1994) 2 HRNZ 24. Indeed, even though the equivalent Australian legislation does not include the word 'undue', Australian Courts have consistently required that hardship beyond that ordinarily contemplated by the operation of the Act is called for, on the basis that otherwise the purpose of the legislation itself would be frustrated: *R v Lake* (1989) 44 A Crim R 63 (CCA NSW); *R v Haddad* (1989) 16 NSWLR 476; 42 A Crim R 304 (CCA NSW)."

'[65] Having considered the Australian authorities cited, I doubt that it is valid in the context of s 48(d)(i) to require undue hardship to be proved when the legislation refers only to "any hardship". Those authorities deal with the issue of forfeiture orders, as does s 15. That section generally contemplates the hardship to the defendant himself or herself, requiring something more than general hardship. In contrast, s 48 of the Act deals specifically with the interests of third parties, of whom a lesser standard of hardship may be required as that would not involve the defendant benefiting, nor allowing the defendant to benefit, from the proceeds of crime by having their interest recognised in the form of a variation to a restraining order.

'[66] Further, third parties who possess a legal interest in the property that is to be forfeited under s 15 have a right to apply for relief against forfeiture (see ss 17 and 18 of the Act). Those sections do not require them to prove hardship of any kind. This suggests that the legislature did not intend to impose a requirement of undue hardship across the board. Where there are different kinds of interest with regard to different kinds of orders, the appropriate standard must have been specifically considered. In s 48(d)(i) the adjective "undue" was not used. Accordingly, I conclude that there is no basis for adding a gloss to the meaning of "any hardship" in that subparagraph.

'[67] If any descriptor is to be added to the word "hardship", I prefer to use the notion of materiality. The need to establish "material hardship" would fit more comfortably with the following qualifier expression of hardship that is reasonably likely to be caused.

'[68] In any event, it is important to recognise that the hardship factor is only one of three non-exhaustive factors which must inform the court's decision as to whether it is satisfied that it is "in the public interest" to make an order excluding an interest from a restraining order.' Solicitor-General v Bartlett [2008] 1 NZLR 87 at [64]–[68], per Stevens J

HOLDS

Canada [Immigration and Refugee Protection Act, s 63(2). A Chinese citizen was issued with a Canadian permanent resident visa which was subsequently revoked but nevertheless travelled to Canada with the revoked visa.] '[4] When Ms Zhang arrived in Canada in February 2004, immigration authorities realized her visa ha[d] been revoked and referred her to an admissibility hearing. On April 3, 2004, an immigration officer found Ms Zhang inadmissible to Canada under paragraphs 20(1)(*a*) and 41(*a*) of the *Immigration and Refugee Protection Act*, SC 2001, c 27 (IRPA), …

'[5] Ms Zhang tried to appeal the officer's decision to the Immigration and Refugee Board's Immigration Appeal Division (the Board). And that is where she ran into problems. The Board has jurisdiction to hear appeals against removal orders from admissibility hearings. However, its jurisdiction is set out specifically at subsection 63(2) of the IRPA, which says:

63. …

   (2) A foreign national who <u>holds a permanent resident visa</u> may appeal to the Immigration Appeal Division against a decision at an examination or admissibility hearing to make a removal order against them. [Emphasis added.]

Thus, the section limits the Board's appeal jurisdiction to foreign nationals who hold permanent resident visas. At Ms Zhang's hearing, the Minister argued the Board had no jurisdiction under subsection 63(2). Because her visa had been revoked, the Minister said she did not "hold" a permanent resident visa.

'[6] The Board agreed with the Minister, relying on *Canada (Minister of Citizenship and Immigration) v. Hundal* [1995] 3 FC 32 (TD). In that case, Justice Marshall Rothstein found four exceptions to the general principle that once a visa is issued, it remains valid. Having one's visa revoked is one of those exceptions. Ms Zhang, for her part, argued the *Hundal* decision was no longer applicable, because it was based on the former *Immigration Act* [RSC, 1985, c I-2]. She claimed the Board had to take note of the differences between subsection 63(2) of the IRPA and its equivalent provision in the former legislation, which said [paragraph 70(2)(*b*) (as am. by RSC, 1985 (4th Supp.), c.28, s 18)]:

70. …

   (2) Subject to subsections (3) and (4), an appeal lies to the Appeal Division from a removal order or conditional removal order made against a person who

     …

   (*b*) seeks landing or entry and, at the time that a report with respect to the person was made by an immigration officer pursuant to paragraph 20(1)(*a*), <u>was in possession of a valid immigrant visa, in the case of a person seeking landing, or a valid visitor's visa, in the case of a person seeking entry</u>. [Emphasis added.]

Since paragraph 70(2)(*b*) of the *Immigration Act* included the word "valid" and subsection 63(2) of the IRPA does not, Ms Zhang argued Parliament intended to remove validity as a prerequisite for the Board's jurisdiction to hear appeals of removal orders.

'[7] The Board [*Zhang v Canada (Minister of Public Safety and Emergency Preparedness)* [2006] IADD No 64 (QL)] rejected Ms Zhang's argument, writing [at paragraph 32], "Surely, one cannot be said to be holding a permanent resident visa where the visa in question is not a valid one? Further, how can one be said to be holding a revoked visa?" While the Board acknowledged the differences between the new and old provisions, it concluded the statutory intent behind the two was largely the same. As such, it refused jurisdiction to hear Ms Zhang's appeal. This is a judicial review of that decision.

ISSUE

Does the Board have jurisdiction, under subsection 63(2) of the IRPA, to hear the appeal of a foreign national whose visa has been revoked?

ANALYSIS

'[8] The question at issue in this application is one of law. Accordingly, the Court will only defer to the Board's reasons if they were correct. Having said that, I am quite confident they were.

'[9] Ms Zhang's submissions to the Court were based on a literal reading of the IRPA. Just as she argued before the Board, she claimed that if legislators intended to limit appeals under subsection 63(2) to foreign nationals with valid permanent resident visas, they would not have cut the word "valid" from the section when they drafted the IRPA. Any case law discussing the notion of validity stemmed from the fact that validity was a legislative requirement at the time — one that no longer exists.

'[10] In compelling submissions, the Minister's counsel went through an extensive analysis of statutory interpretation. He explored the implications of adopting Ms Zhang's interpretation of subsection 63(2) under a textual, contextual and purposive analysis of both the individual provision and the IRPA as a whole. Under each scenario, Ms Zhang's interpretation of the IRPA would be inconsistent with legislative intent.

'[11] For example, under a textual analysis, courts should presume words have their ordinary meaning absent any proof to the contrary. Subsection 63(2) of the IRPA is written in the present tense, whereas the former paragraph 70(2)(*b*) was drafted in the past tense.

That Ms Zhang once "held" a permanent resident visa does not place her within the ambit of subsection 63(2), according to the Minister. The provision only applies to one "who holds" a permanent resident visa. I agree.

'[12] In a contextual analysis, one looks at a provision within the broader scheme of the Act in which it is written. Various sections of the IRPA require foreign nationals to continually demonstrate they are entitled to enter Canada. For example, under subsection 11(1) of the IRPA, a foreign national will only be issued a visa if she is not inadmissible and meets the legislative requirements. Under paragraph 20(1)(a) of the IRPA, foreign nationals trying to enter Canada must show they "hold the visa or other document required under the regulations" or they will be denied entry. Again, I fully agree with the Minister's submission that the Court would be ignoring the IRPA's overall scheme if it found Ms Zhang was someone who "holds" a permanent resident visa, despite the fact that her visa was cancelled and she would otherwise not be admitted into the country.

'[13] Under a purposive approach, one interprets statutory provisions based on Parliamentary intent. Turning to subsection 63(2), Parliament intended to give foreign nationals with legitimate permanent resident visas the chance to appeal removal orders that would have denied them entry despite having the visas. A removal order based on criminality is one example. Parliament can hardly be said to have intended that foreign nationals would be able to use visas revoked by Canadian officials in an attempt to fraudulently enter the country, and then rely on those revoked visas as a basis for their appeal rights.

'[14] As the Minister so deftly argued, Ms Zhang's analysis runs counter to the Supreme Court of Canada's decision in *Rizzo & Rizzo Shoes Ltd (Re)* [1998] 1 SCR 27, because it would lead to two absurd consequences. To find that subsection 63(2) of the IRPA applies to applicants with invalid permanent resident visas would give persons with no right to be in Canada the right to appeal a removal order denying their ability to be in Canada. Further, the same person found to violate paragraph 20(1)(a) of the IRPA for not possessing a permanent resident visa could be deemed to hold a permanent resident visa under subsection 63(2). Their right to appeal the decision would directly contradict the reason they were originally found inadmissible.

'[15] In my view, Ms Zhang's argument is based on the presumption that the best way to interpret subsection 63(2) of the IRPA is to compare it with the equivalent provision in the former *Immigration Act*. While this might be a helpful approach in certain cases, it is by no means the only means of statutory interpretation. And in this particular case, general principles of statutory interpretation make it clear that Ms Zhang's argument must fail.

'[16] If subsection 63(2) applied to "invalid" visas, like those that have been revoked, would it also apply to ones that have expired? This logic defies common sense. From reading Ms Zhang's submissions, it appears that any foreign national holding a visa in his hand would be entitled to an appeal under subsection 63(2), regardless of whether the Canadian government intended to give that document any legal effect. The fact that Ms Zhang still held the physical copy of her visa did not change the legal consequence of its revocation. Rather than pursuing an appeal of the immigration officer's removal order before the Board, she should have sought judicial review of the officer's decision in this Court. That option was still open to her, despite the fact that she did not qualify for an appeal under subsection 63(2).' Zhang v Canada *(*Minister of Citizenship and Immigration*)* [2008] 1 FCR 716, 2007 FC 593, [2007] FCJ No 795 at [4]–[16], per de Montigny J

HOLIDAY

New Zealand '[16] Air New Zealand is in dispute with its pilots over the validity of aspects of their employment agreement. The first and primary issue is whether pilots who are rostered to work on any of the 11 days defined as public holidays by s 44(1) of the Holidays Act 2003 (the Act) must be paid at time and a half. This issue requires consideration of whether those days are always public holidays under the Act. If the day on which an employee works is a public holiday, the employee must be paid at time and a half for working on that day. The debate in this case is about the effect of an agreement under s 44(2), whereby the employee observes a public holiday on another day. Air New Zealand argues that such an agreement transfers public holiday status from the s 44(1) day to the day on which the holiday is to be observed. The pilots contend that the agreement effects no such transfer and simply leads in to the alternative holiday provisions set out later in the subpart. We will refer to the day on which the public holiday is to be observed pursuant to a s 44(2) agreement in deliberately neutral terms as a s 44(2) day.

'[17] Air New Zealand argued successfully in the Court of Appeal (albeit that Court was divided) that the consequence of a s 44(2) agreement is that the day on which the holiday is observed becomes a public holiday and the original s 44(1) public holiday ceases to be a public holiday. Hence employees do not have to be paid at time and a half for working on that day because it is no longer a public holiday. The pilots challenge that interpretation, arguing that on the true construction of the legislation the s 44(1) day does not cease to be a public holiday as a consequence of a s 44(2) agreement.

...

'[55] As we have seen, the principal question is whether s 44(2) should be read as having definitional effect. If Parliament had meant to achieve that outcome we must say that it has made its point (an important one at that) most elusively. Surely if Parliament was intending to set up two materially different consequences for those who work on a s 44(1) day, it would have done so more clearly and directly. The answer must be that Parliament did not intend to achieve the outcome which Air New Zealand's argument ascribes to it. In short, we do not consider the scheme of the Act suggests that a s 44(2) agreement removes public holiday status from a s 44(1) day.

...

'[72] In view of the unfortunate complexity of this issue and the length of our reasons, we will summarise what we see as the key points. Air New Zealand argues that s 44(2) allows an employer and employee to redefine the public holidays listed in s 44(1), thereby removing from the s 44(1) day its status as a public holiday and attaching that status to another day. Thus, every time the Act uses the term "public holiday" it is referring to either a public holiday defined in s 44(1) or another day agreed by the parties under s 44(2). This strikes us as a strained and improbable thing for Parliament to have done.

'[73] First, Parliament has defined the term "public holiday" in very plain terms in s 44(1). If Parliament had intended individual employers and employees to be able to depart from that statutory definition, it would surely have empowered the parties to redefine "public holiday" in similarly clear terms. Section 44(2) does not do this.

'[74] Second, the 2003 Act was intended to herald significant changes to public holiday entitlements. There is a strong focus in the legislation and its history on the need to pay time and a half for working on a public holiday. The introduction of the time-and-a-half entitlement was the source of much debate, yet never was there any suggestion that matters could be arranged so that an employee might work on a public holiday (as defined in s 44(1)) and not be paid time and a half.

'[75] Third, and this is perhaps a rather colloquial point, "public holiday", as commonly understood, means a day on which the public at large have a day's holiday. It is not consistent with this perception to describe 17 July, for example, as a particular employee's "public holiday". There is nothing "public" about that day; it is no more than an alternative holiday. It is awkward, to say the least, to read the term "public holiday", in the 70 or so places it appears in the Act, as including any other day of the year on which a particular employee may have agreed to observe a public holiday. We decline to do so in the absence of a clear statutory direction.

'[76] The effect of Air New Zealand's argument is to undermine the concept of a "public holiday": the days listed in s 44(1) are merely default holidays having no special status. But this is totally at odds with the changes made by the 2003 Act, including the introduction of the purpose in s 3(b) of providing public holidays for the observance of days of national, religious, or cultural significance. The question what interpretation should be placed on s 44(2) is to be determined from its text and in the light of its purpose. Here text and purpose each point in the same direction. The pilots' argument is to be preferred. We cannot therefore agree with the view that prevailed below.' New Zealand Airline Pilots Association International Union of Workers Inc v Air New Zealand Ltd [2007] NZSC 89, [2008] 2 NZLR 1 at [16]–[17], [55], [72]–[76], per Tipping J

I

INCIDENTAL TO

[Supreme Court Act 1981, s 45(4). On the true construction of s 45(4) of the 1981 Act, matters were "incidental to" the jurisdiction of the Crown Court only when the powers to be exercised related to the proper dispatch of the business before it.]

'[23] Section 45 of the Supreme Court Act 1981 is headed "General jurisdiction of Crown Court", and sub-s (4) provides:

> "Subject to section 8 of the Criminal Procedure (Attendance of Witnesses) Act 1965 (substitution in criminal cases of procedure in that Act for procedure by way of subpoena) and to any provision contained in or having effect under this Act, the Crown Court shall, in relation to the attendance and examination of witnesses, any contempt of court, the enforcement of its orders and all other matters incidental to its jurisdiction, have the like powers, rights, privileges and authority as the High Court."

'[24] Mr Nicol submits that the proposed identification of the defendant in the media as the person convicted in the Crown Court is a matter "incidental to its jurisdiction", in that it flows directly from his trial in that court. If, therefore, the proposed identification would infringe the rights of the children under art 8 of the European Convention on Human Rights, s 45(4) confers upon the Crown Court "the like powers ... as the High Court" "in relation to" the proposed identification, in particular the power—indeed presumably by virtue of s 6 of the Human Rights Act 1998, the duty—to restrain it by injunction. Mr Millar, supported by Mr Tomlinson, denies that the proposed identification of the defendant in the media can possibly be described for the purposes of s 45(4) as a matter "incidental to [the] jurisdiction" of the Crown Court.

...

[29] There is a dearth of reported authority on the construction of s 45(4) of the Supreme Court Act 1981. In *Ex p HTV Cymru (Wales) Ltd* [2002] EMLR 184 Aikens J restrained a television company from interviewing witnesses who had given evidence until all the evidence was complete. He pointed out that one witness would have to be recalled, and others might be recalled, and accordingly held that the proposed interviews would constitute a contempt of court pursuant to ss 1 and 2 of the 1981 Act. He proceeded to hold that s 45(4) of the Supreme Court Act 1981 conferred upon the Crown Court the same power to make an injunction as was conferred upon the High Court by s 37 of the same Act. He observed (at [23]):

> "Of course the power of the Crown Court to grant injunctions is strictly limited to the specific matters that are set out in section 45(4). There is no general power in the Crown Court to grant injunctions. But I am satisfied that the Crown Court has the power to grant an injunction to restrain a threatened contempt of court in relation to a matter that is before the Crown Court in question."

This decision seems unimpeachable. Mr Nicol points to Aikens J's use of s 45(4) as a source of power to make an injunction such as can be made in the High Court by virtue of s 37. On the other hand Mr Millar relies on its use "to restrain a threatened contempt of court in relation to a matter that is before the Crown Court". Reasonably enough Mr Nicol responds that the judge"s words were not designed to be prescriptive of the ambit of the subsection, but to identify the particular mischief at which his order was aimed. Nevertheless Mr Millar suggests that this decision provides a prime example of the proper use of the subsection, to ensure the proper despatch of the proceedings.

'[30] In our judgment for the purposes of s 45(4), and for the reasons advanced by Mr Millar and Mr Tomlinson, matters are "incidental to" the jurisdiction of the Crown Court only when the powers to be exercised relate to the proper dispatch of the business before it. We agree with Aikens J that the Crown Court has no "general" power to grant injunctions. There is no inherent jurisdiction to do so on the basis that it is seeking to achieve a desirable, or indeed a "just and convenient" objective. Unless the proposed injunction is directly linked to the exercise of the Crown Court's jurisdiction and the exercise of its statutory functions, the appropriate jurisdiction is lacking. The order was not incidental to the defendant's trial, conviction and sentence. Accordingly, the ambit of s 45(4) of the Supreme Court Act 1981 did not extend to protect the children from the consequences of the identification of their father in the criminal proceedings before the Crown Court.' Re Trinity Mirror plc (A and another (minors acting by the Official Solicitor) intervening) [2008] EWCA Crim 50, [2008] 2 All ER 1159 at [23]–[24], [29]–[30], per Sir Igor Judge P

INSURED BY THE TERMS AND CONDITIONS OF THIS POLICY

[Professional indemnity insurance policy. Extension 3 stated: '3. Grant Thornton International [GTI] is included as an Assured Firm but solely in respect of claims made against [GTI] arising from claims made against a member firm of [GTI] insured by the terms and conditions of this policy.'] '[11] GTI's case is that extension 3 includes GTI as an assured within the insuring clauses—more particularly the second clause found in the third paragraph of part I—and that the wording of extension 3 is to be seen as a shorthand reference to that second insuring clause. "[S]olely" emphasises that GTI's cover is only in respect of that second clause. The words "arising from claims made against a member firm of [GTI]" reflect the limitation of cover under the second clause to legal liability incurred by reason of membership in GTI for any negligent act, etc, on the part of another member firm of GTI. The phrase "insured by the terms and conditions of this policy" limits the member firms of GTI whose negligent act, etc is relevant for this purpose to those insured by the policy, in a manner which, although not express in the reference to "another member firm of [GTI]" in the second clause, applies nonetheless under the second clause as a result of the definition of "Professional Services". The phrase is descriptive, rather than introductory of a positive requirement that either the claim or the member firm should be validly covered.
...
'[14] The rival arguments are finely balanced. This is a claims made policy, as its opening language in capitals emphasises; and the double use of the phrase in extension 3 may be said to point in favour of insurers' construction,

particularly when followed by the final words "insured by the terms and conditions of this policy". The phrase "claims made against a member firm of [GTI]" may be said to suggest a claim made under the policy; and to have no parallel in the second insuring clause, which does not (strictly) require a claim to have been made against the other Grant Thornton member firm, for whose negligent act, etc, the assured firm claiming indemnity is said to be liable "by reason of its membership in [GTI]". The phrase "claims made arising from" can also be read as going wider than the words "by reason of its membership in [GTI] … held liable" in the second insuring clause. The detail of the reference to being "insured by the terms and conditions of this policy" may be said to be surprising if the only intention was descriptive. Mr Colin Edelman QC in his thoughtful argument for insurers relied upon all these factors to differentiate the cover afforded by extension 3 and by the second main insuring clause. If the intention in extension 3 was in effect to add GTI as an additional assured firm under the second main insuring clause, this could, he points out, easily have been done by expanding the wording of that clause. All these are on their face points of some persuasive force.

'[15] Mr Edelman's further argument that the cover intended by extension 3 is essentially parasitic does not appear to me so persuasive. The cover under extension 1, in respect of partners and employees, etc, can be described as parasitic, and it must be limited to claims of a kind in respect of which the relevant assured firm would be insured under one of the main insuring clauses. Such part-ners and employees would have, or be expected to have, cover for other claims under the local policies taken out by member firms such as GT Italy. The effect of extensions 2, 4, 5 and 6 and indeed 8 and 9 is, on the other hand, to define who counts as an assured firm and who can therefore take advantage of the cover afforded by the insuring clauses in respect of claims made directly against them. That it seems to me is also the natural meaning of the opening phrase of extension 3, whereby "[GTI] is included as an Assured Firm".

'[16] While it is true that GTI could have been specifically added into the second insuring clause, extension 3 does not seem to me a surprising place for a provision with similar effect, bearing in mind that GTI is, on any view, only intended to be covered for some and not all policy purposes. Further, on insurers' primary construction, extension 3 does not in-clude GTI as an assured firm under the main insuring clauses, as the opening phrase of extension 3 would lead one to expect; rather it includes GTI at a higher level which requires GTI, before it has any cover, to show that some other GTI member firm has received a claim and is covered under those insuring clauses. (The only alternative proffered by Mr Edelman involved the proposition that the purpose of extension 3 might be to insure GTI as an assured firm under the first main insuring clause, against claims made in respect of international work done by other member firms, who might for this purpose be regarded as persons or entities for whose negligent act, etc, GTI "is legally responsible". Not only is this approach to extension 3 quite inconsistent with insurers' primary approach, it also applies the phrase "is legally responsible" to the relationship between GTI and member firms in an artificial manner which they would certainly not accept as correct, however much a third party might try to allege that it was so.)

'[17] The most cogent consideration on this appeal is, in my opinion, the general nature of the cover that would result from insurers' construction. The Court of Appeal took the view that the second insuring clause was likely only to be relevant in relation to international work as defined in the policy. I am not persuaded by this. Question 18 in the proposal ad-dresses the risk of liability arising from mere association in or with the GTI family. Allegations of vicarious or partnership liability of this nature, however tenuous they might appear to an English lawyer, are a foreseeable risk of such association. (Indeed, in the present New York litigation, GTI is said to be liable "as an entity … in control of [GT Italy]", ie simply because of the association between them within the Grant Thornton family or organisation. There is also a claim against GTI for violating United States securities laws, but GTI does not suggest that that this can be covered by the second insuring clause, read with extension 3.)

'[18] The scheme of the policy appears to be to cover by the first insuring clause claims against an assured firm by reason of its own negligence in respect of international work performed by it, and by the second insuring clause claims by virtue of association in the Grant Thornton family. For the purpose of the first insuring clause, international work is defined quite narrowly, as work performed (a) after being referred by another member firm, or (b) for a client of another mem-ber firm, or (c) for a subsidiary or related company of an accounting

firm after that firm becomes a member firm, or (d) at the request of another member firm, or, finally, (e) consisting in cross border floatation work for the client of another member firm. The second insuring clause provides indemnity only where an assured firm is held liable "by reasons of its membership in [GTI]", in other words where some form of partnership or vicarious liability is held to exist as between the two firms, so that one can be held liable for the other without itself being negligent or indeed having had any involvement at all in the work alleged to have been negligently performed by the latter.

'[19] All that question 18 of the proposal form asks regarding the risk of claims "by virtue of … association with [GTI] or any other member firm" is whether the local policy excludes cover for such claims. On that very limited basis, the sec-ond insuring clause then gives, on its face, full cover for all and any such claims, whatever their nature or origin. I do not think that the risk can be said to be confined to international work, still less to international work in the limited pol-icy sense.

'[20] If individual member firms are as between themselves given full cover in respect of liability for such claims incurred by reason of their membership in GTI, it would seem very odd that GTI itself should not enjoy similarly full cover in re-spect of claims holding it responsible on a vicarious or partnership for or with one of the insured member firms in its international family. The submission that this would not fit, because GTI is not, as the umbrella entity, itself a member of GTI, and that it cannot therefore incur liability "by reason of its membership in [GTI]", is formalistic in the extreme; and anyway ignores the different potential shades of meaning attaching to "[GTI]".

'[21] If insurers are right, then GTI, in respect of the acknowledged risk of claims (however tenuous) made against it, only achieved cover under this policy in two particular situations: one where a member firm received a claim relating to in-ternational work as defined, the other where a member firm was itself the recipient of a claim that it was liable for an-other member firm on some vicarious or partnership basis by reason of its membership in GTI. GTI would then have cover if, "arising from" the claim made against a member firm, GTI itself also received a claim. This limited patchwork cover would mean, on insurers' case, that GTI needed another policy insuring it for vicarious or partnership type claims arising in other circumstances, such as (it appears) the present,

In the vacuum surrounding the present policy, all that can be said is that there is no indication of any relevant gap-filling insurance, and that insurers' construction appears on any view to postulate an unlikely allocation and splitting of insurance risks.

'[22] In these circumstances, I have come to a different conclusion to the Court of Appeal. I consider that GTI's construction of extension 3 is to be preferred. It gives to GTI as an assured firm the protection of the second insuring clause, without any need to show that the claim against GT Italy is itself one which is insured under either of the two insuring clauses. This means that the phrase "insured by the terms and conditions of this policy" do[es] not relate to the earlier words "claims made", but rather to the words "a member firm of [GTI]".' Brit Syndicates Ltd v Italaudit SpA [2008] UKHL 18, [2008] 2 All ER 1140 at [11], [14]–[22], per Lord Mance

INTERNATIONAL EXHIBITION

Australia '[30] The final issue is whether the fair was "international". The ordinary and natural meaning of "international" is "of or relating to different nations or their citizens." Mr McGowan submitted, based on this definition, that an exhibition could be characterised as international either by virtue of the nationality of the goods and exhibitors or by virtue of the nationality of the visitors to the exhibition. Mr Samargis, on the other hand, put the argument that the international character of an exhibition can be determined only by reference to the goods and exhibitors.

'[31] Mr Samargis has the better argument. First, his approach is supported by what little authority there is: see *Bodenhausen* at 151. Second, his argument has the great virtue of certainty and clarity — any prospective design registrant or exhibitor would be able to ascertain with a glance at an exhibition guide or list of exhibitors the nationality of the goods and exhibitors. By contrast, lists of visitors and their nationalities are not so easily or publicly found, if at all. And one must not lose sight of the fact that the exhibitions which were the backdrop to the Paris Convention were international because of their exhibitors.

'[32] In my view an exhibition is international if there are foreign exhibitors exhibiting foreign goods (with foreign being defined as a nationality other than that in which the exhibition is hosted).

'[33] Mr Samargis also submitted that for an exhibition to be truly international it requires exhibitors from at least three nations (that is, the host country and two others). This is a departure from the ordinary dictionary definition of international. But it is an approach that sits comfortably with Professor Bodenhausen's views that for an exhibition to be international "it must include the exhibition of goods coming from foreign countries": *Bodenhausen* at 151.

'[34] … Whatever be the characteristics of an "international exhibition" they are not met by an exhibition which is essentially an Australian exhibition. In my view, for an exhibition to be international in character there must at least be a significant foreign presence.

'[35] I should explain what I mean by "significant foreign presence." First, the quantitative presence of foreign exhibitors, both in relative and absolute terms (here 7 exhibitors out of 257), is a factor. The greater the foreign presence, the more likely it is that an exhibition will be an "international exhibition." Second, the quality of the foreign exhibitors is a factor; and by "quality" I mean both the geographic location and the importance of the foreign state(s) in the relevant industry. For example, if an exhibition is held in Canada and the only foreign exhibitors or goods are from the United States (or if, as in this case, the exhibition is held in Australia and the only foreign exhibitors are from New Zealand), the exhibition is more likely to be a "regional exhibition" rather than an "international exhibition." On the other hand, if a fashion exhibition is held in Australia and the only foreign exhibitors are from Italy or France (or, for example, if a computer software exhibition is held in the US and the only foreign exhibitors are from India or China), the exhibition is likely to be an "international exhibition" due to the importance of those countries in the fashion design field (or computer industry) and the geographic separation between the states involved. This, of course, cannot be, and is not intended to be, an exhaustive list of the factors, or the way they might be applied in combination, to determine whether an exhibition had a "significant foreign presence" so as to make it an international exhibition.' Chiropedic Bedding Pty Ltd v Radburg Pty Ltd [2007] FCA 1869, (2007) 243 ALR 334, (2007) 74 IPR 398, BC200710390 at [30]–[35], per Finkelstein J

INTERVIEW

Australia [Criminal Code (WA) s 579(1).] '[47] Beyond the clarification that "interview" means an "interview with a suspect by … a member of the Police Force", the Criminal Code does not otherwise define the word "interview". The court was taken to a number of dictionary definitions, none of which provided a clear resolution to the present case. The appellant contended that "interview" connoted a "formal, unhurried interrogation procedure directed to the investigation of crime", as opposed to a chat, informal banter, or talk carried out in an atmosphere of informality. In part, this proffered definition was derived from dicta in the judgment of Wright J in *R v McKenzie* [[1999] TASSC 36 at [14]]. In that case certain admissions were ruled inadmissible because they were not recorded by videotape, not for the absence of an "interview".

'[48] The appellant submitted that a mere conversation would not suffice to constitute an "interview". To this end, the appellant pointed to the absence of any definition such as that found in s 74C of the Summary Offences Act 1953 (SA), in which "interview" is defined to include:

(a) a conversation; or
(b) part of a conversation; or
(c) a series of conversations ...

This comparison of the South Australian and Western Australian provisions is of doubtful utility. The South Australian provisions were inserted in 1995 by s 5 of the Statutes Amendment (Recording of Interviews) Act 1995 (SA), well after the enactment in 1992 of the relevant Western Australian provisions. The most that could be said is that the South Australian provision might tend to highlight an ambiguity in the Western Australian one, but it does nothing to resolve that ambiguity one way or the other. The inclusion of conversations in the South Australian definition says nothing about whether they are to be excluded from the Western Australian provision, which is silent on the matter.

'[49] The appellant also contended that the "formality" of an interview required a "meeting of minds" about the nature, context and purpose of the discussion. However, that phrase is more likely to mislead than assist. The absence of a "meeting of minds" might indicate that the appellant's admissions were involuntary, or that they were elicited by unfair deception. Such cases can and should be dealt with under the common law exclusionary rules. They are not matters which touch upon the definition of "interview".

'[50] Even if it be accepted that the term "interview" connotes a degree of formality, it is not apparent where that line is to be drawn. The conversation between the appellant and the police officers in the present case was no mere informal

chit-chat: the police officers fell in with the appellant's style of speech, but they structured the relevant part of the conversation as a patient and deliberate sequence of questions and answers designed to elicit admissions. However, there is much force in the observation of Ormiston J in *R v Raso* [(1993) 115 FLR 319 at 348] that:

> ... it would be difficult to identify that form of questioning which constitutes an "interview" and that which constitutes some less formal kind of questioning in circumstances where the questions are being administered by the police ...

Raso concerned the meaning of s 23V(1) of the Crimes Act 1914 (Cth), which at that time included the phrase "interviewed as a suspect". That legislation concerned the tape recording of such interviews, and Ormiston J considered it (1993) 115 FLR 319 at 348]:

> ... artificial, and possibly conducive to the abuses which the legislation is trying to avert, to draw distinctions between questioning which takes place on a relatively casual basis and questioning which results from some formal or organised interview.

'[51] The same is true of the present case. Contrary to the appellant's submissions, neither logic nor the text of Ch LXA justifies the conclusion that "formality" requires that the suspect appreciate that the conversation was being recorded and that its contents could be used as evidence against him. Rather, in an appropriate case these matters may attract the common law exclusionary rules relating to involuntariness, unfairness or public policy.

'[52] In the absence of textual indicia, the appellant turned to argument based on what was said to be the purpose of Ch LXA. This was said to be "to facilitate formality and propriety throughout the interview ... process" and hence to "serve" the "protection and preservation of the integrity of the interview process generally". The appellant submitted that the "evident policy of the statutory regime" was that evidence of the appellant's admissions be inadmissible, as part of the "broader imperative" of the statute, namely to ensure the "formality" of the interview process and hence its "integrity". The appellant did not otherwise indicate, however, what this formality would require, nor did he indicate how it was to be manifested beyond the suggested requirements that a suspect be cautioned and consent before any interview is videotaped.

'[53] It is difficult to see how any such policy of "formality" is evident either in the statute itself or in the extrinsic legislative materials. The term "interview" is largely undefined and on its face Ch LXA is unconcerned with the conduct of interviews beyond the requirement that they be videotaped if admissions made during them are to be admissible. Contrary to the appellant's contentions, nothing in the text or structure of the Chapter evinces any broader purpose of regulating the conduct of interviews. The textual indicia of Ch LXA all relate to the regulation of *videotapes* — their use, distribution and so forth — but not the regulation of interviews.

'[54] Moreover, a consideration of the relevant extrinsic materials confirms this textual conclusion. In his second reading speech, the Attorney-General stated that the Bill that inserted Ch LXA:

> ... makes provision with respect to the increasing use of video recordings of police interviews for indictable offences ... [and] will ensure that in serious cases an accused's confession will be inadmissible unless it has been videotaped. Exceptions to this rule will be permitted, subject to the court's discretion, to receive evidence of admissions which have not been video-taped, if this is in the interests of justice.

'[55] Further, the appellant did not point to any passage in any of the reports which led to the enactment of legislation similar to s 570D supportive of his submission that their goal was to ensure the "formality" and "integrity" of the interview process.

'[56] Even if the appellant were correct about the policy underlying Ch LXA of the Criminal Code, his construction of the term "interview" is inconsistent with his submission as to that underlying statutory purpose. If indeed Ch LXA is aimed at preserving the integrity of police procedure more generally, it seems odd that the requirement of videotaping should apply only to a vaguely defined subset of interactions between police and suspects, namely "formal" interviews. To the contrary, the text of the statute and its legislative history point towards its purpose as being the encouragement of video recording,

and the expansion — and not restriction — of the circumstances in which video recording was appropriate.

...

'[59] One textual indicium in Ch LXA of this policy is the very choice of the word "interview", rather than merely "admission", in the definition of "videotape". The statutory definition would not be satisfied, for example, by a videotape that recorded only a string of admissions without the surrounding context of the interview during which they were made. In the present case, however, the jury was presented by the playing of Ex 17 with the near entirety of the appellant's interactions with police.

'[60] The consequence of acceptance of the appellant's submissions on the meaning of "interview" would not be that *no* evidence of an admission is admissible unless it be on "videotape". Rather, the consequence would be that the admission might be proved by evidence inferior to and less accurate than a videotape, as long as the prosecution can satisfy the court of the existence of a "reasonable excuse". This result would be to turn the "best evidence rule" on its head.

'[61] The vice to which the appellant's construction leads is that police officers could attempt to evade the statute by informal off-camera discussions with suspects during which unrecorded admissions were made, in the belief that the requirement of videotaping did not apply to "informal" discussions and that the circumstances would provide a "reasonable excuse" within the meaning of para (b) of s 570D(2).

'[62] The appellant's challenge based on the definition of "interview" fails. The Court of Appeal was correct in determining that the meaning of "interview" encompassed any conversation between a member of the police force and a suspect, and included an informal conversation initiated by the suspect.' Carr v Western Australia [2007] HCA 47, (2007) 239 ALR 415, BC200708991 at [47]–[56], [59]–[62], per Gummow, Heydon and Crennan JJ

J

JUDICIAL POWER

Australia [Corporations Act 2001 (Cth), s 657A(2)(b).] '[53] The focus of this appeal is the provision, in s 657A(2)(b), that the panel [the Takeovers Panel] may declare circumstances to be unacceptable circumstances, if it appears to the panel that the circumstances are unacceptable because they constitute a contravention of a provision of Chs 6, 6A, 6B or 6C. The Full Court of the Federal Court of Australia (Gyles and Lander JJ, Finkelstein J dissenting) held that s 657A(2)(b) is invalid because it purports to confer on the panel the judicial power of the Commonwealth. These reasons will show that the impugned provision does not purport to confer on the panel the judicial power of the Commonwealth. ...

'[93] As *Brandy* [*Brandy v Human Rights and Equal Opportunity Commission* (1995) 183 CLR 245, 127 ALR 1, 37 ALD 340, [1995] HCA 10] demonstrated, and has been recognised since the very earliest decisions of this court about Ch III,111 no single combination of necessary or sufficient factors identifies what is judicial power. So much is made plain by the so-called chameleon doctrine [*R v Quinn; Ex p Consolidated Foods Corp* (1977) 138 CLR 1 at 8, 16 ALR 569 at 572, 1A IPR 537 at 547] and the cases in which that doctrine has been engaged.

[94] In *R v Trade Practices Tribunal; Ex parte Tasmanian Breweries Pty* Ltd [(1970) 123 CLR 361 at 374, [1970] ALR 449 at 452] in a passage often since applied in this court, Kitto J said:

[A] judicial power involves, as a general rule, a decision settling for the future, as between defined persons or classes of persons, a question as to the existence of a right or obligation, so that an exercise of the power creates a new charter by reference to which that question is in future to be decided as between those persons or classes of persons. In other words, the process to be followed must generally be an inquiry concerning the law as it is and the facts as they are, followed by an application

of the law as determined to the facts as determined; and the end to be reached must be an act which, so long as it stands, entitles and obliges the persons between whom it intervenes, to observance of the rights and obligations that the application of law to facts has shown to exist.

'[95] In *Tasmanian Breweries*, the legislation in issue (the Trade Practices Act 1965 (Cth)) did not require the relevant tribunal to adjudicate upon any claim of right but did render unenforceable the restriction or practice found to be contrary to the public interest. But as Kitto J went on to say [at CLR 378, ALR 454–455]:

The determination [by the tribunal] itself has no operative effect: it constitutes the factum by reference to which the Act operates to alter the law in relation to the particular case. And an order under s 52 (or an interim restraining order under s 54) is in like case. It presents a direct contrast with an injunction granted by a court as a means of enforcing obligations that have been established by adjudication. The order restrains future conduct, not as being in breach of ascertained obligations, but as being in conformity with ascertained obligations or practices – not in order to ensure observance of them but to prevent observance of them, because it is considered that their observance would be against the public interest. The Act, particularly s 52(7), operates upon the order to give its provisions the force of law, and thus to alter the law for the future in relation to the particular case.

'[96] The features of the legislation in issue in *Tasmanian Breweries* which were identified in that case are also to be observed in the relevant provisions of the Corporations Act. The panel is required to conclude whether a declaration of unacceptable circumstances should be made. If s 657A(2)(b) is engaged, the panel must decide, along the way, whether there has been a contravention of a relevant provision of the Corporations Act. But if it does decide that there has been a contravention, the conclusion to which the panel must ultimately come is whether identified circumstances should be declared unacceptable. In making a declaration, or orders consequent upon a declaration, the panel does not create a charter for the observance of the rights and obligations that attach to the contravention. The panel's powers to make orders expressly exclude the power to make "an order directing a person to comply with a requirement of Ch 6, 6A, 6B or 6C" [s 657D(2)]. The charter that is established by the panel's order is for the observance of the rights and obligations that are created in consequence of a declaration being made. For, if a declaration is made, an order is framed to prevent the consequences of what have been found to be unacceptable circumstances. The order is framed to prevent those consequences by "protect[ing] the rights or interests of any person affected by the circumstances" [s 657D(2)(a)] or by "ensur[ing] that a takeover bid or proposed takeover bid … proceeds (as far as possible) in a way that it would have proceeded if the circumstances had not occurred" [s 657D(2)(b)]. The order constitutes the new charter of rights and obligations of the parties. And the Corporations Act "operates upon the order to give its provisions the force of law, and thus to alter the law for the future in relation to the particular case" [*R v Trade Practices Tribunal; Ex p Tasmanian Breweries Pty Ltd* (1970) 123 CLR 361 at 378, [1970] ALR 449 at 454–455].

'[97] It is then for the courts in the exercise of judicial power to enforce the law as it has been framed by the panel's orders. There is what was identified in *Brandy* [at CLR 261, ALR 11, ALD 348–349] as "an independent exercise of judicial power" to give effect to the panel's orders.'[98] The orders of the panel stand in sharp contrast with the determinations of the Human Rights and Equal Opportunity Commission considered in *Brandy*. By the provisions of the Racial Discrimination Act 1975 (Cth) in issue in *Brandy*, the commission's determination, when registered as it had to be, was binding upon the parties and enforceable as an order of the Federal Court. But the determination remained the determination of the commission and in no sense became the determination of the Federal Court. Under the relevant provisions of the Corporations Act, the

binding effect of the orders of the panel is determined by the court which is called upon to decide whether orders should be made under s 657G to secure compliance with them or to decide whether there has been an offence committed under s 657F by a person contravening a valid order of the panel.

'[99] This analysis of the effect of the relevant provisions requires the conclusion that the panel does not exercise the judicial power of the Commonwealth.

'[100] It is important, however, to notice one further consideration which strengthens the case for validity of the impugned provisions. Although the Corporations Act gives an order of the panel the force of law and makes contravention of the panel's order an offence, an order of the panel is open to challenge. It is open to direct challenge by proceedings under s 75(v) of the Constitution or proceedings seeking relief under s 39B of the Judiciary Act. No less importantly, an order of the panel is open to collateral challenge in other judicial proceedings in which its valid making is an element in issue. That an order of the panel may be challenged in these ways points away from a conclusion that the panel exercises judicial power.

'[101] For these reasons, the Full Court erred in holding that s 657A(2)(b) was invalid as purporting to confer the judicial power of the Commonwealth on the panel.' A-G *(Cth)* v Alinta Ltd [2008] HCA 2, (2008) 242 ALR 1, (2008) 64 ACSR 507, BC200800208 at [53], [93]–[101], per Hayne J

JUSTIFIED

Canada '[40] Subsection 6(2) of the NOC Regulations [Patented Medicines (Notice of Compliance) Regulations, SOR/93–133] require a determination by the Court as to whether the applicant has demonstrated that "none of those allegations is justified."

'[41] The meaning of the word "justified" or in the French language "fondée", was considered by the Federal Court of Appeal in *Procter & Gamble Pharmaceuticals Canada Inc v Canada (Minister of Health)* [2005] 2 FCR 269. It means the ordinary civil burden on a balance of probabilities.' G D Searle & Co v Novopharm Ltd [2008] 1 FCR 477, [2007] FCJ No 120, 56 CPR (4th) 1 at [40]–[41], per Hughes J

L

LEARNING DISABILITY

'Learning disability' means a state of arrested or incomplete development of the mind which includes significant impairment of intelligence and social functioning. (Mental Health Act 1983, s 1(4) (added by the Mental Health Act 2007, s 2(3), as from a day to be appointed))

LIKELY TO BE USEFUL TO A PERSON COMMITTING OR PREPARING AN ACT OF TERRORISM

[Under the Terrorism Act 2000, s 58, a person commits an offence if (a) he collects or makes a record of information of a kind likely to be useful to a person committing or preparing an act of terrorism, or (b) he possesses a document or record containing information.] '[2] Count one of the indictment alleges that on 17 July 2005 the appellant "possessed records containing information of a kind likely to be useful to a person committing or preparing an act of terrorism, namely a CD rom containing a copy of the Al Qaeda training manual". Count two charges the appellant with possession of a copy of a publication called *Zaad-e-Mujahid* on 9 May 2007, count three with possession of a copy of another publication, *The Absent Obligation*, on the same date. Each is alleged to "contain information likely to be useful to a person committing or preparing an act of terrorism".

'[3] The title of the material the subject of the first count speaks for itself. *Zaad-e-Mujahid* is a text directed to the formation and organisation of Jihad movements, to the training requirements for the armed wing of Jihad movements and to the "Attributes and Qualities of Mujahideen". *The Absent Obligation* is in simple terms a text which argues that a Muslim is under an obligation to work for the establishment of an Islamic State.

'[4] It was submitted before the judge that s 58 is insufficiently certain to comply with the common law or with art 7 of the European Convention for the Protection of Human Rights and Fundamental Freedoms 1950 (as set out in Sch 1 to the Human Rights Act 1998), secondly that s 58 was never intended to cover the possession of theological or propagandist material such as *Zaad-e-Mujahid* or *The Absent Obligation*. We have the benefit of a note of the learned judge's ruling. He ruled in relation to the first submission that "likely to be useful to" and "reasonable excuse" are normal everyday terms, that a jury would be perfectly able to determine whether the material, the subject of the counts in the indictment, was material likely to be useful to a terrorist, and possessed by the appellant without reasonable excuse, and that accordingly the offence was sufficiently certain. As to the second submission, the note of his ruling is in the following terms:

'Whether possession of the article crosses the line into illegality depends on the circumstances of the case and is all about the context in which it is found. That is a matter for a jury to decide in each case and not me. Here, the material, the prosecution submit is material capable of amounting to use for a terrorist without reasonable excuse. Whether a jury so find is a matter for them. Counts 2 and 3, the material may be innocent in itself ..."

'[5] In his challenge to the ruling, Mr Moloney, who also appeared for the appellant before Judge Stewart QC, again submitted that that s 58 was insufficiently certain, and that in any event it was never intended to criminalise the possession of theological or propagandist material.

'[6] As to the issue of certainty, he invited our attention to the speech of Lord Bingham of Cornhill in *R v Goldstein, R v Rimmington* [2005] UKHL 63, [2006] 2 All ER 257, [2006] 1 AC 459 in which the relevant principles were addressed at [32]–[35]. In essence Mr Moloney submitted that s 58 is insufficiently certain in its terms for a person to be able to regulate his conduct, even with appropriate advice, so as to ensure that he does not fall foul of the criminal law. He argued that the term "likely to be of use to" is so broad, so undefined in common law or statute, as to criminalise the possession of a myriad items of information. He sought to support his argument by reference to the factual background to the proceedings. The appellant was not initially charged in relation to the material the subject of counts two and three, the additional charges were laid at the committal proceedings at the instigation of the Crown Prosecution Service. Mr Moloney submitted that it was clear from statements made by them in the interviews under caution that the officers from the anti-terrorist branch were uncertain as to whether possession of such publications could found a charge under s 58.

'[7] As to his second submission, namely that s 58 was never intended to embrace the possession of theological or propagandist material, Mr Moloney reminded us that the offences of collecting, recording or possessing information likely to be of use to terrorists have existed for some time in Northern Ireland (see s 21 of the Northern Ireland Prevention of Terrorism (Temporary Provisions) Act 1978 and latterly s 33 of the Northern Ireland (Emergency Provisions) Act 1996). He submitted that there has never been any suggestion that those provisions were designed to criminalise the possession of propaganda or theological material. He also argued that if they had been designed to have such an effect, it is inconceivable that Parliament would have thought it necessary to enact ss 1 and 2 of the Terrorism Act 2006, which created offences relating to the dissemination of terrorist publications.

'[8] We explored with Mr Jonathan Sharp, who appeared both before the judge and us on behalf of the Crown, what the Crown's case was (i) as to the ambit of the phrase 'of a kind likely to be useful to a person committing or preparing an act of terrorism' and (ii) as to the criteria for determining whether the possessor has 'a reasonable excuse for his ... possession'. Regrettably it seemed to us that he was considering these questions for the first time, so that he was not in a position to give us a considered response.

'[9] As to the first question, we asked whether (i) the information had on its face to be the kind of information that would raise a reasonable suspicion that it might be intended to be used for the commission or preparation of an act of terrorism or alternatively (ii) whether it was open to the prosecution to rely on extrinsic evidence to show that the information was intended to be used for the commission of an act of terrorism. Mr Sharp replied that the latter was the Crown's case. Thus an *A to Z* of London

would fall within the scope of the section if the person possessing it intended to provide it to a terrorist so that he could find his way to the place where a planned act of terrorism was to take place. It seems likely that the judge accepted such a submission when he held that whether possession of the article crossed the line into illegality depended on the circumstances of the case and the context in which it was found.

'[10] As to the question of what constituted a reasonable excuse, Mr Sharp submitted that this meant a purpose for possessing the information that was lawful. We asked Mr Sharp whether this meant that a defendant could properly be convicted under s 58 if he explained that he possessed information as to how to make explosives for the purpose of committing a bank robbery. Mr Sharp had no ready answer to that question.

'[11] We had a further question for Mr Sharp that it seemed to us was raised by the facts of this case. Was it the Crown's case that a document that exhorted the reader to commit acts of terrorism fell within the definition of a document "containing information of a kind likely to be useful to a person committing or preparing an act of terrorism"? Mr Sharp replied that it was.

'[12] We do not accept Mr Sharp's submissions as to the scope of s 58. It is helpful to consider them in the light of the provisions of the first part of s 2 of the 2006 Act [Terrorism Act 2006]. This provides:

> "(1) A person commits an offence if he engages in conduct falling within subsection (2) and, at the time he does so—(a) he intends an effect of his conduct to be a direct or indirect encouragement or other inducement to the commission, preparation or instigation of acts of terrorism; (b) he intends an effect of his conduct to be the provision of assistance in the commission or preparation of such acts; or (c) he is reckless as to whether his conduct has an effect mentioned in paragraph (a) or (b).
>
> (2) For the purposes of this section a person engages in conduct falling within this subsection if he—(a) distributes or circulates a terrorist publication; (b) gives, sells or lends such a publication; (c) offers such a publication for sale or loan; (d) provides a service to others that enables them to obtain, read, listen to or look at such a publication, or

to acquire it by means of a gift, sale or loan; (e) transmits the contents of such a publication electronically; or (f) has such a publication in his possession with a view to its becoming the subject of conduct falling within any of paragraphs (a) to (e).

(3) For the purposes of this section a publication is a terrorist publication, in relation to conduct falling within subsection (2), if matter contained in it is likely—(a) to be understood, by some or all of the persons to whom it is or may become available as a consequence of that conduct, as a direct or indirect encouragement or other inducement to them to the commission, preparation or instigation of acts of terrorism; or (b) to be useful in the commission or preparation of such acts and to be understood, by some or all of those persons, as contained in the publication, or made available to them, wholly or mainly for the purpose of being so useful to them …

(5) For the purposes of this section the question whether a publication is a terrorist publication in relation to particular conduct must be determined—(a) as at the time of that conduct; and (b) having regard to both the contents of the publication as a whole and to the circumstances in which that conduct occurs."

'[13] We draw attention to the contrast between sub-ss (3)(a) and (b). On Mr Sharp's submission s 58 of the 2000 Act covers documents described in either sub-s (3)(a) or (b). We consider that it is plain from the language of s 58 that it covers only documents that fall within the description in sub-s (3)(b). A document or record will only fall within s 58 if it is of a kind that is likely to provide practical assistance to a person committing or preparing an act of terrorism. A document that simply encourages the commission of acts of terrorism does not fall within s 58.

'[14] The provisions of s 2 of the 2006 Act, and in particular those of s 2(5), require the jury to have regard to surrounding circumstances when deciding whether a publication is likely to be useful in the commission or preparation of acts of terrorism. Contrary to Mr Sharp's submission, we do not consider that the same is true of s 58 of the 2000 Act. The natural meaning of that section requires that a document or record that infringes it must contain information of such a nature as to raise a reasonable suspicion that it is intended to be used to assist in the preparation or commission of an act of terrorism. It must be information that calls for an explanation. Thus the section places on the person possessing it the obligation to provide a reasonable excuse. Extrinsic evidence may be adduced to explain the nature of the information. Thus had the defendant in *R v Rowe* [2007] EWCA Crim 635, [2007] 3 All ER 36, [2007] QB 975 been charged under s 58, evidence could have been admitted as to the nature of the substitution code possessed by the defendant. What is not legitimate under s 58 is to seek to demonstrate, by reference to extrinsic evidence, that a document, innocuous on its face, is intended to be used for the purpose of committing or preparing a terrorist act.

'[15] As for the nature of a "reasonable excuse", it seems to us that this is simply an explanation that the document or record is possessed for a purpose other than to assist in the commission or preparation of an act of terrorism. It matters not that that other purpose may infringe some other provision of the criminal or civil law.

'[16] If s 58 is interpreted in accordance with this judgment, its effect will not be so uncertain as to offend against the doctrine of legality. It follows that this prosecution does not involve an abuse of process on that ground. …' R v K [2008] EWCA Crim 185, [2008] 3 All ER 526 at [2]–[16], per LORD Phillips of Worth Matravers CJ

M

MANAGEMENT

In connection with the ... management ... of a company

'[11] The power of the court to make an order disqualifying a defendant from acting as a director of a company following conviction on indictment is to be found in s 2(1) of the Company Directors Disqualification Act 1986 which, so far as relevant, provides:

> "The court may make a disqualification order against a person where he is convicted of an indictable offence (whether on indictment or summarily) in connection with the ... management ... of a company."

'[12] Mr Krolick submits that this offence of assisting the retention of criminal property through the client account was not an offence in connection with the management of a company. He says that the appellant was not the manager of the company; he was not convicted of operating either that company or any other company for the purpose of the fraud; he has done no more than to receive sums of money and to shelter them, and that it was immaterial to that offence whether he received them from a company or from an individual criminal.

'[13] The meaning of s 2(1) was carefully considered by this court in *R v Goodman* [1993] 2 All ER 789, [1994] 1 BCLC 349. In the judgment given by Staughton LJ this court said this ([1993] 2 All ER 789 at 792, [1994] 1 BCLC 349 at 352–353):

> "There are three possible ways of looking at the test to be applied. The first might be to say that the indictable offence referred to in the 1986 Act must be an offence of breaking some rule of law as to what must be done in the management of a company or must not be done. Examples might be keeping accounts or filing returns and such matters. It is clear from the authorities that the section is not limited in that way ... Another view might be that the indictable offence must be committed in the course of

managing the company. That would cover cases such as [*R v Georgiou* (1988) 87 Cr App R 207, *R v Corbin* (1984) 6 Cr App R (S) 17 and *R v Austen* (1985) 7 Cr App R (S) 214]. What the defendants in all those cases were doing was managing the company so that it carried out unlawful transactions. The third view would be that the indictable offence must have some relevant factual connection with the management of the company. That, in our judgment, is the correct answer. It is perhaps wider than the test applied in the three cases we have mentioned, because in those cases there was no need for the court to go wider than in fact it did. But we can see no ground for supposing that Parliament wished to apply any stricter test ..."

The precise facts of that case are not greatly analogous with the present. The appellant in that case, who was the chairman of a company, used his knowledge of its affairs to commit an offence of insider trading, but it is to be observed that the offence which he committed was, at least arguably, and in our view plainly, not an offence committed via the management of the company but it nevertheless had a relevant factual connection with the management of the company.

'[14] The question in the present case is whether this sheltering of criminal property by the appellant had a relevant factual connection with the management of Pentagon Securities. It seems to us that it did. What were being sheltered were the criminal proceeds of fraud obtained through the vehicle of the company. Moreover, the relevant factual connection was with the financial management of Pentagon. The appellant made available his client account as a private banking facility for the assets of Pentagon so that those who managed it could manage its affairs by placing its funds there rather than in the bank. The assets were in fact criminal proceeds. He suspected that they were and he received them in circumstances in which no further disbursement of them could be made by those who managed Pentagon's financial (and criminal) affairs without his participation. That as it seems to us is quite sufficient relevant factual connection between the financial management of Pentagon and the offence which the appellant committed. It is not, as *R v Goodman* makes clear, necessary that the offence be committed by the defendant himself using the company as a vehicle for fraud, though that of course is another situation in which a disqualification order is appropriate.

'[15] It follows that our conclusion is that the judge was entitled to disqualify. Mr Krolick alternatively submits that he should not have done so, or not for so long. The appellant is a man of not inconsiderable assets, even after a confiscation order of a little over £1m has been satisfied. Those assets are held, as we understand it, by various private companies controlled and managed by him. The assets are no doubt substantially property and the properties are managed through the companies. Mr Krolick submits that the public do not need any protection from the appellant in the management of those companies. There has never been any criticism of criminal conduct in the course of the management of them. He reminds us of the observations of Potter LJ in *R v Edwards* [1998] 2 Cr App R (S) 213 at 215, namely:

> "The rationale behind the power to disqualify is the protection of the public from the activities of persons who, whether for reasons of dishonesty, or of naivety or incompetence in conjunction with the dishonesty of others, may use or abuse their role and status as a director of a limited company to the detriment of the public."

'[16] It seems to us that the judge was perfectly entitled to say that the appellant fell within that category. It may well be true that there is no criticism of his management of his private companies, but there is every reason to criticise him for other company-related offences. First, the serious money laundering of nearly £1m; and secondly, the offences in New York.' R v Creggy [2008] EWCA Crim 394, [2008] 3 All ER 91 at [11]–[16], per Hughes LJ

MANTRAP

[Offences against the Person Act, 1861, s 31.] '[11] … Mantraps take many forms, although the most common is something like a large bear trap, with steel springs armed with teeth which meet on the victim's leg and trap him. Both spring guns and mantraps appear to involve the deployment of stored energy, and this consideration led Mr Magarian to reject the

suggestion in argument that a disguised deep hole dug in the ground with a vicious spike or spikes fixed at the bottom would constitute a mantrap. While we are inclined to agree that a shallow hole, on its own, might not do so, probably because it would not be calculated to inflict grievous bodily harm, as a matter of statutory construction, notwithstanding the concession by the Crown in *R v Munks* [1963] 3 All ER 757, [1964] 1 QB 304, we entertain no doubt that a deep hole containing potentially lethal spikes would fall within the description "mantrap". The legislation is not confined to objects which operate through "stored energy".' R v Cockburn [2008] EWCA Crim 316, [2008] 2 All ER 1153 at [11], per Sir Igor Judge P

MATERIALLY LARGER

[Under the relevant Green Belt policy for Metropolitan Open Land ('MOL') (Planning Policy Guidance 2: Green Belts (PPG 2)) one category of permitted development was 'limited extension, alteration or replacement of existing dwellings', provided that the new dwelling is not materially larger than the dwelling it replaces (para 3.6 of PPG 2).] '[13] The issue is a short one: whether the "materially larger" test imports, solely or primarily, a simple comparison of the size of the existing and proposed buildings; or whether it requires a broader planning judgment as to whether the new building would have a materially greater impact than the existing building on the interests which MOL policy is designed to protect. Mr Elvin QC's case, in a nutshell, is that, in the context of policies designed to protect the MOL, the development cannot said to be "materially" larger, if the increase has no "material" impact on the objectives of the MOL; or at least that the authority could reasonably take that view.

…

'[33] Mr Elvin's case can be simply and attractively stated. The word "material" is deeply embedded in planning law as meaning "material in planning terms". It is a settled principle that matters of planning judgment, including the weight if any to be given to "material" considerations are for the local planning authority not the courts (see Lord Hoffmann's discussion of "Materiality and planning merits" in *Tesco Stores Ltd v Secretary of State for the Environment* [1995] 2 All ER 636 at 657–658, [1995] 1 WLR 759 at 780–781). The authority correctly identified the increased size of the building, in all its aspects, as a relevant consideration in accordance with the MOL policy, but they decided that on the facts of the case it was not "material". That was a judgment for them, and involves no issue of law justifying the intervention of the court.

'[34] Although I see the force of that submission, it ignores the context in which the word is used. The words "materially larger" in para 3.6 should not be read in isolation. There are two important aspects of the context. First is that para 3.6 is concerned with the definition of "appropriate development", as contrasted with inappropriate development, which is "by definition harmful to the Green Belt" ... This first stage of the analysis is concerned principally with categorisation rather than individual assessment.

'[35] As Mr Elvin points out, the distinction is far from clear-cut. He is able to point, for example, to the sports and cemeteries category ..., where one part of the test is whether the particular uses "preserve the openness of the Green Belt" and "do not conflict with the purposes of including land in it". Even more pertinent, perhaps, is the category of "redevelopment of major existing developed sites". There "appropriateness" depends on meeting the criteria set out in Annex C1 para C4, including a requirement that redevelopment should "have no greater impact than the existing development on the openness of the Green Belt and the purposes of including land in it." To my mind, however, those examples point a contrast with the narrower language of para 3.6. The test is whether the replacement is "materially larger". Had it been intended to make appropriateness dependent on a broad "no greater impact" test, as in Annex C1, the same words could have been used. Instead the emphasis is on relative size, not relative visual impact.

'[36] That leads to the second aspect of the context, which is that of para 3.6 itself. It is part of the test for a category which covers "limited extension, alteration or replacement ...". "Limited" to my mind implies a limitation of size. Paragraph 3.6 deals with both extension and replacement. An extension must be "proportionate" to the size of "the *original* building". The emphasis given to the word "original" shows how tightly this is intended to be drawn, in order presumably to avoid a gradual accretion of extensions, each arguably "proportionate". It would be impossible, in my view, to argue that "proportionate" in this context is unrelated to relative size. For example, an extension three times the size of the original, however beautifully and unobtrusively designed, could not, in my view, be regarded as "proportionate" in the ordinary sense of that word.

'[37] The words "replacement" and "not materially larger" must be read together and in the same context. So read, I do not think that the meaning of the word "material", notwithstanding its use in planning law more generally, can bear the weight which the authority sought to give it. Size as Sullivan J said is the primary test. The general intention is that the new building should be similar in scale to that which it replaces. The *Surrey Homes* case [*Surrey Homes Ltd v Secretary of State for Environment* (18 August 2000, unreported), QBD] illustrates why some qualification to the word "larger" is needed. A small increase may be significant or insignificant in planning terms, depending on such matters as design, massing and disposition on the site. The qualification provides the necessary flexibility to allow planning judgment and common sense to play a part, and it is not a precise formula. However, that flexibility does not justify stretching the word "materially" to produce a different, much broader test. As has been seen, where the authors of PPG 2 intend a broader test, the intention is clearly expressed.

'[38] For these reasons, which are in line with those of Sullivan J, I conclude that the council misunderstood and misapplied MOL policy. Had they properly understood the policy, in my view, they could not reasonably have concluded that a building more than twice as large as the original (in terms of floor space, volume and footprint) was not "materially larger." ' R (on the application of the Heath and Hampstead Society) v Vlachos [2008] EWCA Civ 193, [2008] 3 All ER 80 at [13], [33]–[38], per Carnwath LJ

MENTAL DISORDER

[Note that the definition of 'mental disorder' in the Mental Health Act 1983, s 1(2) is prospectively replaced by the following:

'Mental disorder' means any disorder or disability of the mind; and 'mentally disordered' shall be construed accordingly. (Mental Health Act 1983, s 1(2) (definition substituted by the Mental Health Act 2007, s 1(2), as from a day to be appointed)).]

MENTAL IMPAIRMENT

[Note that the definitions of 'mental impairment' and 'mentally impaired' in the Mental Health

Act 1983, s 1(1) are prospectively repealed by
the Mental Health Act 2007, s 1(3).]

MERCANTILE AGENT

[For 2(1) Halsbury's Laws of England (4th Edn)
(Reissue) para 12 see now 1 Halsbury's Laws
(5th Edn) para 12.]

N

NATURE AND SEVERITY OF THE ACTS COMMITTED

Canada [Immigration and Refugee Protection Act, s 115(2)(b). Judicial review of an opinion of the Minister of Citizenship and Immigration that applicant refugee should not be allowed to remain in Canada as he was a member of gang involved in criminal activities; whether "nature and severity of the acts committed" by criminal organization or by applicant personally shouldbe considered.] '[**Issue No. 3**: Did the Minister err in interpreting paragraph 115(2)(*b*) by considering the "nature and severity of the acts committed" by the criminal organization, as opposed to the applicant personally?

...

'[53] The Minister's opinion, after reviewing the evidence, is set out at paragraph 29 of the opinion:

> Following from the evidence noted above, including Mr Nagalingam's membership and involvement in the A K Kannan [Tamil gang], in my view, the nature and severity of the acts committed by the A K Kannan are serious and significant, and as such Mr Nagalingam should not be allowed to remain in Canada. [Emphasis added.]

'[54] The Minister referred to the acts committed by the applicant at paragraph 27:

> I note that Mr Nagalingam has relatively few criminal convictions as follows: [mischief under $ 5,000; failure to comply with recognizance; assault].

'[55] The issue is whether paragraph 115(2)(*b*) means "the nature and severity of the acts committed" by the criminal organization or by the applicant personally.

'[56] For ease of reference I repeat paragraph 115(2)(*b*) of the Act:

115. ...

(2) Subsection (1) does not apply in the case of a person

...

(*b*) who is inadmissible on grounds of security, violating human or international rights or organized criminality if, in the opinion of the Minister, the person should not be allowed to remain in Canada on the basis of the nature and severity of acts committed or of danger to the security of Canada.

...

'[58] In applying the rules of statutory interpretation to determine whether or not there is an apparent discordance between the French and English versions of the paragraph, it is clear that there is an ambiguity in the English version because the English version does not link the "acts committed" either to the individual or to the criminal organization. That is left vague. The French version is clear. The French text reads: *"il ne devrait pas être présent au Canada en raison soit de la nature et de la gravité de ses actes passés, soit du danger qu'il constitue pour la sécurité du Canada"* [emphasis added]. The literal translation of the French version is "because of the nature and severity of his past acts".

'[59] The Court is satisfied that the common meaning is the French version. It is plain, not ambiguous and narrower. Therefore, according to the rules of statutory interpretation with respect to bilingual statutes, paragraph 115(2)(*b*) means that the Minister must decide whether the applicant should be allowed to remain in Canada on the basis of the nature and severity of his personal acts.

'[60] The second step in the interpretation of paragraph 115(2)(*b*), as stated by the Supreme Court of Canada in *Medovarski*, above [*Medovarski v Canada* (*Minister of Citizenship and Immigration*); *Esteban v Canada* (*Minister of Citizenship and Immigration*) [2005] 2 SCR 539], is that the Court must determine if the common meaning is consistent with Parliament's intent. This principle of statutory construction, described by Elmer Driedger in *The Construction of Statutes* (Toronto: Butterworths, 1974) [at page 87] was adopted by the Supreme Court of Canada in *Re Rizzo & Rizzo Shoes Ltd* [1998] 1 SCR 27, at page 41:

> Today there is only one principle or approach, namely, the words of an Act are to be read in their entire context and in their grammatical and ordinary sense harmoniously with the scheme of the Act, the object of the Act, and the intention of Parliament.

'[61] Considering the words of the paragraph with the scheme of the Act, the object of the Act and the intent of Parliament, the Court concludes Parliament intended that the Minister consider the nature and severity of the acts committed by the person, as opposed to the criminal organization as a whole. The logical reason to examine the nature and gravity of the personal acts committed by the refugee is that the refugee should not be refouled only because he is a member of a criminal organization unless the acts in which he was involved warrant removal. As will be discussed below, the Minister can look at the acts committed by the criminal organization if it is established that the refugee was complicit in those acts, i.e. there are reasonable grounds for believing that the refugee was personally and knowingly involved in these crimes.

...

'[65] Therefore, the proper interpretation of paragraph 115(2)(*b*) is one that requires the Minister to consider the nature and severity of the acts committed personally by the applicant, and by the A K Kannan gang if the applicant was a personal and knowing participant in such acts, ie complicit.' Nagalingam v Canada *(*Minister of Citizenship and Immigration*)* [2008] 1 FCR 87, 2007 FC 229, [2007] FCJ No 295 at [53]–[56], [58]–[61], [65], per Kelen J (revsd on the facts but not on this point, Nagalingam v Canada *(*Minister of Citizenship and Immigration*)* [2008] FCJ No 670, 2008 FCA 153, 165 ACWS (3d) 889: see below)

'[74] Consequently, I endorse the ruling of Justice Kelen that "the logical reason to examine the nature and gravity of the personal acts committed by the refugee is that the refugee should not be *refouled* only because he is a member of a criminal organization unless the acts in which he was involved warrant removal" (Emphasis added) (at paragraph 61 of Reasons for Judgment). The high threshold lies in the nature and severity of the acts committed.

'[75] Therefore, I propose to answer the second certified question as follows:

The exception of paragraph 115(2)(*b*) regarding organized criminality will apply to a Convention refugee or a protected person if, in the opinion of the Minister, that person should not be allowed to remain in Canada on the basis of the nature and substantial gravity of acts committed (in the context of organized criminality) personally or through complicity, as defined by our domestic laws, but established on a standard of reasonable grounds.'

Nagalingam v Canada *(*Minister of Citizenship and Immigration*)* [2008] FCJ No 670, 2008 FCA 153, 165 ACWS (3d) 889 at paras 74–75, per Trudel JA

NEW EVIDENCE

Canada [Meaning of 'new evidence' in Immigration and Refugee Protection Act, SC 2001, c 27, s 113(*a*).] '[23] Paragraph 113(*a*) of the IRPA states as follows:

> **113.** Consideration of an application for protection shall be as follows:
> (*a*) an applicant whose claim to refugee protection has been rejected may present only new evidence that arose after the rejection or was not reasonably available, or that the applicant could not reasonably have been expected in the circumstances to have presented, at the time of the rejection;

'[24] Mr Elezi submits that because the three parts of paragraph 113(*a*) are separated by the word "or," they should be considered three distinct situations in which an applicant can be considered to present "new" evidence. In other words, he argues the test under paragraph 113(*a*) is disjunctive. Applying that notion to this case, he submits the 20 new documents fit within the first branch of paragraph 113(*a*) —"new evidence that arose after the rejection." Thus, according to Mr Elezi's submissions, it does not matter whether the evidence was reasonably available at his hearing, or whether he could have presented it earlier.

'[25] To support this proposition, Mr Elezi relies on the case of *Mendez v Canada* (*Minister of Citizenship and Immigration*) (2005) 42 Imm LR (3d) 130 (FC), in which Justice Douglas Campbell allowed a Mexican claimant's application for judicial review. The new evidence in *Mendez* was documentation from a similarly situated applicant, whose refugee claim had succeeded (the Flores evidence). Mr Mendez tried to submit the Flores evidence in his PRRA application to prove that, contrary to the Board's conclusion, health care professionals in Mexico discriminated against homosexual men with HIV/AIDS. Justice Campbell found that one letter within the package of evidence was dated after the Board's decision in Mr Mendez's case. As such, it was an error to treat that letter the same way as the rest of the Flores evidence. He wrote, at paragraphs 17–18:

> As I expressed during the hearing of the present application, in my opinion, the PRRA Officer made an error in the application of s 113(*a*) with regard to the letter signed by Mr Flores. Section 113(*a*) requires a careful determination on the admissibility of evidence on three available grounds. In my opinion, precision is required in making a finding under this provision since important ramifications follow on the determination of the risk to be experienced by an individual applicant. In my opinion, the PRRA Officer failed to meet this expectation.

> Mr Flores' letter of March 17, 2004 clearly post-dates the Refugee Board's decision in the present case. It appears that the PRRA Officer failed to understand this fact by lumping it in with the tendered evidence which pre-dates the Refugee Board's decision. I find that, as a result of this mistake, the PRRA Officer failed to understand, and consequently reach a clear decision on the Applicant's rectification argument of risk.

'[26] I am prepared to accept that paragraph 113(*a*) refers to three distinct possibilities and that its three parts must be read disjunctively. If the use of the word "or" is to be given meaning, the three parts of paragraph 113(*a*) must clearly be seen as three separate alternatives. While the first part refers to evidence that postdates the Board's decision, the second and third parts obviously relate to evidence that predates its decision. Only evidence that existed before the Board's negative decision requires an explanation before it can be admitted with a PRRA application. As for evidence that arises after the Board's decision, there is no need for an explanation. The mere fact that it did not exist at the time the decision was reached is sufficient to establish that it could not have been presented earlier to the Board.

'[27] That being said, a piece of evidence will not fall within the first category and be characterized as "new" just because it is dated

after the Board's decision. If that were the case, a PRRA application could easily be turned into an appeal of the Board's decision. A failed refugee applicant could easily muster "new" affidavits and documentary evidence to counter the Board's findings and bolster his story. This is precisely why the case law has insisted that new evidence relate to new developments, either in country conditions or in the applicant's personal situation, instead of focusing on the date the evidence was produced: see, for example, *Perez v Canada (Minister of Citizenship and Immigration)* (2006) 59 Imm LR (3d) 156 (FC); *Yousef v Canada (Minister of Citizenship and Immigration)* 2006 FC 864; *Aivani v Canada (Minister of Citizenship and Immigration)* 2006 FC 1231.

'[28] Justice Mosley heard the exact same argument that Mr Elezi's counsel makes now in the case *Raza v Canada (Minister of Citizenship and Immigration)* 2006 FC 1385. Relying on *Mendez*, above, the applicant in *Raza* had submitted that paragraph 113(*a*) provided for the admissibility of three distinct types of new evidence, and that only the second and third types of new evidence called for an explanation why they were not presented to the Board. As for the first type, evidence that arose after the Board's rejection, the applicant argued the only requirement was that it be created after the date of the Board's decision.

'[29] Justice Mosley gave short shrift to that argument. He wrote, at paragraphs 22–23:

> It must be recalled that the role of the PRRA officer is not to revisit the Board's factual and credibility conclusions but to consider the present situation. In assessing "new information" it is not just the date of the document that is important, but whether the information is significant or significantly different than the information previously provided: *Selliah*, above at para 38. Where "recent" information (i.e. information that post-dates the original decision) merely echoes information previously submitted, it is unlikely to result in a finding that country conditions have changed. The question is whether there is anything of "substance" that is new: *Yousef*, above at para 27.

In the present case, though the evidence of the applicant post-dates the refugee determination in time with respect to the date it was written, nothing in the letter, affidavits or articles is substantially different than the information that was before the Board. As noted by the Officer with respect to the letter and affidavits: they "refer only to the applicants' circumstances which were considered by the Board", "no new risk developments are contained", and they contain "essentially a repetition of the same information". In those circumstances, it was not patently unreasonable of the officer to question why they had not been present before. With respect to the articles in particular, the Officer noted that they were "generalized" and did not "address the material elements of the present application".

'[30] I fully agree with Mr Justice Mosley's conclusions and I adopt them. The mere fact that a piece of evidence was created after the Board's rejection of a refugee claim will not, in and of itself, suffice to characterize that evidence as "new" for the purposes of paragraph 113(*a*). There are other factors to take into consideration when assessing whether the evidence sought to be introduced arose after the Board's decision. One should not forget that this provision, like the rest of the IRPA, must be construed and applied in a manner that "ensures that decisions taken under this Act are consistent with the *Canadian Charter of Rights and Freedoms*," and that "complies with international human rights instruments to which Canada is signatory" (paragraphs 3(3)(*d*) and (*f*) of the IRPA).' *Elezi v Canada (*Minister of Citizenship and Immigration*)* [2008] 1 FCR 365, 2007 FC 240, [2007] FCJ No 357, 310 FTR 59 at [23]–[30], per de Montigny J

NORMALLY

[Under the Animals Act 1971, s 2(2), where damage is caused by an animal which does not belong to a dangerous species, a keeper of the animal is liable for the damage if (a) the damage is of a kind which the animal is likely to cause or which, if caused by the animal, is likely to be severe, and (b) the likelihood of the damage or of its being severe is due to characteristics of the animal which are not normally found in animals of the same species or are not normally so found except at particular times or in particular circumstances, and (c) those characteristics were known to that keeper.] '[41] The meaning of s 2(2)(b) has been authoritatively explained by the House of Lords in *Mirvahedy v Henley* [2003] UKHL 16, [2003] 2 All ER 401, [2003] 2 AC 491. The claimant suffered injury when the car he was driving collided with the defendants' horse which had panicked and escaped with others from its field. It was not clear what had frightened the horses. The House held by a majority of three to two that the defendants were liable under s 2(2). To bolt was a characteristic of horses which was normal "in the particular circumstances", these being some sort of fright or other external stimulus. The main issue concerned the true meaning of the second limb of sub-s (2)(b). The majority adopted that favoured by the Court of Appeal in *Cummings v Grainger* [1977] 1 All ER 104, sub nom *Cummings v Granger* [1977] QB 397. Thus the fact that an animal's behaviour, although not normal behaviour generally for animals of the species, is nevertheless normal behaviour for the species in the particular circumstances does not take the case outside s 2(2)(b).

'[42] Lord Nicholls of Birkenhead noted of the *Cummings v Grainger* interpretation that:

"… it is not easy to conceive of circumstances where dangerous behaviour which is characteristic of a species will not satisfy requirement (b). A normal but dangerous characteristic of a species will usually be identifiable by reference to particular times or particular circumstances. Thus the *Cummings* interpretation means that requirement (b) will be met in most cases where damage was caused by dangerous behaviour as described in requirement (a). Requirement (b) will be satisfied whenever the animal's conduct was *not* characteristic of the species in the particular circumstances. Requirement (b) will also be satisfied when the animal's behaviour was characteristic of the species in those circumstances." (See [2003] 2 All ER 401 at [43].)

'[43] The question of what is meant by "normally" was not in issue in *Mirvahedy v Henley* (or any other case that has been cited to us). There are passages in the opinions of their Lordships which, it might be said, suggest that they considered that "normally" means "usually", rather than "conforming to type" or "naturally". The clearest is at para [3], where Lord Nicholls said that the behaviour of the horse in that case was "usual in horses when sufficiently alarmed by a threat". He also said (at [23]) that the horse "was not behaving differently from the way *any* normal horse would have behaved in the circumstances" (my emphasis). But since the meaning of the word "normally" was not in issue, these statements do not provide a secure basis for deciding precisely what it means. In any event, it is plain that, if it is usual for horses to bolt when sufficiently alarmed, it is also natural and conforming to type for horses to bolt in such circumstances. But it does not necessarily follow that, if it is unusual for horses to bolt when sufficiently alarmed, it is abnormal for them to bolt in such circumstances.

'[44] The *Oxford English Dictionary* provides a definition of "normal" as being "according to or squaring with a norm; constituting, conforming to, not deviating from a type or standard; regular, usual 1828". A "norm" is defined as a "rule or authoritative standard". "Abnormal" is defined as "Deviating from the ... type; contrary to rule or system ... unusual [1835 ...]". Depending on the context, therefore, "normal" can mean "conforming to a type" or "usual". The latter meaning connotes a greater degree of regularity or frequency of occurrence than the former. But even the former must connote some frequency of occurrence. If a characteristic is rarely found in animals of the same species, it may be difficult to say that the characteristic conforms to the type of animal in question.

'[45] In some contexts, it is clear that the word "normally" means "usually". If I say: "I normally travel to work on the No 18 bus," I am saying that I usually travel to work on that bus. I may occasionally travel to work by different means, but that is an exception to my usual practice. In other contexts, however, the position is different. It is a proper use of language to say "horses will most often turn and flee when faced with a frightening stimulus, but it also normal for them to rear in such circumstances". It is normal for horses to rear when frightened in such circumstances, because it is natural for them to do so, although rearing may be a less usual response than turning and fleeing. Another way of making the same point is to say that it is not abnormal (even if it is unusual) for horses to rear when frightened.

'[46] It seems to me that the core meaning of "normal" is "conforming to type". If a characteristic of an animal is usual, then it will certainly be normal. The best evidence that a characteristic conforms to the type of animals of a species is that the characteristic is usually found in those animals.

'[47] I can find nothing in the context of sub-s (2)(b) to suggest that Parliament did not intend "normally" to bear this core meaning. It is difficult to see why Parliament should have intended to exclude from the ambit of sub-s (2)(b) cases where the relevant characteristic is natural, although unusual, in the animal which has caused the damage. There is no need for such a narrow interpretation because a claim will not succeed unless the knowledge requirement in sub-s (c) is also satisfied. To adopt the language of Lord Walker of Gestingthorpe in *Mirvahedy v Henley* [2003] 2 All ER 401 at [157], [2003] 2 AC 491, if s 2(2)(b) is interpreted in this way, there is nothing unjust or unreasonable, as between the keeper (who can decide whether "to run the unavoidable risks involved in keeping horses" and whether or not to insure against those risks) and the victim of the horse's behaviour, in requiring the keeper to bear the loss.' Welsh v Stokes [2007] EWCA Civ 796, [2008] 1 All ER 921 at [41]–[47], per Dyson LJ

NOTICE

Of intended prosecution

[For 40(2) Halsbury's Laws of England (4th Edn) (Reissue) para 728 see now 40(2) Halsbury's Laws (4th Edn) (2007 Reissue) para 1028.]

O

OBTAINS PROPERTY

[Proceeds of Crime Act 2002, ss 329, 340.] '[6] Section 329 of the 2002 Act reads: "(1) A person commits an offence if he—(a) acquires criminal property; (b) uses criminal property; (c) has possession of criminal property."

'[7] Relevant definitions are to be found in s 340:

> "(3) Property is criminal property if—(a) it constitutes a person's benefit from criminal conduct or it represents such a benefit (in whole or part and whether directly or indirectly); and (b) the alleged offender knows or suspects that it constitutes or represents such a benefit …
>
> (5) A person benefits from conduct if he obtains property as a result of or in connection with the conduct …
>
> (8) If a person benefits from conduct his benefit is the property obtained as a result of or in connection with the conduct …
>
> (10) The following rules apply in relation to property— (a) property is obtained by a person if he obtains an interest in it … (d) references to an interest, in relation to property other than land, include references to a right (including a right to possession)."

'[8] The essential submissions made in the skeleton argument for the applicant were that the person who stole the motorcycle in the course of the burglary did not obtain an "interest" in it within the meaning of s 340(10)(a), since "interest" must mean a lawful interest, and did not therefore obtain property within the meaning of that provision; by working through the earlier provisions of s 340, it followed that the motorcycle in this case was not "criminal property"; and the applicant could not therefore have been guilty of acquiring criminal property even if he was the thief or a handler of the motorcycle.

'[9] Those arguments were met by written submissions from Mr Perry QC, for the Crown, contending that a thief does obtain an "interest", within the meaning of s 340(10), in the property he steals, because he obtains a right to possession of that property. Mr Perry relied on *Costello v Chief Constable of Derbyshire Constabulary* [2001] EWCA Civ 381, [2001] 3 All ER 150, [2001] 1 WLR 1437. In that case the claimant was found to be in possession of a motor car which was to his knowledge stolen. The police seized the car from him pursuant to s 19 of the Police and Criminal Evidence Act 1984 and retained it pursuant to s 22 of the 1984 Act since the owner was unknown. The claimant brought an action against the chief constable for delivery up and damages. The Court of Appeal held that the statutory provisions vested in the police no title to the property seized but only a temporary right to retain it for specified purposes; and that when that right expired, the police were obliged to return the car to the claimant since he had a possessory title in it even though it was stolen. Lightman J, with whom the other members of the court agreed, expressed his conclusion on that issue as follows (at [31]):

> "In my view on a review of the authorities, (save so far as legislation otherwise provides) as a matter of principle and authority possession means the same thing and is entitled to the same legal protection whether or not it has been obtained lawfully or by theft or by other unlawful means. It vests in the possessor a possessory title which is good against the world save as against anyone setting up or claiming under a better title. In the case of a theft the title is frail, and of likely limited value (see e g *Rowland v Divall* [1923] 2 KB 500, [1923] All ER Rep 270), but none the less remains a title to which the law affords protection … This conclusion is in accord with that long ago reached by the courts that even a thief is entitled to the protection of the criminal law against the theft from

him of that which he has himself stolen (see eg Smith and Hogan *Criminal Law* (9th edn, 1999) p 522."

'[10] Mr Perry submitted that, applying that principle to the facts of the present case, the applicant clearly acquired criminal property and was properly convicted of an offence contrary to s 329 of the 2002 Act. The motorcycle was stolen in the course of a burglary. The thief obtained an interest in it, namely a right to possession. It followed that the motorcycle was property obtained by him as a result of criminal conduct and constituted his benefit from such conduct. It was therefore criminal property.
...

'[12] ... In our judgment there is no answer to Mr Perry's submissions. The stolen motorcycle was property obtained by the thief, within the meaning of s 340(10)(a), since the thief obtained a right to possession of it and, by s 340(10)(d), an interest includes a right to possession; and it was self-evidently obtained as a result of or in connection with criminal conduct. It therefore constituted the thief's benefit from criminal conduct. It follows that the first part of the definition of criminal property, in s 340(3)(a), was satisfied. The second part, in s 340(3)(b), depended on whether the applicant knew or suspected that it constituted or represented such a benefit. That was an issue that the recorder properly left to the jury and that the jury decided against the applicant. The recorder, who did not have the benefit of Mr Perry's argument, based his rejection of the submission of no case on a construction of s 340(10) that Mr Perry has not sought to uphold; but his instincts were sound and his conclusion was correct. His directions to the jury captured the substance of the matter accurately and no complaint has been made about them.

'[13] A question was raised as to whether s 340(10) is an exhaustive definition of when a person "obtains property" as a result of or in connection with criminal conduct. It may be arguable that, as a matter of simple language, a thief or handler "obtains" stolen property even if he does not obtain an interest in it or come within any of the other specific provisions of s 340(10). However, in the light of the clear conclusion we have reached on the application of s 340(10) in this case, that is not a question that we need decide.' R v Rose; R v Whitwam [2008] EWCA Crim 239, [2008] 3 All ER 315 at [6]–[10], [12]–[13], per Richards LJ

OCCUPATION (OF PROPERTY)

[A college, which made exempt supplies for value added tax (VAT) purposes and was unable to recover input tax on goods and services supplied to it, gave notice of election to waive exemption under the Value Added Tax Act 1994, Sch 10 para 2 which applies to buildings and land. It built a new library and granted a lease of the library, giving exclusive possession, to a company in which the college held all the shares and members of the college formed the board of directors, intending that the effect would be that the lease to the company would be a taxable supply and the college would be entitled to recover all the input tax it had paid in relation to building the library. The college also entered into an agreement with the company by which it sold all the books, fixtures, fittings and equipment in the library to the company, and the company agreed in return for a fee to provide the college with services including the provision of books on hire to the college for the use of senior and junior members. The Value Added Tax Act 1994, Sch 10 para 2(3AA) provides that where an election to waive exemption had been made in relation to any land 'a supply shall not be taken by virtue of that election to be a taxable supply if—(a) the grant giving rise to the supply was made by a person ("the grantor") who was a developer of the land; and (b) at the time of the grant ... it was the intention or expectation of ... the grantor ... that the land would become exempt land'. Paragraph 3A(7) provides that for the purposes of para 2(3AA) land is exempt land if the grantor is in occupation of the land. The Revenue and Customs Commissioners considered that the college, as the developer, had remained in occupation of the library, that the library was therefore exempt land and accordingly the grant of the lease had not been a taxable supply. The Value Added Tax and Duties Tribunal dismissed the college's appeal. The Court of Appeal allowed the college's appeal, referring to authority of the Court of Justice of the European Communities in relation to Sch 9 to the 1994 Act (which implemented European law relating to letting or leasing of immovable property) that 'occupation' meant the right to occupy property as if that person were the owner and to exclude any other person from enjoyment of such a right. The commissioners appealed to the House of Lords, contending that cases on the meaning of 'occupy' for the purposes of Sch 9 had no application to the meaning of 'occupation' in Sch 10 para 3A(7) and that as an anti-avoidance provision para 3A(7) should be given a wide meaning and be interpreted to mean any physical presence on the land by which the grantor continued to use it.

'[6] These are very detailed provisions but the issue to which they give rise in this case is relatively straightforward. The college, as grantor of the lease, was the developer of the land. If, since the grant of the lease, it has been "in occupation" of the library within the meaning of para 3A(7), the library is "exempt land" as defined in that paragraph and the grant of the lease is not a taxable supply. So the question is whether the college is "in occupation" of the library, either alone or together with the company.

...

'[9] The question, therefore, is whether the college is in occupation of the library. For this purpose one must, I think, begin by considering what the statute means by "occupation". It has often been remarked that this is a word which can mean different things in different contexts: see, for example, Viscount Cave in *Madrassa Anjuman Islamia of Kholwad v Municipal Council of Johannesburg* [1922] 1 AC 500 at 504 ("a word of uncertain meaning") and Lord Mustill in *Southern Water Authority v Nature Conservancy Council* [1992] 3 All ER 481 at 487–488, [1992] 1 WLR 775 at 781. I start, therefore, with the context in which the word is used.

'[10] Paragraph 2 of Sch 10 operates as an exception to the general provision in Group 1, para 1 of Sch 9 which provides that "The grant of any interest in or right over land or of any licence to occupy land" shall be an exempt supply. The election under para 2(1) of Sch 10 has effect only if the grant would otherwise have fallen within para 1 of Group 1. This context suggests that a "licence to occupy" in Sch 9 and "occupation" in Sch 10 refer to the same concept.

'[11] On the question of what amounts to a licence to occupy within Sch 9, we have the recent guidance of the Court of Justice in *Sinclair Collis Ltd v Customs and Excise Comrs* Case C-275/01 [2003] STC 898, [2003] ECR I-5965. The question in this case was whether the grant of a right to maintain a cigarette vending machine in a public house was a "letting of immovable property" within art 13B(b) of the Sixth Directive [EC Council Directive 77/388 of 17 May 1977 on the harmonisation of the laws of the member states relating to turnover taxes—common system of value added tax: uniform basis of assessment (OJ 1977 L145, p 1)]. This concept had been transposed in Sch 9 to include a "licence to occupy land". The Court of Justice decided that

it was not. It stated the principle (see [2003] STC 898, [2003] ECR I-5965, para 25 of the judgment):

"25.... . The fundamental characteristic of a letting of immoveable property for the purposes of art 13B(b) of the Sixth Directive lies in conferring on the person concerned, for an agreed period and for payment, the right to occupy property as if that person were the owner and to exclude any other person from enjoyment of such a right ..."

'[12] In formulating the test in this way, the Court of Justice was echoing the opinions expressed by Lord Nicholls of Birkenhead, Lord Millett and Lord Scott of Foscote when the case was before the House of Lords: see [2001] UKHL 30, [2001] STC 989. Lord Nicholls said (at [35]) that the licence was "more naturally to be regarded as a licence to use land rather than a licence to occupy land." Lord Scott (at [77]) gave the example of a right to use a safe deposit box in a bank. The bank remained in occupation of the whole of its premises, including the space taken up by the box:

"[77] ... The customer has no more than a right to put things in the box and is not, in any meaningful sense, in occupation of the space taken up by the box."

'[13] The same distinction between occupying land and merely using it had previously been made by Advocate General Jacobs in *Swedish State v Stockholm Lindöpark AB; Stockholm Lindöpark AB v Swedish State* Case C-150/99 [2001] STC 103, [2001] ECR I-493. Lindöpark owned golf courses and provided golfing facilities for the staff and clients of companies who joined and paid a fee. The question was whether this was a letting of the golf course within the meaning of art 13B(b). The Advocate General thought it was not (see [2001] STC 103, [2001] ECR I-493, paras 34–35 of the opinion):

"34.... . Where ... an individual pays an entrance fee to gain transient access, amongst other individuals, to a public swimming pool, it would be stretching the concept beyond any reasonable limit to regard such a transaction as leasing or letting.

35.... . If a person or entity were to pay for the exclusive use of a course for a specified period—say, in order to organise a tournament or championship—with a concomitant right to charge entrance fees for players and/or spectators, that would appear to partake fairly clearly of the nature of a lease or let. The same would not apply, however, to the casual golfer or group of golfers coming to play a round ... A golfer may be thought of not as occupying the course in any sense but as traversing it ..."

'[14] The Court of Justice agreed. More recently, in *Belgian State v Temco Europe SA* Case C-284/03 [2005] STC 1451, [2004] ECR I-11237 it summed up these cases (para 20 of the judgment) by saying that it was necessary to distinguish the "relatively passive" activity of letting immoveable property from transactions which—

> "have as their subject matter something which is best understood as the provision of a service rather than simply the making available of property ..."

'[15] The Commissioners say that these cases on the meaning of "occupy" for the purposes of Sch 9 have no application to the meaning of "occupation" in para 3A(7) of Sch 10. The latter is an anti-avoidance provision which should be given a wide meaning. The policy of the 1997 amendments was that exempt suppliers should not be able to create a taxable supply of the land by the grant of a lease and still use it for the purposes of making exempt supplies. "Occupation" should therefore be interpreted to mean any physical presence on the land by which the grantor continues to use it.

'[16] I do not agree. In choosing the concept of occupation, Parliament must have been aware that it came with a well-understood meaning. The Commissioners say that it was only after 1997 that the concept was clarified in cases like *Lindöpark* and *Sinclair Collis*. But I do not think that there was ever a time when a mere physical presence on land for the purpose of making use of it, like playing a round of golf, would have been regarded as occupation. Furthermore, other parts of Sch 10 show the Parliament was well aware that "occupation" of land and "use" of land are different concepts. For example, in para 5(5), (which was in the original 1994 Act), the definition of a developer of a building or work includes a person who constructs it—

> "with a view to granting an interest in, right over or licence to occupy it (or any part of it) or to occupying or using it (or any part of it) for his own purposes."

'[17] The question is therefore whether the college has, as the Court of Justice said in the *Sinclair Collis* case (see [2003] STC 898, [2003]

ECR I-5965, para 25 of the judgment), "the right to occupy property as if that person were the owner and to exclude any other person from enjoyment of such a right." For this purpose it is necessary to examine the arrangements under which its members are able to use the library. This appears from the lease, four agreements made between the college and the company on 2 July 2001 and the unchallenged evidence of the college bursar, Mr du Quesnay, who is also a director of the company.

...

'[23] Despite the close links between the college and the company, the Commissioners do not suggest that the separate personality of the company should be ignored or that the agreements should not be taken at face value. On that basis, it seems to me clear that the college is entitled to the provision of services for its members but cannot be said to be in occupation of the library. There is nothing in the arrangements, whether in law or in practice, which contradicts or displaces the right of exclusive occupation granted to the company by the lease. The practical physical control of the library premises is in the hands of the librarian and her staff, who act on behalf of the company. It is they who have the right to admit or exclude persons from the library and they do not share this right with the college. The college is contractually entitled to have its members in good standing admitted and provided with books and other services, but these rights cannot be characterised as rights of occupation any more than the rights of the Swedish golfers or their companies to the use of the course. The services provided by the company to the college are by no means "relatively passive": acquiring and cataloguing the books, maintaining them upon the shelves and assisting the users are activities which require the full time services of the librarian, her two assistants and a graduate trainee. In my opinion it is impossible to say that the college either had in law or exercised in practice "the right to occupy [the] property as if [it] were the owner and to exclude any other person from enjoyment of such a right". The essence of the right conferred on the college is the right to the use of the books. The right to enter on the premises for the purpose of taking them out or consulting them is only ancillary to this primary right.

...

'[27] In my opinion a decision as to whether acts attributable to a body like the school or college amount to occupation of premises is a question of degree, sensitive to the particular constellation of facts. An appellate court must pay considerable respect to the opinion of the fact-finding body: compare *Designers Guild Ltd v Russell Williams (Textiles) Ltd* [2001] 1 All ER 700, [2000] 1 WLR 2416. I would therefore not question the decision of the tribunal in the *Brambletye School Trust* case [*Brambletye School Trust Ltd v Customs and Excise Comrs* (2002) VAT Decision 17688]. In this case, the tribunal did not really consider whether the facts amounted to occupation by the college rather than (or in addition to) occupation by the company because they simply lumped the two bodies together. The Court of Appeal (see [2006] STC 1010), however, did consider this question and came to the conclusion that occupation by the college had not been established. I would not have disturbed this judgment, even if I had been inclined myself to take a different view. In fact, however, I am on complete agreement with the judgment of Chadwick LJ, whose reasoning is largely reflected in this opinion. I would therefore dismiss the appeal.' Revenue and Customs Commissioners v Newnham College, Cambridge [2008] UKHL 23, [2008] 2 All ER 863 at [6], [9]–[17], [23], [27], per Lord Hoffmann

'[29] The question is whether the college remained in "occupation" of the library for the purposes of para 3A(7) of Sch 10 to the Value Added Tax Act 1994 after granting the lease to the company. If it did, the land is exempt land for the purposes of para 2(3AA) and the grant of the lease is not to be taken as a taxable supply notwithstanding the college's election under para 2(1) of the schedule that its grant of the land to the company was to be a taxable supply. As Lord Hoffmann has explained, the Commissioners have not argued that the transaction was a sham or that the college was abusing the legislative provisions which allow taxpayers who make exempt supplies to opt for taxation in relation to any land. The Commissioners do not seek to uphold the reasoning of the Value Added Tax and Duties Tribunal (the tribunal) (see (2005) VAT Decision 18936) in so far as it may have been influenced by the fact the college was plainly seeking to avoid tax. Their case is that the exemption was designed to prevent tax avoidance, that it must be strictly construed, and that the disqualification from the exemption which it creates applies here. The scheme that was entered into, which was specific to the use by an academic institution of land for academic purposes, failed to satisfy the conditions of the exemption.

'[30] Although the legislative provisions are rather complicated, the issue in the end turns on the meaning that is to be given in this context to the words "in occupation of the land" in para 3A(7). Mr Pleming QC, for the Commissioners, submitted that they meant that a grantor who was intended or expected at the time of the grant to be physically present on the land was to be taken to be in occupation of it. This reading of the words gave effect to the central policy objective of the value added tax (VAT) system that persons making exempt supplies should not recover VAT incurred by them in the course of their businesses. The college was in occupation of the land by means of the physical presence in the library of its fellows, students, staff and other persons authorised by the college to be there. This was part of the package of the exempt services that were provided to them by the college. The fact that they were there in the enjoyment of those services was sufficient. It would be wrong in this context to confine the concept of occupation to the meaning that would be given to it in other contexts, such in the phrase "licence to occupy" as used in item 1 of Group 1 in Sch 9 to describe exempt supplies in relation to land.

'[31] I do not think that there is much doubt about what the word "occupation" means, although it may be more difficult to apply its ordinary meaning to the facts in some contexts than it is in others. In its ordinary meaning it requires more than just a right to use the land or to enjoy the facilities that are to be found there. Physical presence is an essential element. But there is more to it than that. It requires actual possession of the land, and the possession must have some degree of permanence. In the Court of Appeal (Sir Andrew Morritt C, Chadwick and Lloyd LJJ) (see [2006] EWCA Civ 285 at [36], [2006] STC 1010 at [36]) Chadwick LJ drew on the guidance that the House derived from decisions of the Court of Justice of the European Communities about the meaning to be given to the concept in the context of the Council Directive (EC) 77/388 of 17 May 1977 on the harmonisation of the laws of the member states relating to turnover taxes—common system of value added tax: uniform basis of assessment (OJ 1977 L 145 p 1) (the Sixth Directive) in *Customs and Excise Comrs v Sinclair Collis Ltd* [2001] UKHL 30, [2001] STC 989. He said that to be in "occupation" of land for the purposes of para 3A(7) requires more than a right to use that land. He then added this important sentence (at [36]):

"It requires some degree of control over the user by others—that is to say, some degree of control over what those who are not also in occupation of the land can do on the land."

'[32] The sentence which I have quoted directs attention to what I would regard as the central issue in this case. The question is not whether the college is in control of the company. It is whether the college is to any degree in control of the use of the land. This is not an insignificant test. Paragraph 3A(13) of Sch 10 provides that, for the purposes of the paragraph, a person is to be taken to be in occupation of any land whether he occupies it alone or together with one or more other persons and whether he occupies all of that land or only part of it. Its effect is to remove the requirement of exclusive occupation which is usually inherent in a grant of an interest in or a right over land or a licence to occupy. The usual requirement of exclusive occupation would be too easy for tax avoidance. So occupation by the college to any extent will be sufficient to disqualify the scheme from the exemption.

'[33] The college and the company both, to some degree, have a presence on the land. The land is the building that contains the library. The college, through its members, goes to the library to make use of its services. The company, through the librarian and other members of the staff seconded to it by the college, provides the services that are available there. The lease gives the company the exclusive right to occupy the land, and the college sold all its books and other library assets to the company. The company entered into a back-to-back agreement to provide those books on hire to the college or other persons or authorities nominated by it, along with other incidental services. The arrangements that it entered into between the company and the college for the use of the library must be seen as a whole. The question which they give rise to is this. Was there a sufficient element of control by the college over access to and use of the land to show that, to some degree at least, the college was in occupation of it?

'[34] As Lord Russell of Killowen observed in *Westminster City Council v Southern Railway Co* [1936] 2 All ER 322 at 326, [1936] AC 511 at 529, in every case where there may be a rival occupancy in some person who to some extent may be thought to have occupancy rights over the premises, the question is one of fact. The issue there was whether the railway company or the various companies to whom they were let out were in rateable occupation of bookstalls and other tenements within the area of a railway station. Here too the question is essentially one of fact, once the right test has been identified. And, in contrast to the rating cases, exclusive occupation is not required. Mr Pleming, very properly, did not seek to rely on the decision of the tribunal on the facts, although it was in the Commissioners' favour. This was because the tribunal may have been unduly influenced by its view that the scheme was an abuse. The Court of Appeal also held that its reasons were unsatisfactory, so it formed its own judgment on the issue. I would be reluctant to interfere with that decision as our function is to deal with issues of law, not issues of fact. But, like Lord Hoffmann, I agree with it.

'[35] The Commissioners submit that, if control is an element of "occupation" for the purposes of para 3A(7), a sufficient degree of control was retained by the college by means of the individual members of the college who use the library for study or research and by its librarian and other members of the library staff who run the library. But, as Chadwick LJ pointed out ([2006] STC 1010 at [37]), the members of the college have no control over access to and use of the library by others. The library is under the day-to-day control of the librarian and her staff, and admission of others is at her discretion and under her control. The college bursar described how the system works in practice in his witness statement. Only persons authorised by her can use the proximity cards that open the doors of the library during staff hours. She can add or remove names from the library's database. Users who are in breach of the rules of the library may be removed by the library staff, and their authorisation to use it may be withdrawn by the librarian. Members of the college who are present in the library every day have no control over these arrangements.

'[36] The contractual position between the college and the company as to the librarian and her staff provides the answer to the question whether the college is in control of these arrangements. Under the secondment agreement the library staff were retained in the employment of the college. This was to maintain their existing employment status, including their membership of the pension scheme. But, as the bursar explained, they are for all practical purposes under the control and direction of the company. The contractual change which this brought about was described in a letter which the college wrote to the librarian when, on the date when the various agreements were entered into, she was invited to accept secondment to the company. She was told that she would resume her duties as librarian for the college on the termination of the secondment, but that during the secondment she was to act as librarian for the company.

'[37] The effect of this arrangement was that during the period of the secondment her duties as librarian were to be carried out under the direction of the board of directors of the company. She was to be answerable to the company, and not the college, for the way she controlled access to the library. The Commissioners say that the college retained ultimate control because the librarian and the staff are their employees and because the books were hired back to the college. But access to the books is controlled by the librarian, and the secondment agreement places the day-to-day control over her activities and those of her staff in the hands of the company. The fact that the company is controlled by the college does not permit one to ignore the effect of this agreement. The college and the company are separate entities. I would give all the weight that is due to this concept, which lies at the heart of the entire arrangement. In my opinion the college is not to any degree in occupation of the library.' Revenue and Customs Commissioners v Newnham College, Cambridge [2008] UKHL 23, [2008] 2 All ER 863 at [29]–[37], per Lord Hope of Craighead

Reasonable for him to continue to occupy

[Under the Housing Act 1996, s 175(3) a person is not to be treated as having accommodation unless it is accommodation which it would be 'reasonable for him to continue to occupy'. The local council notified an applicant for housing assistance of its decision that he was not homeless because he was entitled to occupy accommodation at his family home in Uganda, which it had concluded was reasonable for him and his family to occupy since he had not identified any problem with living in it. The applicant requested a review of the decision, reiterating that he lived in England and not Uganda. One question which arose was whether the inclusion of the words 'to continue' in s 175(3) has the effect that the subsection can only apply if the person is in actual occupation of the relevant accommodation.] '[37] On the assumption that the council was entitled to decide that the property in Kampala was available to Mr Maloba, did it follow that he was not to be treated as homeless or threatened with

homelessness within the meaning of s 175, regardless of whether it was reasonable to expect him to occupy it?

'[38] On first impression, it would be surprising if the answer were yes. This would seem to go against the grain of Parliament's intention in providing that a person is not to be treated as having accommodation unless it is accommodation which it would be reasonable for him to continue to occupy. However, in *Begum*'s case [*Begum v Tower Hamlets London Borough Council* [2000] 1 WLR 306, CA] a majority of the court considered that the inclusion of the words "to continue" in s 175(3) had the effect that the subsection could only apply if the person was in actual occupation of the relevant accommodation. On this reading, if at the time of the council's decision a person was in occupation of accommodation which it would not be reasonable for him to continue to occupy, the fact that he was living there would not prevent him from being homeless within the meaning of the Act; but the opposite would apply if he had left the property, so long as it remained available for his occupation. In the latter case, in order to qualify for help under the Act he would have to take up the accommodation which it would not be reasonable for him to continue to occupy, whereupon he would become statutorily homeless.

'[39] In reaching this conclusion Sedley LJ referred ([2000] 1 WLR 306 at 325–326) to the history of the legislation, which led him to the view that s 175(3) stood apart from s 175(1) and (2), and that they could not be read together. He considered that the theoretical possibility of an applicant being required to move into accommodation available to him, but which was unfit, could properly be regarded as unreal, since no responsible local authority would ever contemplate expecting an applicant to act in that way.

'[40] Auld LJ took a different approach. He interpreted the words 'to continue to occupy' in s 175(3) as follows (at 319):

"In my view, it is plain that Parliament was not using continued occupation in the sense of continuance of an actual occupation at the time of the application, but of continuance stemming from one of the entitlements to occupy specified in section 175(1)."

'[41] On the facts of *Begum*'s case, the difference between Auld and Sedley LJJ on this point made no difference to the outcome. The appeal was originally heard by them as a two-judge court, but it was adjourned for further argument before a three-judge court on an unrelated point. On the adjourned hearing, presided over by Stuart-Smith LJ, the argument was limited to that other point, but in his judgment Stuart-Smith LJ expressed his agreement with Sedley LJ's analysis of s 175. He added that in his view it made no practical difference because no responsible authority would be likely to take the point that an applicant was homeless where the only accommodation available to him was not reasonable for him to occupy.

'[42] Ms Bretherton relied on the opinions of the majority regarding the interpretation of s 175(3) as persuasive but not binding authority. The issue was academic in *Begum*'s case, but it is not academic in this case.

'[43] In my view the grammatical argument which found favour with the majority is outweighed by other factors which support Auld LJ's approach. These relate to the coherence of the statute and the reasonableness of the result.

...

'[46] The construction preferred by the majority in *Begum*'s case leads to this paradox: a person who has left accommodation in circumstances which did not make him homeless intentionally under the provisions of s 191 and s 177, because it was unreasonable to expect him to remain there, is nevertheless not homeless at all if he is able to return to the property which he reasonably left. This would produce statutory incoherence and cannot have been Parliament's intention.

...

'[49] Linked with the question of coherence is the question of reasonableness. In general terms, the provision of ss 175, 177, and 191 point towards a policy that in deciding whether a person is homeless or, if homeless, has become homeless intentionally, no regard should be had to property available or previously available to the applicant if it would not be reasonable to expect the applicant to occupy it or to have occupied it for a continuing period.

'[50] As Sedley LJ noted, the provision now contained in s 175(3) was introduced by the Housing and Planning Act 1986 by amendment to the Housing (Homeless Persons) Act 1977 following the decision in *Puhlhofer v Hillingdon London BC* [1986] 1 All ER 467, [1986] AC 484 (together with the provision now contained in s 177(2)).

...

'[56] I do not believe that Parliament can have positively intended by the language used in the amendments to create a distinction between a person with unfit accommodation available to him who was living in it and one who was not—a distinction so unreasonable that the majority in *Begum*'s case did not consider that any responsible authority could properly take the point. It is impossible to see any policy reason for such a distinction. Indeed, if there were a policy reason and Parliament positively intended to create such a distinction, then a responsible council could not be criticised for following it.

'[57] There remains the question whether the language used by Parliament nevertheless has the unavoidable effect for which the council contends. I would reach that result only if the words used were incapable of any other construction. In my view they are not. Good sense can be made of s 175(3) by construing the words "reasonable for him to continue to occupy" as synonymous with "reasonable for him to occupy for a continuing period", ie for the future, whether or not he is in occupation at the moment of the application or the decision.

'[58] This construction also "produces symmetry between the key concept of homelessness ... and intentional homelessness", to which Lord Hoffmann referred in *Awua v Brent London BC* [1995] 3 All ER 493 at 497, [1996] AC 55 at 67–68. He observed that if accommodation is so bad that leaving it for that reason would not make one intentionally homeless, then one is in law already homeless. Logic and justice suggests that the same should apply if a person has for the same reason not occupied accommodation which is physically available to him.' Maloba v Waltham Forest London Borough Council [2007] EWCA Civ 1281, [2008] 2 All ER 701 at [37]–[43], [46], [49]–[50], [56]–[58], per Toulson LJ

OFFENCE

Motoring offence

[For 40(2) Halsbury's Laws of England (4th Edn) (Reissue) para 680 see now 40(2) Halsbury's Laws (4th Edn) (2007 Reissue) para 971.]

OFFICIAL

Australia '[24] The result is that s 47(1) [of the Designs Act 1906 (Cth)] should be read so that the publication of a design at either: (1) an official exhibition; or (2) an officially recognised international exhibition is not a novelty-destroying prior publication.

'[25] I do not, however, accept that an official exhibition includes an exhibition organised by a private person or body, such as a private trade association. First, it does not conform with the meaning of Art 11(1) [of the Paris Convention for the Protection of Industrial Property]. Second, it lacks any limiting principle. If "official" is taken to implicate any body having officers (as Mr McGowan would have it), an exhibition organised by a large private corporation, which of course has officers, might qualify. So also might exhibitions organised by small corporations or neighbourhood associations. At a minimum, the approach proposed by Mr McGowan would entangle the courts in difficult issues of fact while robbing designers and exhibitors of certainty as to whether a particular exhibition did or did not qualify for s 47(1) protection. The net effect would be to encourage litigation without concomitantly encouraging designers to Ex or test their designs.

'[26] The only suggestion that "official" is not intended to refer to the involvement of a government is in Phillips, *Protecting Designs: Law on Litigation* (1994). There (at 287) the author suggests with regard to s 47 that "arguably an exhibition organised by [a] relevant trade or industry association will come within [the] ambit" of those terms. The history to which I have referred does not bear this out. The use of the word "official" is designed, in my opinion, to draw a distinction between public and privately organised exhibitions. It refers to an exhibition that is organised by a government: see *Oxford English Dictionary* definition of "official" at [4a]. The "government" may be federal or state or a local government authority.

'[27] In the instant case, the fair was organised by an industry association, the FIAA, and not by a government authority. Accordingly, it cannot qualify as an official exhibition for the purposes of s 47(1).' Chiropedic Bedding Pty Ltd v Radburg Pty Ltd [2007] FCA 1869, (2007) 243 ALR 334, (2007) 74 IPR 398, BC200710390 at [25]–[27], per Finkelstein J

OFFICIALLY RECOGNISED

Australia [Designs Act 1906 (Cth), s 47(1).]
'[28] This still leaves open the possibility that the fair was an "officially recognised international exhibition." "Officially recognised" can be defined in opposition to "official," which effectively means "officially organised". An

exhibition will be "officially recognised" if it is recognised by the federal or state government or any local government authority. Two obvious indicia of governmental recognition are: (1) the provision of public funds to fund the exhibition, particularly if given upon terms and conditions; and (2) the open participation of one or more ranking government officials at the opening, closing, or other formal ceremony or proceeding of the exhibition. While there will be other indicia of government recognition, it is neither necessary nor possible to provide an exhaustive list. The best indicia is that which may be readily ascertained ex ante from public information and thus provide prospective exhibitors with sufficient certainty as to whether an exhibition could qualify for protection under s 47(1).

'[29] In the present case, the fair was funded by a $200,000 grant from the Victorian government upon various conditions, including that the exhibition be opened to the general public for at least 1 day and that no goods be sold to the public. The fair was opened by the Minister for Small Business. On these facts, it is clear that the fair was an officially recognised exhibition.' Chiropedic Bedding Pty Ltd v Radburg Pty Ltd [2007] FCA 1869, (2007) 243 ALR 334, (2007) 74 IPR 398, BC200710390 at [28]–[29], per Finkelstein J

OPPORTUNITY

Opportunities for casino gambling

New Zealand '[1] This appeal concerns the meaning of the term "opportunities for casino gambling" which appears in ss 11, 12 and 139(2)(d) of the Gambling Act 2003 (the 2003 Act). This has particular importance for the appellants (to which we will refer collectively as "Skycity") because the prohibition in s 11 of the 2003 Act of any increase in gambling opportunities significantly affects Skycity's casino business. Skycity says that the phrase "opportunities for casino gambling" relates only to the number of casino games and/or the number of player positions associated with casino games in a particular casino. The Gambling Commission, which is the body charged with the regulating of casinos under the 2003 Act, contends that "opportunities for casino gambling" has a much broader meaning. The issue for determination is whether the narrow interpretation suggested by Skycity is correct.

...

'[76] Having carefully evaluated all of the arguments put to us by Skycity, we are unable to conclude that Parliament's intention in outlawing any increase in the opportunities for casino gambling can be read down as meaning simply a freezing of the maximum number of persons permitted to gamble in a casino at any one time (and the maximum number of gaming tables). The term "opportunities" is vague, but it strains the language of the provision too far to say that a change such as the speeding up of a game so that many more hands per hour occur than previously did is not, in conceptual terms, a[n] increase in the opportunities for gambling. We do not underestimate the difficulties which the Commission will face in assessing such matters, when it has no statistical base from which to make the assessment, nor do we underestimate the degree to which this involves what Skycity called "micro-management" by the Commission. On the other hand, if the legislature had intended only to prevent any increase in the maximum number of persons gambling in a casino at any one time, it is hard to see what role could have been envisaged for the Commission, other than a purely arithmetic one: s 12(1) would be redundant, because no "decisions" by the Commission would be required.

'[77] Ultimately, we are unable to accept Skycity's contention that matters other than the maximum number of persons permitted to gamble at any one time in a casino (and the maximum number of table games) should be excluded from consideration. We would not go as far as Cooper J in saying that anything could be relevant to an inquiry as to whether there has been an increase in the opportunities for casino gambling.'
Skycity Auckland Ltd v Gambling Commission [2007] NZCA 407, [2008] 2 NZLR 182 at [1], [76]–[77], per O'Regan J

ORDER

Order made by the court at trial

Australia [Sentencing Act 1989 (NSW), s 13A.]
'[20] As a result of changes made by the 1997 Act [Sentencing Legislation Further Amendment Act 1997 (NSW)], an eligibility requirement of service of at least 20 years of the sentence was imposed upon those the subject of a "non-release recommendation": s 13A(3)(b). This expression was now defined in s 13A(1) as meaning: "a recommendation or observation, or an expression of opinion, by the original sentencing court that (or to the effect that) the person should never be released from imprisonment". When considering an application in such cases the Supreme Court, if it were to accede to the application, had to be satisfied that there existed "special reasons" to justify the making of a determination: s 13A(3A).

'[21] In *Baker* [v R (2004) 223 CLR 513 at 532 [43], 210 ALR 1 at 14, [2004] HCA 45], this selection by the 1997 Act of a "non-release recommendation" was characterised as the creation of a criterion as the "trigger" for a particular legislative consequence. The relevant consequence concerned satisfaction of the eligibility requirement for application to the Supreme Court for determination of a minimum term and an additional term.

'[22] It is against that background that there falls to be considered the submission by the appellants that the remarks made by Newman J acquired with the enactment of the 1997 Act the character of an "order" within the definition of "sentence" in the Criminal Appeal Act. Of that submission, Spigelman CJ referred to the characterisation in *Baker* of the inclusion of non-release recommendations as a criterion for the operation of the 1997 Act. His Honour held that this was inconsistent with the proposition that the legal consequence of a non-release recommendation now could be said to arise from anything done "by" the court of trial within the meaning of the definition of "sentence" in s 2(1) of the Criminal Appeal Act. His Honour added that at the time Newman J made his recommendation it had no legal effect and that its subsequent legal effect was not something occasioned by anything done "by" the court of trial. We agree.

'[23] The same conclusion applies to the further change to the legislation made subsequently to the decision in *Baker*. Apparently for more abundant caution, it was provided by the Crimes (Sentencing Procedure) Amendment (Existing Life Sentences) Act 2005 (NSW) (the 2005 Amendment) that the definition of existing life sentence:

> … includes any such recommendation, observation or expression of opinion that (before, on or after the date of assent to the [2005 Amendment]) has been quashed, set aside or called into question …

…

'[24] The effect of the 2005 Amendment was to continue the adoption of non-release recommendations as a criterion for the operation of the amended Supreme Court review structure, notwithstanding curial disapproval or criticism of a particular recommendation. This did not have the consequence that the recommendation in question in this case had now acquired the character of an order by the court of trial.

'[25] It follows that leave to pursue out of time a sentencing appeal under s 5(1)(c) of the Criminal Appeal Act with respect to the recommendation made by Newman J was correctly refused and on a fundamental basis. This is that the recommendation never was and did not subsequently acquire the character of an "order made by the court of trial", with the result that the Court of Criminal Appeal lacked jurisdiction to entertain the proposed appeal.' Elliott v R *(No S215 of 2007)* [2007] HCA 51, (2007) 239 ALR 651, BC200709514 at [20]–[25], per Gummow, Hayne, Heydon, Crennan and Kiefel JJ

P

PARTISAN POLITICAL VIEWS

[The Education Act 1996, s 406 is headed 'Political indoctrination' and requires the local education authority, governing body and head teachers to forbid the promotion of 'partisan political views' in the teaching of any subject in the school.] '[11] ... Although there was some earlier suggestion on behalf of the defendant that *"partisan"* might relate to "party political", it soon became clear that it could not be and is not so limited. Mr Downes pointed to dictionary definitions suggesting the relevance of commitment, or adherence to a cause. In my judgment, the best synonym for it might be "one sided". Mr Downes, in para 27 of his skeleton argument, helpfully suggested that there were factors that could be considered by a court in determining whether the expression or promotion of a particular view could evidence or indicate *"partisan promotion"* of those views:

"(i) A superficial treatment of the subject matter typified by portraying factual or philosophical premises as being self-evident or trite with insufficient explanation or justification and without any indication that they may be the subject of legitimate controversy; the misleading use of scientific data; misrepresentations and half-truths; and one-sidedness.

(ii) The deployment of material in such a way as to prevent pupils meaningfully testing the veracity of the material and forming an independent understanding as to how reliable it is.

(iii) The exaltation of protagonists and their motives coupled with the demonisation of opponents and their motives.

(iv) The derivation of a moral expedient from assumed consequences requiring the viewer to adopt a particular view and course of action in order to do 'right' as opposed to 'wrong'."

This is clearly a useful analysis.' R *(on the application of Dimmock)* v Secretary of State for Education and Skills [2007] EWHC 2288 (Admin), [2008] 1 All ER 367 at [11], per Burton J

PECUNIARY ADVANTAGE

New Zealand '[6] The grounds on which Ms Hayes was granted leave to appeal on this aspect of the case were:[4]

(a) Whether, in terms of s 229A, now replaced by s 228, of the Crimes Act "pecuniary advantage" includes a situation where there is an avoidance of the risk of losing a compensation benefit under accident compensation legislation.

(b) Whether the trial Judge erred in law in not directing the jury in respect of the legislative provisions relating to continuing entitlement to a compensation benefit.

'[7] The concept of pecuniary advantage first entered New Zealand law in 1973 with the enactment of s 229A by s 4 of the Crimes Amendment Act 1973. Its source was the Theft Act 1968 (UK). The English authorities on pecuniary advantage do not assist because of the definition which applied to its use there and the way it was interpreted. In New Zealand the expression is not defined.

'[8] The issue, as the Court of Appeal saw it, was whether, in order to obtain a pecuniary advantage, the accused had to obtain compensation payments to which she was not entitled; or whether a pecuniary advantage included the situation where she avoided the risk of losing compensation. In the former case, the question of the accused's entitlement to compensation would be a material issue and the Judge's failure to direct the jury on that issue would have been a material error. The Court of Appeal concluded that a pecuniary advantage included Ms Hayes avoiding the risk that, on a reassessment, compensation payments would have been stopped. On this premise the Judge was justified in not directing on the question of entitlement. Ms Hayes' stance, in this Court and below, was that for her to gain a pecuniary advantage the Crown had to show more than the avoidance of the risk of the payments being stopped. It had to show she had gained an actual monetary advantage to which she had no entitlement. The Judge had therefore erred in not directing the jury on that basis.

'[9] The way in which the argument developed in the Court of Appeal, and indeed in this Court, was substantially influenced by previous decisions of the Court of Appeal on the subject of pecuniary advantage. Those decisions held that obtaining something to which the accused is entitled cannot amount to obtaining a pecuniary advantage. Hence the Crown must show lack of entitlement.

'[10] In *R v Firth* [[1998] 1 NZLR 513] the Court of Appeal said [at 516]:

"We have not been referred to any case which specifically discusses the point but we think it is implicit in the term 'advantage' that if a defendant were legally entitled to receive the money in question, he has not obtained a pecuniary advantage to which he was not entitled. In *Ruka v Department of Social Welfare* [1997] 1 NZLR 154 at p 163 this Court recorded, seemingly without argument on the point, that that was the position in regard to the Social Welfare benefit there in issue."

'[11] The passage in *Ruka v Department of Social Welfare* [1997] 1 NZLR 154 to which the Court was referring is contained in the judgment of Blanchard J in which Richardson P joined. Their Honours there said [at 163] of charges under s 229A:

"Miss Ruka was charged that with fraudulent intent she used applications under the Social Security Act for the purpose of obtaining a pecuniary advantage. If, as we have concluded, she qualified for the benefits in question because she was not in a relationship in the nature of marriage, it follows that she did not, whatever her intent, use a document to obtain an advantage; that is, something to which she had no entitlement."

'[12] We consider the approach taken in *Ruka* and followed in *Firth* does not reflect either the text or the purpose of the legislation. In its terms the legislation does not require proof of lack of entitlement. The concept of entitlement can arise, if at all, only by implication from the word "advantage". But if a person seeking to obtain a pecuniary advantage uses a document with intent to defraud (s 229A), or dishonestly and without claim of right (s 228), we do not consider it is any defence to say that the user of the document was entitled to the advantage. The statutory purpose is to criminalise the use of dishonest means directed to gaining the advantage even if the accused is otherwise entitled to it. Questions of actual entitlement may well be relevant to sentence, but they are not relevant to guilt, save that a belief in entitlement will, of course, be relevant to mens rea.

'[13] In view of the tenor of some of the submissions, it is worth stating at this point that for present purposes an unsuccessful use of a document is just as much a use as a successful one. An unsuccessful use must not be equated conceptually with an attempted use. The concept of attempt relates to use, not to the ultimate obtaining of a pecuniary advantage, which is not a necessary ingredient of the offence. Because the use does not have to be successful it may be difficult to draw a clear line between use and attempted use. That seems to be why attempts have been brought within the definition of the offence ("uses or attempts to use any document"), rather than being left to be dealt with, as is usual, under s 72 of the Crimes Act. This supports the view that the offence is directed at the dishonest conduct by means of which the pecuniary advantage is sought.

'[14] Both s 229A and s 228 use the expression "pecuniary advantage" in conjunction with the expression "valuable consideration". The composite expression is "pecuniary advantage or valuable consideration". The second part of this conjunction does not say or *other* valuable consideration. That must, however, be the effect of the terms pecuniary advantage and valuable consideration when they are read together in their statutory context. Leaving aside the other concepts addressed in the sections, the statutory purpose must have been to encompass anything capable of being valuable consideration, whether of a monetary kind or of any other kind; in short, money or money's worth.

'[15] The construction we would adopt of the expression "pecuniary advantage" in ss 229A and 228 also derives support from the fact that if the charges against Ms Hayes had been framed on the basis that her purpose or intent was to obtain valuable consideration as opposed to pecuniary advantage, the implicit comparison with entitlement said to be inherent in the word "advantage" could not be present. It is self-evident that the weekly compensation payments represented valuable consideration, irrespective of entitlement. The same can be said of the concepts of property and service, which are also found in s 228. The more is this so because property is defined in s 2 as including money. Hence money is actually included within three of the four concepts covered by s 228. It cannot be right that the question of entitlement should be regarded as relevant on the basis of one framing of the charges and not on the basis of another. Whether the recipient is entitled to receive the weekly compensation payments does not make them any more or less property or valuable consideration; nor should it make them any more or less a pecuniary advantage.

'[16] This Court is not bound by the decisions in *Ruka* and *Firth*. We respectfully consider they should not be followed on this point. As already foreshadowed there is a different way of construing the expression "pecuniary advantage" which better reflects both the statutory language and purpose and does not involve the difficulties inherent in an approach which has been held to require consideration of entitlement to and risk of losing compensation. The preferable construction treats the expression "pecuniary advantage" as meaning simply anything that enhances the accused's financial position. It is that enhancement which constitutes the element of advantage. If what the accused person is seeking to obtain is of that kind, it does not matter whether he or she is entitled to it, or may be trying to avoid the risk of not continuing to receive it. It follows that even if the person from whom the pecuniary advantage is sought has an obligation to supply it to the recipient, that will not prevent the use of dishonest means to procure the advantage from being an offence.

'[17] As the Court of Appeal put it in *R v Thomas* [(Court of Appeal, CA 71/00, 7 June 2001, McGrath, Ellis and McGechan JJ)], a pecuniary advantage advances the economic interests of the recipient. Some of the submissions seem to have proceeded on the assumption that somehow the continuation of the weekly compensation payments could not in itself be an advantage. It must have been for this reason that the argument focused on questions such as the risk of the compensation being stopped or being lost. On the view we take, each weekly payment of compensation, which it was Ms Hayes' purpose to obtain, constituted a pecuniary advantage to her.

'[18] This approach overcomes what we see as a potentially difficult aspect of the Court of Appeal's reasoning in *Firth*. Immediately after the passage cited above the Court said that it did not necessarily follow that in all cases the Crown must establish that the accused was not entitled to the advantage. The Court then gave as an example a case (*R v Gunthorp* [2003] 2 NZLR 433, date of judgment 9 June 1993))] in which the concept of entitlement could not apply. The advantage in that case was attaining better loan terms than were available in the marketplace. The concept of legal entitlement could not apply to such an advantage. The difficulty is twofold. First, it seems unlikely that Parliament envisaged that lack of legal entitlement would be a formal ingredient of the offence in some situations but not others. Second, *Firth* raises the potential for uncertainty as to when entitlement is an issue and when it is not. We consider that the example given and this uncertainty both demonstrate that the concept of advantage should not be construed as involving a comparative notion, that is, obtaining a better financial outcome than that to which you are entitled in law. The underlying notion is practical rather than comparative. By practical we mean simply getting something which enhances your financial position. As we have said, this construction better aligns the concept of pecuniary advantage with the cognate concepts of property, service and valuable consideration found in s 228.

'[19] Support for the approach we are taking also comes from the decision of the Court of Appeal for England and Wales in *Re Attorney-General's Reference (No 1 of 2001)* [[2003] 1 WLR 395]. In that case the defendants were the parents of a young woman who had been arrested overseas and charged with a criminal offence. A trust fund was established to assist the family with the proceedings. Contributions were made by members of the public. Some money which had been donated to the defendants personally, to use as they chose, was mistakenly paid into the trust fund. The defendants presented a forged invoice to the trustees of the fund seeking payment for accommodation expenses they had never incurred. The trustees paid the invoice.

'[20] The defendants were charged with dishonestly furnishing false information with a view to gain for themselves, contrary to s 17 of the Theft Act (UK). The trial Judge held that since at least some of the money in the trust fund "must have belonged" to the defendants they could not be said to have acted with a view to gain for themselves. He accordingly directed that they be acquitted.

'[21] The Attorney-General referred the point to the Court of Appeal, which held that, even if the accused were entitled to payment, they still committed an offence because of the dishonesty with which they sought to procure it. In the course of giving the judgment of the Court, Kennedy LJ said [at paras [27]–[28]]:[2]

"The successful submission focused on the words 'with a view to gain for themselves'. 'Gain' is defined in s 34(2)(a) as including 'a gain by keeping what one has as well as a gain by getting what one has not'. In relation to blackmail, which is also governed by s 34, the question has arisen whether a person demanding money undoubtedly owed to him did have a view to gain. In *R v Parkes* [1973] Crim LR 358 that question was answered by Judge Dean QC in the affirmative. As he put it, by intending to obtain hard cash as opposed to a mere right of action in respect of the debt the defendant was getting more than he already had, and in his commentary on that case Professor Smith submitted that gain means acquisition, whether at a profit or not. That was the intention of the Criminal Law Revision Committee's Eighth Report on Theft and Related Offences (1966) (Cmnd 2977), which in para 121 stated: 'the person with a genuine claim will be guilty unless he believes that it is proper to use the menaces to enforce his claim.' ...

"[28] In our judgment, *R v Parkes* [1973] Crim LR 358 was rightly decided, and it follows that on the facts of the present case, contrary to what was decided by the trial judge, there was clear evidence that [the defendants] were acting with a view to gain for themselves. Even if they had a valid claim to some of the money in the trust fund on the basis that the money should never have gone into the fund, and even recognising that they were beneficiaries under the trust, makes no difference, because none of that relates to what they were doing at the material time: they were dishonestly making use of a false invoice to substantiate a claim for expenses, and thus to extract from the trustees a cheque for £9113.50. As Judge Dean QC put it in *R v Parkes*, they were seeking to obtain hard cash as opposed to a mere right to claim."

There is a sufficient conceptual parallel between "advantage" and "gain" to make the Court of Appeal's reasoning helpful in the resolution of the case before us.

'[22] On this basis, it is not necessary to discuss the reasoning of the Court of Appeal or the submissions which were made in this Court seeking to attack or uphold that reasoning. It is, however, appropriate to record that the Court of Appeal was not asked, nor was it free, to depart from the view that has hitherto been taken about the role that the question of entitlement should play in construing the term "pecuniary advantage". Our focus from this point on will necessarily depart somewhat from the precise formulation of the first ground of appeal with its reference to "risk of losing" a compensation benefit. We return to the circumstances of this case on that basis.

'[23] The offence created by s 229A, as it related to Ms Hayes' case, involved proof that:
  (1) with intent to defraud;
  (2) she used a document;
  (3) which was capable of being used to obtain a pecuniary advantage;
  (4) for the purpose of obtaining a pecuniary advantage.

The offence created by s 228 involved proof that:
  (1) Ms Hayes used a document;
  (2) dishonestly and without claim of right;
  (3) with intent to obtain a pecuniary advantage.

'[24] The crucial elements for present purposes are, respectively, the fourth and the third; specifically, whether Ms Hayes had the purpose of obtaining or the intent to obtain something that constituted a pecuniary advantage when she used the medical certificates by supplying them to ACC. As documents the medical certificates were clearly capable of being used to obtain a pecuniary advantage. Ms Hayes' purpose and intent when using them was undoubtedly to obtain weekly compensation payments. What she was endeavouring to obtain was unquestionably a pecuniary advantage in that its receipt would enhance her financial position. Provided she had an intent to defraud, or acted dishonestly and without claim of right, Ms Hayes therefore committed offences against s 229A and s 228.

'[25] When the essential elements of the offences are analysed as they should be, there is nothing to support the contention that the trial Judge erred in not directing the jury on the legislative provisions concerning what entitlement

Ms Hayes may or may not have had. Proof that her purpose was to obtain the pecuniary advantage of weekly compensation did not require any examination of her legal entitlement to that compensation. She committed an offence if she used the medical certificates for the purpose of obtaining weekly compensation and with the requisite dishonest mind. The actus reus of the offence was constituted by her use of the relevant document for the purpose of obtaining a pecuniary advantage. The Crown was required to prove that purpose, but not that she actually obtained a pecuniary advantage. The weekly compensation monies she was seeking were in themselves a pecuniary advantage, irrespective of entitlement. The trial Judge did not therefore err by failing to direct on the subject of entitlement.' R v Hayes [2008] NZSC 3, [2008] 2 NZLR 321 at [6]–[25], per Tipping J

PERSON IN AUTHORITY

Canada

'[34] The confessions rule ensures that statements made out of court by an accused to a person in authority are admissible only if the statements were voluntary. The relevant principles were canvassed by this Court in *R v Hodgson* [1998] 2 SCR 449, and *R v Oickle* [2000] 2 SCR 3, 2000 SCC 38. In *Oickle*, at paras 47–71, the Court set out the factors relevant to the voluntariness inquiry. The issue argued on this appeal by the appellant was whether the impugned statements were made to a "person in authority" within the meaning of *Hodgson*, and not whether they were free and voluntary within the meaning of *Oickle*.

'[35] The rule, the policies supporting it, and the definition of "person in authority", were all considered in *Hodgson*, Cory J expressed the rule's rationale as follows:

> The rule is based upon two fundamentally important concepts: the need to ensure the reliability of the statement and the need to ensure fairness by guarding against improper coercion by the state.
> ...
> It cannot be forgotten that it is the nature of the authority exerted by the state that might prompt an involuntary statement ... . In other words, it is the fear of reprisal or hope of leniency that persons in authority may hold out and which is associated with their official status that may render a statement involuntary ... . This limitation [ie, the

person in authority requirement] is appropriate since most criminal investigations are undertaken by the state, and it is then that an accused is most vulnerable to state coercion. [paras 48 and 24]

The underlying rationale of the "person in authority" analysis is to avoid the unfairness and unreliability of admitting statements made when the accused believes himself or herself to be under pressure from the uniquely coercive power of the state. In *Hodgson*, although explicitly invited to do so, the Court refused to eliminate the requirement for a "person in authority" threshold determination. As Cory J stated, were it not for this requisite inquiry,

> all statements to undercover police officers would become subject to the confessions rule, even though the accused was completely unaware of their status and, at the time he made the statement, would never have considered the undercover officers to be persons in authority. [para 25]

'[36] There is no doubt, as the Court observed in *Hodgson*, at para 26, that statements can sometimes be made in such coercive circumstances that their reliability is jeopardized even if they were not made to a person in authority. The admissibility of such statements is filtered through exclusionary doctrines like abuse of process at common law and under the *Canadian Charter of Rights and Freedoms*, to prevent the admission of statements that undermine the integrity of the judicial process. The "abuse of process" argument was, in fact, made by Mr Grandinetti at trial, but was rejected both at trial and on appeal, and was not argued before us.

'[37] In *Hodgson*, the Court delineated the process for assessing whether a confession should be admitted. First, there is an evidentiary burden on the accused to show that there is a valid issue for consideration about whether, when the accused made the confession, he or she believed that the person to whom it was made was a person in authority. A "person in authority" is generally someone engaged in the arrest, detention, interrogation or prosecution of the accused. The burden then shifts to the Crown to prove, beyond a reasonable doubt, either that the accused did not reasonably believe that the person to whom the confession was made was a person in authority, or, if he or she did so believe, that the statement was made voluntarily. The question of voluntariness is not relevant unless the threshold determination has been made that the confession was made to a "person in authority".

'[38] The test of who is a "person in authority" is largely subjective, focusing on the accused's perception of the person to whom he or she is making the statement. The operative question is whether the accused, based on his or her perception of the recipient's ability to influence the prosecution, believed either that refusing to make a statement to the person would result in prejudice, or that making one would result in favourable treatment.

'[39] There is also an objective element, namely, the reasonableness of the accused's belief that he or she is speaking to a person in authority. It is not enough, however, that an accused reasonably believe that a person can influence the course of the investigation or prosecution. As the trial judge correctly concluded:

> [R]eason and common sense dictates that when the cases speak of a person in authority as one who is capable of controlling or influencing the course of the proceedings, it is from the perspective of someone who is involved in the investigation, the apprehension and prosecution of a criminal offence resulting in a conviction, an agent of the police or someone working in collaboration with the police. It does not include someone who seeks to sabotage the investigation or steer the investigation away from a suspect that the state is investigating.

(Alta QB, No 98032644C5, April 30 1999, at para 56)

'[40] Although the person in authority test is not a categorical one, absent unusual circumstances an undercover officer will not be a person in authority since, from the accused's viewpoint, he or she will not usually be so viewed. This position is supported by precedent. As Cory J explained in *Hodgson*:

> The receiver's status as a person in authority arises only if the accused had knowledge of that status. If the accused cannot show that he or she had knowledge of the receiver's status (as, for example, in the case of an undercover police officer) ..., the inquiry pertaining to the receiver as a person in authority must end. [para 39]

See also *Rothman v The Queen* [1981] 1 SCR 640, at p 664; *R v Todd* (1901) 4 CCC 514 (Man KB), at p 527.

'[41] The appellant conceded that undercover officers are usually not persons in authority. His position is that although undercover officers are not usually persons in authority, when an undercover operation includes as part of its ruse a suggested association with corrupt police, who the accused is told could influence the investigation and prosecution of the offence, the officers qualify as persons in authority.

'[42] However, under the traditional confession rule,

> a person in authority is a person concerned with the prosecution who, in the opinion of the accused, can influence the course of the prosecution.

(*R v Berger* (1975) 27 CCC (2d) 357 (BCCA), at p 385, cited in *Hodgson*, at para 33).

'[43] This, it seems to me, is further elaborated in *Hodgson* by Cory J's description of a person in authority as someone whom the confessor perceives to be "an agent of the police or prosecuting authorities", "allied with the state authorities", "acting on behalf of the police or prosecuting authorities", and "acting in concert with the police or prosecutorial authorities, or as their agent" (paras 34–36 and 47). He amplified this theory as follows:

> Since the person in authority requirement is aimed at controlling coercive state conduct, the test for a person in authority should not include those whom the accused unreasonably believes to be acting on behalf of the state. Thus, where the accused speaks out of fear of reprisal or hope of advantage because he reasonably believes the person receiving the statement is acting as an agent of the police or prosecuting authorities and could therefore influence or control the proceedings against him or her, then the receiver of the statement is properly considered a person in authority. In other words, the evidence must disclose not only that the accused subjectively believed the receiver of the statement to be in a position to control the proceedings against the accused, but must also establish an objectively reasonable basis for that belief ... .
> ...
> ... there is no catalogue of persons, beyond a peace officer or prison guard, who are automatically considered a person in authority solely by virtue of their status. A parent, doctor, teacher or employer all may be found to be a person in authority if the circumstances warrant, but their status, or the mere fact that they may wield some personal authority over the accused, is not

sufficient to establish them as persons in authority for the purposes of the confessions rule ... . [T]he person in authority requirement has evolved in a manner that avoids a formalistic or legalistic approach to the interactions between ordinary citizens. Instead, it requires a case-by-case consideration of the accused's belief as to the ability of the receiver of the statement to influence the prosecution or investigation of the crime. That is to say, the trial judge must determine whether the accused reasonably believed the receiver of the statement was acting on behalf of the police or prosecuting authorities. [paras. 34 and 36]

'[44] The appellant believed that the undercover officers were criminals, not police officers, albeit criminals with corrupt police contacts who could potentially influence the investigation against him. When, as in this case, the accused confesses to an undercover officer he thinks can influence his murder investigation by enlisting corrupt police officers, the state's coercive power is not engaged. The statements, therefore, were not made to a person in authority.' R v Grandinetti [2005] 1 SCR 27, 2005 SCC 5 at [34]–[44], per Abella J

PRACTICABLE

As far as is practicable

Australia '[35] The obligation imposed on Airservices by s 9(2) of the Air Services Act [1995 (Cth)] is intended to assist in the protection of the environment from the direct and indirect effects of the operation and use of aircraft, "as far as is practicable". *The Macquarie Dictionary* (revised 3rd ed) gives a fuller meaning of the word "practicable" as:

> ... capable of being put into practice, done, or effected, *especially with the available means or within reason or prudence; feasible*. [Emphasis added.]

What is "practicable" includes consideration of Airservices' available means to perform the relevant function and the nature of the task itself.

'[36] Airservices' function of "promoting and fostering civil aviation" in Australia under s 8(1)(b) raises the possibility that there may be an expansion of civil aviation over time to meet the changing needs and demands of the people of Australia. None the less, s 9(2) recognises that that activity has an environmental consequence. Thus, s 9(2) requires Airservices to take measures, in a way that is reasonable and prudent, to adopt a means of promoting and fostering civil aviation that is to be the least harmful, and will offer the greatest protection, to the environment. However, s 9(2) does not impose on Airservices an absolute obligation to protect the environment. Rather the section imposes a condition on the exercise of the functions entrusted to Airservices.

'[37] And s 16(1) is a power of the minister to give directions to Airservices relating to the performance of its existing functions or the exercise of its existing powers. When Airservices exercises a function in a manner directed by the minister under s 16, s 16(3) requires it give effect to the policy objectives of the executive government.

'[38] The manner in which Airservices performs the function or exercises the power the subject of a s 16 direction is further qualified by the words "as far as is practicable" in s 9(2). What is "practicable" for the purposes of s 9(2) can be affected by the resources available to Airservices with which it can perform its functions. ...' The Village Building Co Ltd (ACN 056 509 025) v Airservices Australia [2007] FCA 1242, (2007) 241 ALR 685, BC200706932 at [35]–[38], per Rares J

PREMISES

Any premises in which the tenant's flat is contained

[Under the Leasehold Reform, Housing and Urban Development Act 1993, s 47, the court can by order declare that the right to acquire a new lease is not exercisable by a tenant by reason of the landlord's intention to redevelop 'any premises in which the tenant's flat is contained'. The landlord intended to redevelop the 'premises' by combining the tenant's flat with a flat owned by a subsidiary of the landlord and situated immediately below the tenant's flat to form a single duplex apartment. Before the judge it contended that the two flats constituted 'premises' in which the tenant's flat was contained within s 47(2)(b). The judge held that, for the purposes of s 47(2), the premises in which the tenant's flat was contained had to be the whole block or at least some self-contained part of the block. He therefore dismissed the landlord's application. The Court of Appeal allowed the landlord's appeal, holding that any part of the block which comprised contiguous flats could constitute 'premises' in which, for s 47(2) purposes, each of the flats was contained. The tenant appealed to the House of Lords contending that 'premises' must be a physical space which is objectively recognisable at the time when the tenant serves his notice and not a notional space defined by the landlord in whatever way it chooses.] '[37] There can be no doubt about what the 1993 Act was designed to achieve. It was designed to give long-leaseholders of flats rights as close as possible to those of freeholders, at a price approximating to the market price, though subject to some statutory assumptions. That purpose would be frustrated if the landlord could defeat either of those rights by proposing to do comparatively minor works to the building involved. I accept that the definition of premises in Ch I is not applied in Ch II, but it is legitimate to look at the scale of redevelopment which would defeat the right of collective enfranchisement in Ch I in order to consider what scale of redevelopment would defeat the right to a new lease in Ch II. Section 23(2) is in almost identical terms to s 47(2). It contemplates demolition or reconstruction of or substantial works of construction to a whole or a substantial part of a whole building or self contained part of a building. These are major works, requiring a large investment in proportion to the value of the premises, not simply the reconstruction of a small part for the purpose of making a profit on that part.

'[38] Nor can it have been Parliament's intention to allow the landlord to define the "premises" for itself. That would in many cases allow it to defeat the right to a new lease. The purpose of granting the right to buy a new lease was to support the value of the old. The final years of long leases can now be bought and sold with a reasonable expectation that they can be extended when they come to an end. There has to be some objective way of estimating how likely it is that the landlord will be able to prevent that.

'[39] Hence it seems to me clear that "any premises in which the flat is contained" must be an objectively recognisable physical space, something which the landlord, the tenant, the visitor, the prospective purchaser would recognise as "premises". In common with Lord Scott, I have little doubt that, if one asked a visitor, "in which premises is flat 77, Boydell Court, contained?", the visitor would say "Block B". The visitor would not further sub-divide the space. In a row of terraced houses, or in a pair of

semi-detached houses, the visitor would regard each house as the "premises". In a single block of flats with several entrances leading to separate staircases, the visitor might also say "Block B" rather than the whole building. Much would depend upon the physical facts on the ground. This is a much more objective test than that proposed by the landlord and in most cases would lead to very similar results to those in collective enfranchisement cases in Ch I.

'[40] It has hitherto been taken for granted that, if the premises are Block B, then two flats out of the fifty do not constitute "a substantial part of" the premises. Were it otherwise there would have been no point in the appellant pursuing matters to this House. The respondent has not hitherto sought to argue otherwise. In my view, it was right not to do so. "Substantial" is a word which has a wide range of meanings. Sometimes it can mean "not little". Sometimes it can mean "almost complete", as in "in substantial agreement". Often it means "big" or "solid", as in a "substantial house". Sometimes it means "weighty" or "serious", as in a "substantial reason". It will take its meaning from its context. But in an expression such as a "substantial part" there is clearly an element of comparison with the whole: it is something other than a small or insignificant or insubstantial part. There may be both a qualitative element of size, weight or importance in its own right; and a quantitative element, of size, weight or importance in relation to the whole. The works intended by this landlord are substantial in relation to each of the flats involved, but those flats do not in my view constitute a substantial part of the whole premises. ...' Majorstake Ltd v Curtis [2008] UKHL 10, [2008] 2 All ER 303 at [37]–[40], per Baroness Hale of Richmond

PRIMA FACIE GROUND

New Zealand [Under the Judicature Act 1908, s 88B(2), leave for a vexatious litigant to pursue a proceeding is not to be granted unless the court is satisfied that the proceeding is not an abuse of the process of the court and that there was prima facie ground for the proceeding.] '[8] The key requirements are that the court must be satisfied that the proposed proceeding is not an abuse of the process of the court and that there is prima facie ground for the proceeding.

'[9] It is well settled that the discretion to grant leave to institute or continue proceedings by a vexatious litigant is a jurisdiction to be exercised very carefully since, as Davies LJ said in writing for the English Court of Appeal in *Becker v Teale* [1971] 3 All ER 715 at p 716:

> "Ex hypothesi the person has already 'habitually and persistently and without any reasonable ground instituted vexatious proceedings' ..."

'[10] Davies LJ added that there is a "high onus" cast on such a person seeking leave under the English statute which was, at that time, in terms virtually identical to s 88B of the Judicature Act.

'[11] There are, however, competing interests to be considered, including the fact that a refusal to grant leave amounts to a denial of every citizen's usual right of access to the courts. As Staughton LJ said in *Attorney-General v Jones* [1990] 1 WLR 859 at p 865:

> "The power to restrain someone from commencing or continuing legal proceedings is no doubt a drastic restriction of his civil rights, and is still a restriction if it is subject to the grant of leave by a High Court Judge. But there must come a time when it is right to exercise that power for at least two reasons. First, the opponents who are harassed by the worry and expense of vexatious litigation are entitled to protection; secondly the resources of the judicial system are barely sufficient to afford justice without unreasonable delay to those who do have genuine grievances, and should not be squandered on those who do not."

'[12] In England, the previous legislation considered in *Becker v Teale* has been replaced by s 42 of the Supreme Court Act 1981 (UK). The term "prima facie ground" has been replaced with "reasonable ground". But in *Re C* (1989) Times, 14 November, Brooke J (as he then was) sitting in the Queen's Bench Division, did not consider there to be a material difference between the two terms.

'[13] In New Zealand, there is relatively little authority on the threshold prescribed by the expression "prima facie ground". In *Black, White and Grey Cabs Ltd v Hill* (High Court, Auckland, CP 1013/91, 10 December 1993), Barker J discussed *Becker v Teale* and stated at p 10:

> "The requirement of a prima facie case is higher than the current test for the grant of an interim injunction; that is, a serious question to be tried. Authorities on a prima facie case show that the plaintiff must show 'probable cause for relief at the hearing'; *Republic of Peru v Dreyfus Brothers and Co* (1888) 38 Ch D 348 at p 362, or 'it is likely

to succeed'; *Harman Pictures v Osborne* [1967] 2 All ER 324 at p 336. Add to that the views expressed in *Becker v Teale* that this particular jurisdiction should be 'very carefully exercised' with 'a high onus' cast on the applicant."

'[14] More recently, Fogarty J considered another application for leave by the present applicant Mr Collier in a proposed proceeding against five named defendants. Fogarty J granted leave in a reserved judgment (*Re Collier* [2004] NZAR 472). Fogarty J found at para [7] on the facts of the case before him that there was a material difference between the standard identified by Barker J in *Black, White and Grey Cabs Ltd v Hill* and the standard of "prima facie ground". Fogarty J stated at para [6]:

> "... I interpret the prima facie test in the traditional way of the Court being satisfied, without hearing the other side, that the plaintiff has a good reason to start or continue a proceeding."

'[15] I agree with Fogarty J that the tests of "probable cause for relief" or "likely to succeed" referred to by Barker J in *Black, White and Grey Cabs Ltd* are not apt in the context of s 88B(2). The expression "prima facie ground" must be applied to the facts of the case in accordance with its usual meaning. Spiller, *Butterworths New Zealand Law Dictionary* (6th ed, 2005), defines "prima facie case" as:

> "A serious, as opposed to a speculative case.
>
> A litigating party is said to have a prima facie case when the evidence in his or her favour is sufficiently strong for his or her opponent to be called on to answer it."

'[16] This definition adequately captures the flavour of the expression "prima facie ground" in s 88B(2), focusing on the strength of the evidence, which must reach a sufficiently high threshold to require the potential defendant to respond to it. But the threshold to be established before leave may be given under s 88B(2) is not to be confused with the level of scrutiny required in respect of the claim. The "careful scrutiny" test remains apposite and the court is not bound to accept uncritically the assertions made by the vexatious litigant seeking leave. Where relevant, the background leading to the making of the order declaring the applicant a vexatious litigant is to be considered. The court may also require the applicant to produce appropriate evidence in support of the claim as Fogarty J did in connection with the application Mr Collier made in 2004.' Re Collier [2008] 2 NZLR 505 at [8]–[16], per Randerson J (Chief High Court Judge)

PROMOTION

[The Education Act 1996, s 406 is headed "Political indoctrination" and requires the local education authority, governing body and head teachers to forbid the 'promotion' of partisan political views in the teaching of any subject in the school.] '[12] Mr Downes submits that, if the film [former United States Vice-President Al Gore's film, 'An Inconvenient Truth'], which is sent to schools in order to facilitate its showing, is itself a partisan political film, one that "*promotes partisan political views*", and if schools then make available such film to its teachers, and if teachers then show such film to their pupils, then inevitably there is the "*promotion of partisan political views*" in the teaching of any subject in the school, which is thus not only not being "*forbidden*" by the local education authority (and the DES), but being positively facilitated by them. Thus he submits, irrespective of any publication of guidance, the breach of the statute is, as he puts it, irremediable. I do not agree, and prefer the submissions of Mr Chamberlain. The statute cannot possibly mean that s 406 is breached whenever a partisan political film is shown to pupils in school time. Mr Downes has to assert that there is, depending on the context, an exception that can be made in respect of the teaching of history, but I cannot see how, on his interpretation of the statute, any such exception can be carved out. It must be as much of a breach of the statute, on his construction, for the school or a teacher to show in a history class a film for example of Nazi or Leninist/Stalinist propaganda, or for that matter to make available such literature in documentary form, or to show a racist or an anti-racialist film in a history or a citizenship class, as it is to show or distribute any other film or document which promotes partisan political views. Such an approach however construes the word "promotion" as if it meant nothing more than "presentation". What is forbidden by the statute is, as the side heading makes clear, "political indoctrination". If a teacher uses the platform of a classroom to *promote* partisan political views *in the teaching of* any subject, then that would offend against the statute. If on the other hand a teacher, in the course of a school day and as part of the syllabus, presents to his pupils, no doubt with the appropriate setting and with proper

tuition and debate, a film or document which itself promotes in a partisan way some political view, that cannot possibly in my judgment be the mischief against which the statute was intended to protect pupils. It would not only lead to bland education, but to education which did not give the opportunity to pupils to learn about views with which they might, vehemently or otherwise, either agree or disagree. I conclude that the mere distribution by the defendant to schools to facilitate their showing the film, and accompanied by guidance, to which I shall refer, is not per se, or irremediably, a promotion of those partisan political views.' R (on the application of Dimmock) v Secretary of State for Education and Skills [2007] EWHC 2288 (Admin), [2008] 1 All ER 367 at [12], per Burton J

PSYCHOPATHIC DISORDER

[Note that the definition of 'psychopathic disorder' in the Mental Health Act 1983, s 1(1) is prospectively repealed by the Mental Health Act 2007, s 1(3).]

PUBLIC

Avaliable to the public

Canada '[14] Paragraph 17(2)(*d*) of the *Statistics Act* [RSC, 1985, c S-19] provides that the Chief Statistician may authorize the disclosure of information "available to the public" under any statutory or other law. Paragraph 8(2)(*k*) of the *Privacy Act* [RSC, 1985, c P-21] allows the disclosure of personal information to "any aboriginal government, association of aboriginal people, Indian band, government institution or part thereof, or to any person acting on behalf of such government, association, band, institution or part thereof." Does this limited segment of the population amount to "public" within the meaning of paragraph 17(2)(*d*) of the *Statistics Act*? The applications Judge concluded that it does and I agree.

'[15] The applications Judge held that the word "public" in the phrase "available to the public" is a noun, which, according to the *Canadian Oxford Dictionary*, has three meanings, referring to either the entirety of the community, to members of the community, or to a section of the community sharing a common status or interest. The applications Judge concluded that "[e]ach of these meanings is sufficient to meet the definition of public in paragraph 17(2)(*d*) of the *Statistics Act*" (paragraph 53). With respect to the words "information available to the public" [underlining added], the applications Judge stated that these words denote "records capable of being obtained by the entire general public, or by members or sections thereof" (paragraph 54). Based on this interpretation, the applications Judge concluded that the census information requested by the Algonquin bands "is exactly the type of information which Parliament intended under [paragraph 8(2)(*k*) of] the *Privacy Act* may be disclosed to an Aboriginal people or Indian band" (paragraph 56).

'[16] The appellant submits that the term "available to the public" refers "to the community at large." In making this submission, the appellant argues that "disclosure in accord[ance] with paragraph 8(2)(k) — which only contemplates discretionary disclosure to certain people for a specific purpose — cannot be the same as 'public availability' within the meaning of paragraph 19(2)(*b*) [of the *Access to Information Act* [RSC, 1985, c A-1]]" adding that "[t]here is no reason why the concept of "available to the public" should be interpreted differently in paragraph 17(2)(*d*) of the *Statistics Act* than in subsection 19(2) of the [*Access to Information Act*]*."

'[17] The respondent submits that there are compelling reasons why the concept of the public may vary in scope in these two legislative provisions. The respondent points out that the statutory language is not identical in both provisions: while paragraph 19(2)(*b*) of the *Access to Information Act* contemplates disclosure "if ... the information is publicly available / *dans les cas où [...] le public y a accès*", paragraph 17(2)(*d*) of the *Statistics Act*, in turn, authorizes disclosure of "information available to the public under any statutory or other law / *les renseignements mis à la disposition du public en vertu d'une loi ou de toute autre règle de droit*." The respondent further submits that the meaning of "the public" under paragraph 17(2)(*d*) of the *Statistics Act* can be contrasted with subsection 2(2) of the *Access to Information Act* where the wording is "available to the general public" [underlining added] ("*à la disposition du grand public*") [underlining added]. This demonstrates that when Parliament intended to limit the scope of the noun "the public" to mean only the public in its entirety rather than particular segments of it, it used legislative language that clearly demonstrates this intent.

'[18] In my view, even if paragraph 19(2)(*b*) of the *Access to Information Act* and

paragraph 17(2)(*d*) of the *Statistics Act* were interpreted to mean the same thing, as the appellant suggests, not much turns on the argument. What still needs to be determined is the scope intended by the use of the word "public." In that respect, I agree with the applications Judge that, to give effect to paragraph 8(2)(*k*) of the *Privacy Act*, the words "available to the public" under paragraph 17(2)(*d*) of the *Statistics Act* must be interpreted to mean a segment of the population, such as Aboriginal groups, as opposed to the entire population.

'[19] The appellant further submits that the discretion under paragraph 17(2)(*b*) of the *Statistics Act* can only be exercised to disclose information to which the public already has a right of access from another source. In support of this submission, the appellant compares the English and French versions of paragraph 17(2)(*d*): the English version refers to any "information available to the public under any statutory or other law" whereas the French versions refers to "*les renseignements mis à la disposition du public en vertu d'une loi ou de toute autre règle de droit*." In the appellant's view, the exception, especially when considering the words "*mis à la disposition du public en vertu d'une loi*" in the French version, requires the information to be already accessible or obtainable.

'[20] In reading the English and French versions of paragraph 17(2)(*d*), I can see the subtle distinction the appellant is trying to make but, from a practical point of view, the argument cannot stand. The appellant is reading the statutory provision as requiring the information to be "already" accessible, as opposed to simply being accessible. In my opinion, if a statutory provision allows for the disclosure of information to the public, as does paragraph 8(2)(*k*) of the *Privacy Act*, then the information is "available" to the public or "*mis à la disposition du public*". There is no requirement that the information be "already" in the public domain.' Canada *(*Information Commissioner*) v Canada *(*Minister of Industry*) [2008] 1 FCR 231, 284 DLR (4th) 293, [2007] FCJ No 780, 2007 FCA 212 at [14]–[20], per Richard CJ

PURPOSE

For all purposes

Australia [Easement granted 'to go, pass and repass at all times and for all purposes with vehicles to and from the said lots benefited or any such part thereof across the lots burdened'.]

'[19] In its submissions, Westfield stressed the significance for the construction of the instrument of the phrase therein "for all purposes". This was said to be plainly apt to encompass the purpose of accessing Skygarden, the dominant tenement, and from there travelling to some further property.

'[20] The phrase "for all purposes" appears also in the statutory formulation which has been included in the Conveyancing Act since the commencement of the 1930 Act [Conveyancing (Amendment) Act 1930 (NSW)]. Before 1930 it had appeared in easements the construction of whose terms had come before the courts.

'[21] One such case was *Thorpe v Brumfitt* [(1873) LR 8 Ch App 650]. There, a grant of a right of way "for all purposes" across the servient tenement did not plainly identify any dominant tenement. Did the grant fail as being an attempt to create an easement in gross? As a matter of construction James LJ and Mellish LJ avoided that result. Mellish LJ construed the phrase "for all purposes" as identifying all purposes which made it necessary to pass between the servient tenement and a triangular parcel of land indicated in the conveyance creating the easement. This decision is significant in two respects. First, it illustrates the importance of the legislative requirement imposed in New South Wales by s 88 of the Conveyancing Act (also introduced by the 1930 Act) for identification of the lands comprising the dominant and servient tenements. Second, it emphasises that the "purposes", extensive as they may be, must confer what the law regards as a benefit on the dominant tenement, by making it "a better and more convenient property"; this is something more than a "personal advantage" to the owner of the tenement for the time being.

'[22] More recently, in *Peacock v Custins* [[2002] 1 WLR 1815; [2001] 2 All ER 827] the English Court of Appeal considered the phrase "a right of way at all times and for all purposes" in favour of the dominant tenement (the red land) the owners of which also owned adjacent land (the blue land). After reviewing many authorities, including *Harris v Flower* [(1904) 74 LJ Ch 127], Schiemann LJ (delivering the judgment of the court also comprising Mance LJ and Smith J) concluded that the terms of the grant did not permit the extended user in favour of the blue land and, further, that this user could not reasonably be described as "ancillary" to the use of the red land.

'[23] The reference in *Peacock* to user which could be described as "ancillary" to the grant appears to have identified the line of cases holding that, on general principles of conveyancing, the grant of an easement carries with it those ancillary rights which are necessary for the enjoyment of the rights expressly granted. For example, Warner J held in *National Trust for Places of Historic Interest or Natural Beauty v White* [[1987] 1 WLR 907] that use by visitors of a car park adjacent to an Iron Age hill fort in Wiltshire known as the Figsbury Ring was an "ancillary" user in the required sense. However, it is not necessary for the enjoyment of the rights granted for access to the Skygarden land that those using that access be at liberty to pass beyond Skygarden to other land.

'[24] It should be added that if the construction of the instrument urged by Westfield were accepted, and the grant extended to permit use of Glasshouse to pass across Skygarden to other parcels of land, then a further question would arise. This would be whether a grant in those terms would be appurtenant to Skygarden in the sense of the authorities, or be but a personal advantage accruing to Westfield as the present owner of Skygarden. It is unnecessary to determine such a question. This is because the easement, upon the proper construction of the terms of the grant, does not extend to user of the type for which Westfield contends.

'[25] The most recent edition of *Gale on Easements* [17th ed, Sweet & Maxwell, London, 2002, p 334 [9–27]] states:

> The general rule is that a right of way may only be used for gaining access to the land identified as the dominant tenement in the grant.

There follows a detailed analysis of the English authorities, which begins with remarks to that effect by Romer LJ in *Harris* [at 132].

'[26] The decision in that case has been much discussed in later authorities both in England and Australia, a number of which were reviewed by Brereton J at first instance. His Honour concluded that *Harris* stands for the proposition that:

> ... use of an easement cannot be extended, beyond the scope of the grant, to impose a burden greater than that which the servient owner agreed to accept.

'[27] That statement accords with the following analysis of *Harris* which is offered in *Gale on Easements* [p 470 [12–79]] and which we would adopt:

In *Harris v Flower & Sons* the excessive user by which it was attempted to impose an additional burden on the servient tenement consisted in the use of a right of way for obtaining access to buildings erected partly on the land to which the right of way was appurtenant and partly on other land. A claim was put forward on behalf of the plaintiffs that the right of way had been abandoned, on the ground that, as it was practically impossible to separate the lawful from the excessive user, the right of way could not be used at all. This contention failed, however, the court holding that there had been no abandonment, but that the user of the way for access to the buildings so far as they were situate upon land to which the right of way was not appurtenant was in excess of the rights of the defendants, and a declaration was made accordingly, with liberty to apply. [Footnote omitted.]

'[28] However, Brereton J went on to hold:

> [62] ... It is not in excess of the grant to use a right of way to access the dominant tenement for those purposes that were contemplated at the time of the grant.

The difficulty is in the phrase "that were contemplated". Contemplated by whom? By what evidentiary means is this contemplation later to be revealed to the court? How do these steps accommodate the Torrens system? To these matters it will be necessary to return.

'[29] At this stage in the reasons it is important to remark that care certainly must be taken lest the statement in *Gale on Easements* set out above be elevated to the status of a "rule", whether of construction or substantive law. What the statement does provide is a starting point for consideration of the terms of any particular grant. The statement is consistent with an understanding that the broader the right of access to the dominant tenement granted by the easement, the greater the burden upon the proprietary rights in the servient tenement.

'[30] We return to the terms of the easement. The access is to go, pass and repass to and from Skygarden and across Glasshouse. The terms do not speak of going, passing and repassing to and from and across Skygarden, and across Glasshouse. The term "for all purposes" encompasses all ends sought to be achieved by those utilising the easement in accordance with its terms.' Westfield Management Ltd v Perpetual Trustee Co Ltd [2007] HCA 45, (2007) 239 ALR 75, BC200708402 at [19]–[30], per Gleeson CJ, Gummow, Kirby, Hayne and Heydon JJ

For the purposes of the mediation

[Under the Employment Relations Act 2000, s 148, any statement, admission, or document created or made 'for the purposes of the mediation' must be kept confidential.] '[21] The [Employment] Court concluded that Mr Jesudhass was entitled to adduce evidence to establish that communications between the parties at mediation, other than those made in an attempt to resolve his employment relationship problem, should be admissible at the hearing of his personal grievance. Whether or not the communications adduced were "for the purposes of the mediation" was a matter for the trial judge to determine, and the onus would be on the plaintiff to satisfy the judge that the evidence should be admitted.

'[22] Mr Gilkison submitted that the Employment Court misinterpreted the intention of Parliament in enacting s 148 of the Employment Relations Act. Counsel contended that the words of the section mean what they say, and that the legislative intention was to remove, rather than preserve, the limited exceptions to the principle of confidentiality in mediation created by *Crummer* [*v Benchmark Supplies Ltd* [2000] 2 ERNZ 22].

...

'[27] For the respondent, Mr Corkill QC submitted that the Employment Court's interpretation was correct. To promote the purposes of the Act as a whole and for reasons of public policy, s 148(1) should be construed as protecting only communications for the "proper" purposes of a mediation. Because it is not proper to act illegally, any evidence of illegal conduct (whether criminal or otherwise) is outside the scope of s 148 and therefore not protected by it.

...

'[31] We do not see any ambiguity in the words of s 148(1). All communications "for the purposes of the mediation" attract the statutory confidentiality, except possibly ... where public policy dictates otherwise.

'[32] In accordance with the ordinary meaning of the word "purpose", that of the intended object of an activity, a communication (written or oral) is protected unless it is created or made independently of the mediation.

'[33] Documents which are prepared for use in or in connection with a mediation therefore come within the ambit of s 148(1). So do statements and submissions made orally at the mediation, or a record thereof. Only documents which come into existence independently of the mediation are excluded.

'[34] There is nothing surprising in this conclusion. To the contrary, it reflects the desirability of encouraging the parties to a mediation to speak freely and frankly, safe in the knowledge that their words cannot be used against them in subsequent litigation if the dispute does not prove capable of resolution at mediation.

...

'[37] Section 148(6)(a) provides that nothing in s 148 prevents the discovery or affects the admissibility of evidence which exists "independently of the mediation process". This wording strongly supports the interpretation of s 148(1) which we are adopting. The obvious implication of s 148(6)(a) is that communications at a mediation which do not exist independently of it will not be discoverable or admissible. There is no reason why such evidence should not be discoverable or admissible unless it attracts the confidentiality conferred by subs (1). All evidence which does not exist independently of the mediation process is therefore evidence created or made "for the purposes of the mediation".

'[38] As we noted at paras [17] and [18], the Employment Court held that s 148(1) only protected communications that were "genuinely" for the purposes of settling an employment dispute (at para [56]), or for the "legitimate" purposes of the mediation (at para [59]). In defending that position, Mr Corkill submitted that the section should be read as referring to the "proper" purposes of the mediation and argued that this imposed a high threshold for scrutiny. We disagree. Such concepts could be applied only after a detailed examination of what occurred at a mediation. Such a retrospective examination, based on a mere allegation of illegitimate or improper purpose or of non-genuine use, would effectively defeat the protection that s 148(1) seeks to provide.' Just Hotel Ltd v Jesudhass [2007] NZCA 582, [2008] 2 NZLR 210 at [21]–[22], [27], [31]–[34], [37]–[38], per Wilson J

Q

QUALIFYING BODY

'[4] On 26 February 1998 Mr Ahsan made a complaint to an employment tribunal, alleging that the Labour Party had discriminated against him on racial grounds, contrary to s 12(1) of the Race Relations Act 1976:

"It is unlawful for an authority or body which can confer an authorisation or qualification which is needed for, or facilitates, engagement in a particular profession or trade to discriminate against a person–(a) in the terms on which it is prepared to confer on him that authorisation or qualification; or (b) by refusing, or deliberately omitting to grant, his application for it; or (c) by withdrawing it from him or varying the terms on which he holds it."

'[5] By s 3, "discriminate" means to discriminate on racial grounds and by s 78(1), "profession" is defined to include "any vocation or occupation". Mr Ahsan says that being a councillor is a profession, or at any rate an occupation, and that the Labour Party is able to confer its authorisation to stand as a Labour candidate, which he needs to be elected or which will facilitate his election.

'[6] The Labour Party objected that s 12 did not apply to them. They said they did not confer authorisations or qualifications within the meaning of the Act. Section 12 is headed "Qualifying bodies" and appears in Pt II of the Act, which is headed "Discrimination in the Employment Field". It is, they said, concerned with vocational or professional qualifications and not with politics.

...

'[18] My Lords, it seems to me that logically the first question to be answered is whether the Labour Party is a qualifying body for the purposes of s 12. In my opinion, for the reasons given by Peter Gibson LJ in *Triesman v Ali* [[2002] EWCA Civ 93, [2002] IRLR 489], it is not. The notion of an "authorisation or qualification" suggests some kind of objective standard which the qualifying body applies, an even-handed, not to say "transparent", test which people may pass or fail. The qualifying body vouches to the public for the qualifications of the candidate and the public rely upon the qualification in offering him employment or professional engagements. That is why s 12 falls under the general heading of discrimination "in the Employment Field". But that is far removed from the basis upon which a political party chooses its candidates. The main criterion is likely to be the popularity of the candidate with the voters, which is unlikely to be based on the most objective criteria. That will certainly be true of selection by vote of the branch and I doubt whether greater objectivity can be expected of a selection committee. The members or selection panel want to choose the candidate who, for whatever reason, seems to them most likely to win or at least put up a respectable showing in the election.

'[19] That does not mean that a political party is entitled to discriminate on racial grounds in choosing its candidates. It would be most surprising if it could lawfully do so. But the relevant prohibition is to be found, not in s 12, but in s 25, which deals with discrimination by associations against members or prospective members ...' Ahsan v Watt (formerly Carter) (sued on behalf of the Labour Party) [2007] UKHL 51, [2008] 1 All ER 869 at [4]–[6], [18]–[19], per Lord Hoffmann

R

REFUGEE

Canada '[10] State protection is an issue that arises from the very definition of a refugee. A refugee is a person who has "a well-founded fear of persecution" and is "unable or, by reason of that fear, unwilling" to obtain protection from their country of nationality (paragraph 96(*a*), *Immigration and Refugee Protection Act*, SC 2001, c 27 ...). The definition contains both subjective and objective elements: the claimant must actually fear persecution and that fear must be well founded.

...

'[13] The burden of proof lies on claimants to show that they meet the definition of a refugee. To do so, they must prove that they actually fear persecution and that their fear is "well founded." To establish a well-founded fear, refugee claimants must show that there is a "reasonable chance," a "serious possibility" or "more than a mere possibility" that they will be persecuted if returned to their country of nationality (*Adjei v Canada (Minister of Employment and Immigration)* [1989] 2 FC 680 (CA)). (By contrast, a person who claims to be in danger of being tortured, killed or subjected to cruel and unusual treatment must establish his or her claim on the balance of probabilities: *Li v Canada (Minister of Citizenship and Immigration)* [2005] 3 FCR 239 (FCA).) In respect of particular underlying facts, the claimant shoulders a burden of proof on the balance of probabilities (*Adjei*, above, at page 682)." Carrillo v Canada *(*Minister of Citizenship and Immigration*)* [2008] 1 FCR 3, 2007 FC 320, [2007] FCJ No 439 at [10], [13], per O'Reilly J (decision revsd Carrillo v Canada *(*Minister of Citizenship and Immigration*)* [2008] FCJ No 399, 2008 FCA 94, 69 Imm LR (3d) 309, FCA)

REINSTATEMENT

[New Roads and Street Works Act 1991 ss 70 (duty to reinstate), 71 (standard of reinstatement). Hertfordshire County Council laid a large number of informations against National Grid Gas plc (the defendant) alleging various breaches of duty under the New Roads and Street Works Act 1991 in respect of the reinstatement of the street following the replacement of a gas main, including 23 informations alleging breaches of the duty under s 71(2) to ensure that the reinstatement conforms to prescribed performance standards.] '[46] In the case stated the judge sets out her conclusion as follows:

"I was of the opinion that s 70 should be seen to refer to reinstatement to the required standard and would therefore continue to apply after a 'works closed' notice has been served if further works are required by the authorities following inspection by them. I was of the opinion therefore that the summonses under s 70(2) were properly brought and that the section applied to works required to be done by [the council] after the service of a 'works closed' notice; that there was no distinction to be drawn between works done prior to the notice being served and works later required by the authorities and described by [the defendant] as 'remedial' works."

'[47] The question she has posed for the opinion of this court is:

"Was I right to conclude that there was a case for [the defendant] to answer in respect of three alleged contraventions of s 70(2) of the New Roads and Street Works Act 1991 on dates between 11 February 2005 and 8 November 2005 on the ground that s 70(2) can relate to delay in commencing 'remedial' works in the street?"

'[48] Before us, Mr Bradnock has repeated the defendant's submissions to the judge. He says that the council has conflated the two separate concepts of reinstatement and remedial works. Reinstatement refers purely to the act of finishing street works so that the street is left in useable condition: it may be applied to the original works or to remedial works as the case may be. It is an essential part of any street works involving an excavation and cannot exist independently of such works. Remedial works, by contrast, are street works in themselves. They are necessitated by a failure of reinstatement, as s 72(2) makes clear. It is apparent from Mr Castleman's witness statement that the council's allegation is that the defendant failed to begin remedial works with appropriate dispatch, not that reinstatement (whether as part of the substantive works or the remedial works) was delayed. Reinstatement of the substantive works was carried out in 2004. Once a purported reinstatement has been completed, as indicated by the filing of a "works closed" notice under s 70(3), the authority is at liberty to inspect it; and if it does not meet the required standard, an offence will have been committed under s 71. That section creates a continuing offence and any delay can be reflected by the authority laying a suitable number of s 71 informations to cover the entire period for which the undertaker fails to remedy the defects in reinstatement.

'[49] Mr Bradnock further submits that if the judge's interpretation of s 70(2) were correct, reinstatement could never be said to be complete until the "guarantee" period (ie the prescribed period under s 71(2)) for the work carried out had expired without further works being required–in the case of failure to meet required performance standards, two years after the "works closed" notice or two years after the authority's requirement for further works to be undertaken, whichever is the later. Any requirement to carry out further work would prolong the guarantee period and therefore the period of reinstatement. Such an interpretation would render the "works closed" notice meaningless and would make s 71 allegations all but impossible for prosecutors to prove: if street works remained open for the purposes of s 70 even after purported reinstatement had been concluded, an allegation that the relevant standards of workmanship and materials had not been met could be successfully defended by the argument that the defects were merely temporary and reinstatement was not yet complete.

'[50] For the council, Mr Reed submits that the judge was right to consider that "reinstatement" means proper reinstatement or reinstatement not requiring remedial works; and if she was right on that, then the defendant's case falls down, since on that basis delays in remedial works are necessarily delays in the overall reinstatement under s 70(2). First, "reinstatement" is defined in s 105(1) as including "making good", which indicates that reinstatement is not achieved until remedial works

are carried out. Second, in the *British Telecommunications* case [*British Telecommunications plc v Nottinghamshire CC* [1998] All ER (D) 478, DC] it was held that "reinstate" means "reinstate properly" (and the same decision undermines the defendant's argument based on the existence of the guarantee period). Third, the purpose of the section is to ensure that the completion of the relevant works is carried out in a manner to enable the proper use of the street in good time, and it is consistent with that aim that "reinstatement" should include the totality of the works required to be carried out to achieve it. Further, the issue of a "works closed" notice does not mean that reinstatement is completed, which is a question of fact. The requirement to give notice under s 70(3) is simply a mechanism to ensure that the authority is aware of the progress of the works. As to the possibility of a prosecution under s 71 for delays in remedial works, that is a tortuous means of interpreting the legislation so as to achieve a result which can be achieved more simply under s 70(2).

'[51] For my part, if I had come to this issue free from existing authority, I would have been doubtful about the correctness of the judge's decision. In my view there is much to be said for the view that the 1991 Act provides in Pt 3 a staged approach. The first stage, so far as relevant to the present dispute, relates to the execution of the street works of which notice has been given under s 54 or s 55. Where those street works are of a kind mentioned in s 66(1), there is a duty to carry on and complete the works with all such dispatch as is reasonably practicable. The next stage is the reinstatement of the street, pursuant to the duty under s 70(1). That duty is engaged as the street works are completed: the undertaker is required by s 70(2) to begin the reinstatement as soon after the completion of any part of the street works as is reasonably practicable, and then to carry on and complete the reinstatement with all such dispatch as is reasonably practicable. When the reinstatement is completed, there is a duty to inform the street authority pursuant to s 70(3). The completed reinstatement is required to meet the standards in s 71. If it fails to do so, the undertaker is liable to prosecution under that section. The street authority can carry out the investigatory works referred to in s 72(1), with the costs consequences referred to in that subsection and in s 72(2). By notice under s 72(3) the authority can also require the undertaker to carry out any necessary remedial works; and if the undertaker fails to comply with the notice, the authority can carry out the necessary works and recover from the undertaker the costs reasonably incurred in doing so. On the face of it, that is an intelligible and workable scheme, and it does not require "reinstatement" in s 70 or s 71 to be interpreted as meaning proper reinstatement or reinstatement not requiring remedial works. If the completed reinstatement is defective, remedies are available both in the form of prosecutions and in the form of the street authority's power to get remedial works carried out.

'[52] That is not, however, the approach that has been taken in the decided cases. Of particular importance is *British Telecommunications plc v Nottinghamshire CC* [1998] All ER (D) 478, in which the essential question for decision was whether the duty to reinstate in accordance with the specification under s 71(1) continues indefinitely so that failure to reinstate in accordance with the specification constitutes a continuing offence for which the undertaker may be prosecuted at any time until the street is reinstated in accordance with the specification. Lord Bingham of Cornhill CJ said that he had found this a difficult question and that his mind had altered more than once in the course of argument. On balance, however, he had concluded that there was a continuing offence, for these reasons:

> "It seems to me important that the overriding duty to reinstate in s 70(1) of the Act is expressed in wholly general terms and without any qualification whatever as to time, albeit the undertaker is required to give notice to the street authority. Furthermore, the duty laid on an undertaker in s 71(1) is again an obligation to reinstate properly, there being no limitation of time whatever attached to that duty. Mr Treacy is, I think, entitled to submit that 'reinstate' means 'reinstate properly', both because the definition section refers to the street being made good and because the code of practice which is incorporated by reference indicates that compliance with proper standards is inherent in the concept of reinstatement. It does not appear to me that s 71(2) undermines that conclusion since, although it refers to what is in effect a guarantee period, that would be applicable in a case where the work had initially been done properly but had developed defects during the two-year period.

Furthermore it seems to me very difficult, as it seemed to Henry LJ in [*Camden London BC v Marshall* [1996] 1 WLR 1345], to give any effect to s 95(2) if there is not, in fact, a continuing duty. It was the language of s 376(2) that was the crucial factor leading to his decision. It seems to me difficult to construe s 95(2) on the premise that a duty ends on the completion of reinstatement, even if that reinstatement is defective. It is scarcely possible as it seems to me to envisage any prosecution being begun before purported completion of the reinstatement, but on BT's argument the duty to reinstate properly would have come to an end on purported completion, yet here in s 95(2) we find reference to a failure to comply with a duty being continued after conviction and that seems to me to point strongly towards the continuation of the duty …

I would accordingly conclude that the failure to reinstate in accordance with the Act and prescribed standards and the specification creates a continuing offence which may be the subject of prosecution unless and until the time comes when the reinstatement is properly carried out. If further proceedings are brought after a conviction then the matter is covered by s 95(2)."

'[53] Collins J agreed, stating that the duty in s 71(1) is to reinstate properly and that "a reinstatement which is not done properly, and in respect of which there is a breach of s 71(1), can be the subject of a prosecution, notwithstanding that the contractor in question has purported to complete the reinstatement".

'[54] In *Thames Water Utilities Ltd v Bromley London BC* [2000] All ER (D) 459 the undertaker had informed the street authority of the completion of an interim reinstatement but had thereafter done nothing. Informations alleging failure to complete the permanent reinstatement as soon as practicable and in any event within six months, as required by s 70(4), were laid over a year later. The issue was whether they were out of time. The court followed the reasoning in the *British Telecommunications* case in holding that they were not. A suggestion that Lord Bingham had perhaps overlooked the significance of s 72(3) was rejected, and the reasoning of Lord Bingham in relation to s 95(2) was described as wholly convincing.

'[55] In my judgment, the *British Telecommunications* case is neither irrelevant nor distinguishable, as submitted by

Mr Bradnock, and I am satisfied that this court should follow the reasoning in it. The doubts I have expressed come nowhere near satisfying the conditions set out in *R v Greater Manchester Coroner, ex p Tal* [1984] 3 All ER 240 at 248, [1985] QB 67 at 81, for a departure by one Divisional Court from a prior decision of another Divisional Court. The fact that there are now two prior decisions and that the first of them was by a court which included Lord Bingham, and on an issue that he considered difficult, makes it all the more appropriate that a consistent line should be taken.

'[56] On that basis it seems to me that the matters relied on by the council were properly included in informations alleging a breach of the duty under s 70(2). "Reinstatement" must be given the same meaning in s 70 as in s 71, and in each case it must be taken to mean "proper reinstatement", ie a reinstatement meeting the requirements of s 71. The issue of a "works closed" notice under s 70(3) marks the point where the undertaker has purported to complete the reinstatement, but the contractor's view of the matter tells one nothing about whether there

has in fact been a proper reinstatement. The reinstatement will not have been completed for the purposes of the statute unless and until it is a proper reinstatement meeting the s 71 requirements. Where it does not meet those requirements, the carrying out of remedial works to correct the defects forms part of the continuing process of reinstatement and is subject to the duty under s 70(2) to carry on and complete the reinstatement with all such dispatch as is reasonably practicable. It follows that it was open to the council to bring a prosecution on the basis that the process of reinstatement continued during the periods specified in the three informations and that reinstatement was not carried on and completed with all such dispatch as was reasonably practicable during those periods.

'[57] I would therefore give an affirmative answer to the judge's question on s 70(2) and would dismiss the defendant's appeal on this issue.' Hertfordshire County Council v National Grid Gas plc [2007] EWHC 2535 (Admin), [2008] 1 All ER 1137 at [46]–[57], DC, per Richards LJ

S

SEVERE MENTAL IMPAIRMENT

[Note that the definitions of 'severe mental impairment' and 'severeley mentally impaired' in the Mental Health Act 1983, s 1(2) are prospectively repealed by the Mental Health Act 2007, s 1(3).]

SIGNIFICANT

'[31] This appeal raises the important point of the meaning of "significant" injury in [the Limitation Act 1980] s 14(2). Section 14(1) provides that the "date of knowledge" is the date upon which the claimant first had knowledge of various facts, including "that the injury … was significant". A "significant injury" is defined by s 14(2):

> "For the purposes of this section an injury is significant if the person whose date of knowledge is in question would reasonably have considered it sufficiently serious to justify his instituting proceedings for damages against a defendant who did not dispute liability and was able to satisfy a judgment."

'[32] Section 14(3) then provides that, for the purpose of deciding whether the claimant had knowledge of the various matters listed in s 14(1), including the fact that the injury was significant, one should take into account not only his actual knowledge but also what is usually called his imputed or constructive knowledge. That is defined as "knowledge which he might reasonably have been expected to acquire (a) from facts observable or ascertainable by him; or (b) from facts ascertainable by him with the help of medical or other appropriate expert advice which it is reasonable for him to seek."

'[33] The question which has arisen is whether the definition of significance in s 14(2) allows any (and if so, how much) account to be taken of personal characteristics of the claimant, either pre-existing or consequent upon the injury which he has suffered. This question was first considered in *McCafferty v Metropolitan Police District*

Receiver [1977] 2 All ER 756 at 775, [1977] 1 WLR 1073 at 1081, soon after the 1975 Act [Limitation Act 1975] had come into force. After reading the then equivalent of sub-s 14(2), Geoffrey Lane LJ said:

> "[T]he test is partly a subjective test, namely: 'would this plaintiff have considered the injury sufficiently serious?' and partly an objective test, namely: 'would he have been reasonable if he did not regard it as sufficiently serious?' It seems to me that the subsection is directed at the nature of the injury as known to the plaintiff at that time. Taking that plaintiff, with that plaintiff's intelligence, would he have been reasonable in considering the injury not sufficiently serious to justify instituting proceedings for damages?"

'[34] I respectfully think that the notion of the test being partly objective and partly subjective is somewhat confusing. Section 14(2) is a test for what counts as a significant injury. The material to which that test applies is generally "subjective" in the sense that it is applied to what the claimant knows of his injury rather than the injury as it actually was. Even then, his knowledge may have to be supplemented with imputed "objective" knowledge under s 14(3). But the test itself is an entirely impersonal standard: not whether the claimant himself would have considered the injury sufficiently serious to justify proceedings but whether he would "reasonably" have done so. You ask what the claimant knew about the injury he had suffered, you add any knowledge about the injury which may be imputed to him under s 14(3) and you then ask whether a reasonable person with that knowledge would have considered the injury sufficiently serious to justify his instituting proceedings for damages against a defendant who did not dispute liability and was able to satisfy a judgment.

'[35] It follows that I cannot accept that one must consider whether someone "with [the] plaintiff's intelligence" would have been reasonable if he did not regard the injury as sufficiently serious. That seems to me to destroy the effect of the word "reasonably". Judges should not have to grapple with the notion of the reasonable unintelligent person. Once you have ascertained what the claimant knew and what he should be treated as having known, the actual claimant drops out of the picture. Section 14(2) is, after all, simply a standard of the seriousness of the injury and nothing more. Standards are in their nature impersonal and do not vary with the person to whom they are applied.

...

'[39] The difference between s 14(2) and 14(3) emerges very clearly if one considers the relevance in each case of the claimant's injury. Because s 14(3) turns on what the claimant ought reasonably to have done, one must take into account the injury which the claimant has suffered. You do not assume that a person who has been blinded could reasonably have acquired knowledge by seeing things. In s 14(2), on the other hand, the test is external to the claimant and involves no inquiry into what he ought reasonably to have done. It is applied to what the claimant knew or was deemed to have known but the standard itself is impersonal. The effect of the claimant's injuries upon what he could reasonably have been expected to do is therefore irrelevant.' A v Hoare [2008] UKHL 6, [2008] 2 All ER 1 at [31]–[35], [39] per Lord Hoffmann

SPEAK

Canada '[34] The verb "to speak" refers to more than the faculty of speech. *The Canadian Oxford Dictionary*, 2nd ed., also defines it as:

> ... **2. transitive** a utter (words). **b** make known or communicate (one's opinion, the truth, etc.) in this way (*never speaks sense*). **3 intransitive** a ... hold a conversation (*spoke to him for an hour, spoke with them about their work*). **b** ... mention in writing etc. (*speaks of it in his novel*). **c** ... articulate the feelings of (another person etc.) in speech or writing (*speak for our generation*). **4 intransitive** a ... address; converse with (a person etc.) ... .'

Knopf v Canada (Speaker of the House of Commons) [2008] 2 FCR 327, [2007] FCJ No 1474, 2007 FCA 308 at [34], per Trudel JA

SPRING GUN

'[11] A spring gun can be described as a gun, often a shotgun, rigged up so as to fire when a string or other triggering device is tripped by contact of sufficient force to "spring" the trigger. Someone stumbling over or treading on the string or triggering device causes it to be discharged and in consequence is wounded. ...' R v Cockburn [2008] EWCA Crim 316, [2008] 2 All ER 1153 at [11], per Sir Igor Judge P

STATE PROTECTION

Canada '[10] State protection is an issue that arises from the very definition of a refugee. A refugee is a person who has "a well-founded fear of persecution" and is "unable or, by reason of that fear, unwilling" to obtain protection from their country of nationality (paragraph 96(*a*), *Immigration and Refugee Protection Act*, SC 2001, c 27 ...). The definition contains both subjective and objective elements: the claimant must actually fear persecution and that fear must be well founded.

'[11] The issue of state protection arises within the objective branch of the definition of a refugee. Simply put, a person's fear of persecution is not well founded if state protection is available. The contrary is also true — a person's fear of persecution is well founded if state protection is unavailable (see *Ward [Canada (Attorney General) v Ward* [1993] 2 SCR 689] at page 726). Further, the definition of a refugee goes on to refer explicitly to the person's inability or unwillingness, out of fear, to secure state protection. Accordingly, the issue of state protection can arise in more than one way but, practically speaking, it usually comes up in the consideration of the well-foundedness of a claim (*Zhuravlvev v Canada (Minister of Citizenship and Immigration)* [2000] 4 FC 3 (TD), at paragraph 18).

'[12] The question of state protection generally arises only in cases where the person alleges persecution by persons who are not state agents. In those cases where the person claims persecution by the state itself, it can usually be assumed that no state protection is available (*Zhuravlvev*, above, at paragraph 19).

'[13] The burden of proof lies on claimants to show that they meet the definition of a refugee. To do so, they must prove that they actually fear persecution and that their fear is "well founded." To establish a well-founded fear, refugee claimants must show that there is a "reasonable chance," a "serious possibility" or "more than a mere possibility" that they will be persecuted if returned to their country of nationality (*Adjei v Canada (Minister of Employment and Immigration)* [1989] 2 FC 680 (CA)). (By contrast, a person who claims to be in danger of being tortured, killed or subjected to cruel and unusual treatment must establish his or her claim on the balance of probabilities: *Li v Canada (Minister of Citizenship and Immigration)* [2005] 3 FCR 239 (FCA).) In respect of particular underlying facts, the claimant shoulders a burden of proof on the balance of probabilities (*Adjei*, above, at page 682).

'[14] In most situations, decision makers are entitled to presume that states are able to protect their citizens (*Ward*, above). Justice La Forest, in *Ward*, stated for the Court: "Absent some evidence, the claim should fail, as nations should be presumed capable of protecting their citizens" (at page 725). The exception is where there has been a complete breakdown of a state's apparatus (*Canada (Minister of Employment and Immigration) v Villafranca* (1992) 99 DLR (4th) 334 (FCA)).

'[15] However, from my reading of the cases, the concept of the "presumption of state protection" does not mean that there is a higher burden of proof on claimants in cases involving the question of state protection. It simply means that, in those cases, claimants must tender reliable evidence on the point or risk failing to meet the definition of a refugee. In other words, the presumption is not a special hurdle that refugee claimants must overcome where the issue of state protection arises — rather, it simply establishes a starting point for analysing the well-foundedness of a claim.' Carrillo v Canada *(*Minister of Citizenship and Immigration*)* [2008] 1 FCR 3, 2007 FC 320, [2007] FCJ No 439 at [10]–[15], per O'Reilly J (decision revsd Carrillo v Canada *(*Minister of Citizenship and Immigration*)* [2008] FCJ No 399, 2008 FCA 94, 69 Imm LR (3d) 309, FCA)

STRUCTURE

Canada '[121] *"Structure"* means [TRANSLATION] "organization of the parts of a whole" (*Trésor de la langue française*); [TRANSLATION] "complex and extensive organization, considered in its essentials" (*Le Nouveau Petit Robert*).' Quebec *(*Attorney General*)* v Canada [2008] 2 FCR 230, [2007] FCJ No 1086, 2007 FC 826 at [121], per Lemieux J

SUBSTANTIAL REASON

Australia '[83] In *McGinty* [*v Western Australia* (1996) 186 CLR 140 at 170, 134 ALR 289 at 296, [1995] HCA 46] Brennan CJ considered the phrase "chosen by the people" [in the Commonwealth Constitution ss 7, 24] as admitting of a requirement "of a franchise that is held generally by all adults or all adult citizens unless there be substantial reasons for excluding them". This proposition reflects the understanding that representative government as that notion is understood in the Australian constitutional context comprehends not only the bringing of concerns and grievances to the attention of legislators but also the presence of a voice in the selection of those legislators. Further, in the federal system established and maintained by the Constitution, the exercise of the franchise is the means by which those living under that system of government participate in the selection of both legislative chambers, as one of the people of the relevant state and as one of the people of the Commonwealth. In this way, the existence and exercise of the franchise reflects notions of citizenship and membership of the Australian federal body politic.

'[84] Such notions are not extinguished by the mere fact of imprisonment. Prisoners who are citizens and members of the Australian community remain so. Their interest in, and duty to, their society and its governance survives incarceration. Indeed, upon one view, the Constitution envisages their ongoing obligations to the body politic to which, in due course, the overwhelming majority of them will be returned following completion of their sentence.

'[85] The question with respect to legislative disqualification from what otherwise is adult suffrage (where 18 is now the age of legal majority throughout Australia) thus becomes a not unfamiliar one. Is the disqualification for a "substantial" reason? A reason will answer that description if it be reasonably appropriate and adapted to serve an end which is consistent or compatible with the maintenance of the constitutionally prescribed system of representative government. When used here the phrase "reasonably appropriate and adapted" does not mean "essential" or "unavoidable". Rather, as remarked in *Lange* [*v Australian Broadcasting Corp* (1997) 189 CLR 520, 145 ALR 96, [1997] HCA 25], in this context there is little difference between what is conveyed by that phrase and the notion of "proportionality". What upon close scrutiny is disproportionate or arbitrary may not answer to the description reasonably appropriate and adapted for an end consistent or compatible with observance of the relevant constitutional restraint upon legislative power.' Roach v

Electoral Commissioner [2007] HCA 43, (2007) 239 ALR 1, BC200708182 at [83]–[85], per Gummow, Kirby and Crennan JJ

SUFFICIENT CONSIDERATION

Australia [Whether the expression "sufficient consideration", as it occurs in the Confiscation Act 1997 (Vic), s 52(1)(a)(v), includes the consideration of "natural love and affection".]
'[60] If property is forfeited under s 35, s 51 permits a person (other than the defendant) who claims an interest in such property to make an application for an exclusion order within 60 days or otherwise with the leave of the court. The application is for "an order under s 52" which provides for "an order excluding property in which the applicant claims an interest from the operation of s 35". Section 52 contains the conditions for the grant of such an order ...

...

'[103] Because the wife obtained her joint interest in the apartment from her husband, she had to satisfy the court that her interest was acquired for "sufficient consideration". This expression, which occurs in s 52(1)(a)(v) (and also in s 52(1)(b)(ii) and in ss 21, 22, 24, 50 and 54), is not defined in the Act.
'[104] The DPP submitted that the policy of the Act is to ensure that criminals, their associates and dependants forfeit the proceeds of crime. It was contended that the policy supported the submission that "sufficient consideration" means "adequate consideration", which in turn means money or money's worth. Otherwise, it was contended, criminals could subvert the Act by transferring property to a spouse, partner, child or other relative in order to put the property beyond the reach of the Act. Analogies with bankruptcy legislation and cognate confiscation legislation in other jurisdictions were also relied upon.
'[105] The wife sought to sustain the conclusion of all members of the Court of Appeal that "sufficient consideration" includes "valuable consideration" and "good consideration" but not "nominal consideration".
'[106] The general obligations or duties of support owed by married couples to each other, reaffirmed recently in the United Kingdom, often entail legal and equitable joint ownership of marital property such as the matrimonial home. This gives rise to a separate point. In finding that the husband's transfer to the wife of a "moiety" of his interest in the real property "was no more than fulfilling a matrimonial obligation", the

primary judge treated "natural love and affection" as adequate consideration in all the circumstances of this case.
'[107] This court has recognised that consideration may have different meanings in different contexts, and that it has a wider meaning or operation in conveyancing than it does in simple contracts. The "wider" meaning is that in conveyancing consideration is not treated as requiring consideration sufficient to support a contract.
'[108] Speaking generally, and without reference to exceptions, a promise will not be legally binding unless made in a deed or supported by consideration. As Professor Treitel states [G H Treitel, *The Law of Contract*, 11th ed, Sweet & Maxwell, London, 2003, p 67]:

> This doctrine [of consideration] is based on the idea of reciprocity: "something of value in the eye of the law" must be given for a promise in order to make it enforceable as contract. [Footnote omitted.]

'[109] Because consideration of "natural love and affection" is commonly referred to in deeds of gift or voluntary settlements, a reference to the phrase "strongly suggests a gift" [*Mansukhani v Sharkey* [1992] 2 EGLR 105 at 106 per Fox LJ]. There are older cases in which it was recognised that "natural love and affection" was not "sufficient consideration" to ground an assumpsit, although it was sufficient to raise a use.
'[110] While natural love and affection may not be sufficient consideration to support a contract, it is settled that, at common law, "[a]n antenuptial agreement to settle property in consideration of marriage is backed by good consideration, and may be specifically enforced by the husband, wife and issue of the marriage" [R P Meagher, J D Heydon and M J Leeming, *Meagher, Gummow and Lehane's Equity: Doctrines and Remedies*, 4th ed, 2002, LexisNexis, Sydney, p 654 [20–025] citing *Re Cook's Settlement Trusts* [1965] Ch 902 at 915–916, [1964] 3 All ER 898 at 904. See also *Attorney-General v Jacobs Smith* [1895] 2 QB 341 at 353 per Kay LJ].
'[111] The situation is more complicated in relation to post-nuptial settlements of property, although some post-nuptial promises have been considered to constitute "valuable consideration" or "good consideration".
'[112] Marriage has long been considered "valuable consideration" in the specific context of conveyancing. The principle has been given statutory force and has been reconfirmed on many occasions. In the factual circumstances of

the present case, where Mr Le and the wife were married, it is unnecessary to explore the extent to which, in contemporary social circumstances, that learning applies to other marriage-like relationships.

'[113] The phrase "sufficient consideration" generally means legally sufficient to enforce a promise; it is specifically defined in a number of cognate acts to exclude certain forms of consideration which, otherwise, might have been thought sufficient.

'[114] In the Court of Appeal, Maxwell P and Chernov JA (with whom Neave JA agreed on this point) noted:

[41] The term "sufficient consideration" is not defined in the Act, although courts have sometimes used it as a synonym for adequate or "valuable" consideration. Thus, for example, in describing as "sufficient" the valuable consideration given by the promisee in *Wigan*, Mason J meant no more than that the consideration was adequate to impose on the promisor an enforceable obligation. [Footnote omitted.]

'[115] While the courts have at times used the terms "valuable consideration" and "sufficient consideration" interchangeably, it seems well recognised in the context of contract law that the term "sufficient consideration" can be contradistinguished from the term "adequate consideration", as noted by Professors Carter and Harland [J W Carter and D J Harland, *Contract Law in Australia*, 4th ed, Butterworths, Sydney, 2002, p 112 [323]]:

The rule that consideration must be sufficient requires that what is put forward as consideration reach a threshold of legal recognition. But once this threshold is reached no inquiry is required into how valuable the consideration is. Thus, the rule is frequently expressed in the form "consideration must be sufficient but need not be adequate".

'[116] Similarly, Dr Robinson notes that "valuable consideration" has a particular meaning when used in contradistinction to "good consideration" [S Robinson, *The Property Law Act Victoria*, Law Book Co, Sydney, 1992, p 408]:

Formerly no distinction was drawn between "valuable consideration" and "good consideration" … However when contrasted with "valuable consideration", the expression "good consideration" generally means

natural affection towards a member of the settlor's family. [Footnote omitted.]

'[117] In support of the submission that "sufficient consideration" in this Act should be construed as "adequate", which would mean money's worth, the DPP submitted that the policy considerations underpinning the Act were more closely aligned with policy considerations relevant to the Bankruptcy Act 1966 (Cth) than they were with policy considerations informing stamp duties and similar legislation. Particular reliance was placed on s 121 of the Bankruptcy Act as it stood prior to its amendment in 1996. That provided that a disposition which was not "for valuable consideration" was void against the trustee in bankruptcy. Section 121(1) was construed in *Cannane v J Cannane Pty Ltd* (*in liq*) [(1998) 192 CLR 557 at 573 [37], 153 ALR 163 at 173–174, 27 ACSR 603 at 613–614, [1998] HCA 26 per Gummow J] in the light of the principle that fraudulent dispositions made for the purpose of delaying creditors should be set aside. The principle derived from the Statute of Elizabeth (13 Eliz I c 5), which was enacted in 1570. Bankruptcy provided a special context in which "valuable consideration" was construed as consisting of "real and substantial value, and not [consideration] which is merely nominal or trivial or colourable" [*Re Abbott* [1983] Ch 45 at 57, [1982] 3 All ER 181 at 186–187 per Sir Robert Megarry VC]. By way of contrast, the legislation under consideration in this appeal is relatively new. An applicant for an exclusion order must satisfy a court of his or her non-involvement with criminal conduct before an exclusion order will even be considered. Further, like cognate confiscation provisions, s 121(6)(d) of the Bankruptcy Act as it currently stands expressly provides that "love or affection" has no value as consideration.

'[118] The DPP also urged that "sufficient consideration" should be construed in conformity with cognate statutes in other jurisdictions, which reflect similar policy considerations.

'[119] In *New South Wales Crime Commission v Mahoney* [(2003) 142 A Crim R 409 at 419 [52], [2003] NSWSC 1030], Grove J construed the term "sufficient consideration" as it appears in s 9(5) of the Criminal Assets Recovery Act 1990 (NSW) as requiring "adequacy … that is to say, something more than nominal". However, it should be noted that that Act expressly provides [s 4(2)] that:

(2) A reference in this Act to acquiring an interest in property for sufficient consideration is a reference to acquiring

the interest for a consideration that, having regard solely to commercial considerations, reflects the value of the interest.

'[120] Legislation of the Commonwealth dealing with the proceeds of crime [the Proceeds of Crime Act 2002 (Cth), s 338] specifically provides that whether or not there has been "sufficient consideration" is to be assessed "having regard solely to commercial considerations".

'[121] The provisions of s 52(1)(a)(i)–(v) inclusive, operating together, support the policy considerations identified by the DPP. They ensure that in circumstances such as those here, an exclusion order will only be made in favour of an applicant found innocent of any involvement in the commission of a Sch 2 offence and found to have no knowledge of circumstances leading to a property being "tainted property".

'[122] Given that "natural love and affection" is "sufficient consideration" for conveyancing purposes, and given the mutual obligations of support of spouses, if a purpose of the legislation is to provide for the forfeiture of a joint interest in real property of an innocent spouse (who acquired the interest as the wife did here), that would need to be expressly provided. As mentioned above, there are express provisions in cognate legislation, and in s 4(3) of the Confiscation Amendment Act 2007 (Vic), which define "sufficient consideration" to exclude "love and affection".

'[123] In the absence of an express limitation on the meaning of sufficient consideration, the legislative history of the Act "is of insufficient weight ... to displace the considerations of justice and fairness which ordinarily attend the administration of a new remedy" [*Mansfield v DPP (WA)* (2006) 226 CLR 486 at 497 [27], 228 ALR 214 at 221, [2006] HCA 38 per Gleeson CJ, Gummow, Kirby, Hayne and Crennan JJ].

'[124] The Court of Appeal did not err in construing "sufficient consideration", as it occurred in s 52(1)(a)(v), as encompassing "natural love and affection" in the circumstances of this case.' Director of Public Prosecutions (Vic) v Le [2007] HCA 52, (2007) 240 ALR 204, BC200709716 at [60], [103]–[124], per Kirby and Crennan JJ

T

TILLAGE

[For 1(2) Halsbury's Laws of England (4th Edn) (2007 Reissue) para 301 see now 1 Halsbury's Laws (5th Edn) para 365.]

TIMBER

[For 19(1) Halsbury's Laws of England (4th Edn) (Reissue) para 32 see now 19(1) Halsbury's Laws (4th Edn) (2007 Reissue) para 55.]

TONTINE

[For 19(1) Halsbury's Laws of England (4th Edn) (Reissue) para 107n see now 50 Halsbury's Laws (5th Edn) para 2087n.]

U

USE (VERB)

Canada [The Official Languages Act, s 4(1), provides that the English and French are the official languages of Parliament, and everyone has the right to 'use' either of those languages in any debates and other proceedings of Parliament.] '[5] The appellant opines that a witness before a parliamentary committee has the right to submit documents in either official language for contemporaneous distribution to committee members as part of his or her testimony. ...

...

'[12] The applications Judge is of the opinion that subsection 4(1) of the Act protects an individual's right to use the official language of his or her choice. It does not dictate the form of the individual's interaction with the Committee:

> Mr Knopf was entitled to speak to the Committee in the official language of his choice. That right was respected. Mr Knopf's request that his documents be circulated did not fall within the parameters of the right enshrined in subsection 4(1) of the OLA. Rather, it was a challenge to the manner in which the Committee conducts its business. It was a challenge to the procedure adopted by the Committee regarding the distribution of documents. This is not, in my view, a language rights issue.

'[13] Citing section 133 of the *Constitution Act, 1867*, she further states that [at paragraph 36] "In the context of proceedings before Parliament, the word 'use' provides Mr Knopf with the right to speak in the official language of his choice," thus concluding that Mr Knopf's choice of addressing the House Committee in either English or French was respected.

'[14] The appellant argues that the first Judge erred in law in failing to declare a violation of his rights under the Act, the Charter, and the *Constitution Act, 1867*. Contrary to a finding of the Federal Court, he states that his application is not the result of his disappointment because the Committee did not consider his submission sufficiently. He declares that it involves a language right, not a political right.

'[15] In his opinion, it is an error to limit the meaning of the word "use" in subsection 4(1) of the Act to oral speech excluding the right, for a witness, to make written submissions or present written material in either official language as an integral part of his or her testimony.

...

'[31] As mentioned earlier, the appellant submits that by referring to the verb "to speak," Justice Layden-Stevenson limited the meaning of the word "use" in subsection 4(1) of the Act and the relevant legislation to oral speech. He suggests that it includes also the right to make written submissions or present written material in either official language as an integral part of one's testimony.

'[32] A careful reading of the first judgment does not warrant the appellant's interpretation. The first judgment and the authorities cited by the applications Judge do not suggest such a restriction.

'[33] In all fairness, one has to read Justice Layden-Stevenson's finding entirely. She writes [at paragraph 36]:

> In short, an individual has the choice of addressing the House in either English or French. In the context of proceedings before Parliament, the word "use" provides Mr Knopf with the right to speak in the official language of his choice.

'[34] The verb "to speak" refers to more than the faculty of speech. *The Canadian Oxford Dictionary*, 2nd ed., also defines it as:

> ... **2. transitive** a utter (words). **b** make known or communicate (one's opinion, the truth, etc.) in this way (*never speaks sense*). **3 intransitive** a ... hold a conversation (*spoke to him for an hour, spoke with them about their work*). **b** ... mention in writing etc. (*speaks of it in his novel*). **c** ... articulate the feelings of (another person etc.) in speech or writing (*speak for our generation*). **4 intransitive** a ... address; converse with (a person etc.) ... .

'[35] Justice Layden-Stevenson does not restrict the word "speak" to oral speech. Rather, she states that subsection 4(1) of the Act provides the appellant with a right to address the House in the language of his choice. She is of the opinion that the appellant's request that his documents be circulated does not fall within the parameters of subsection 4(1) of the Act. For the following reasons, I agree with her finding.

'[36] It is trite law that language rights have to be interpreted purposively and liberally (*Doucet-Boudreau v Nova Scotia* (*Minister of Education*) [2003] 3 SCR 3; *Arsenault-Cameron v Prince Edward Island* [2000] 1 SCR 3; *R v Beaulac* [1999] 1 SCR 768).

'[37] This purpose is to be sought by reference to the character and the larger objects of the Charter and the Act, the historical origins of the concepts enshrined, the manner in which the right is expressed and the implications to be drawn from the context in which the right is to be found, including other parts of the Charter or the Act (*R v Big M Drug Mart Ltd et al* [1985] 1 SCR 295, at page 344; *Re BC Motor Vehicle Act* [1985] 2 SCR 486, at pages 499–500; Peter W Hogg, *Constitutional Law of Canada*, 2006 Student ed (Scarborough, Ont: Thomson Carswell, 2006), at page 770; Henri Brun and Guy Tremblay, *Droit Constitutionnel*, 4th ed (Cowansville, QC: Éditions Y Blais, 2002), at page 929).

'[38] Subsection 4(1) of the Act reiterates the right first recognized by section 133 of the *Constitution Act, 1867* and reaffirmed by subsection 17(1) of the Charter. These three sections recognize the right of any person participating in parliamentary proceedings "to use" (*d'employer*) English or French. Subsection 4(1) of the Act, as well as subsection 17(1) of the Charter create a scheme of unilingualism at the option of the speaker or writer, who cannot be compelled by Parliament to express himself or herself in another language

than the one he or she chooses (See *MacDonald v City of Montreal et al* [1986] 1 SCR 460, at page 483).

'[39] However, in some other language rights provisions, such as subsection 20(1) of the Charter and section 25 of the Act, the legislator chose the term "to communicate" (*communiquer*). In my opinion, this is not accidental.

'[40] To "communicate" presupposes interactions, bilateral actions between the parties. The verb "to use" does not encompass such interaction. The right is unilateral: one has the right to address the House of Commons in the official language of his choice. In the case at bar, Mr Knopf made his opinion known on particular topics of interest to the Committee and filed his documents. There stops his right under subsection 4(1) of the Act.

'[41] I do not read into subsection 4(1) of the Act any requirement for a Committee to distribute documents to its members in one official language. Subsection 4(1) of the Act provides the appellant with a right to address the Committee in the language of his choice only. Once this right has been exercised, subsection 4(1) of the Act does not compel the Committee to act in a certain way with the oral or written information provided to it.

'[42] Justice Layden-Stevenson was right in finding that the distribution of documents does not fall within the scope of subsection 4(1) of the Act. The right to use an official language of choice does not include the right to impose upon the Committee the immediate distribution and reading of documents filed to support one's testimony. The decision on how and when to treat the information received from a witness clearly belongs to the Committee. I find, therefore, that the appellant's language rights were not infringed upon.' Knopf v Canada (Speaker of the House of Commons) [2008] 2 FCR 327, [2007] FCJ No 1474, 2007 FCA 308 at [5], [12]–[15], [31]–[42], per Trudel JA

W

WAR CRIME

Canada [On an application for judicial review of a decision of the Immigration and Refugee Board that the applicant was excluded from refugee protection under the United Nations Convention Relating to the Status of Refugees (28 July 1951, [1969] Can TS No 6) art 1F(a) because there were serious grounds to believe that he committed or was complicit in the commission of war crimes against Peruvian guerrillas during his time in the Peruvian armed forces, one question to be decided was whether, for the purposes of exclusion under art 1F(a), war crimes could be committed during an internal conflict.] '[10] The parties agree that the question of whether the meaning of war crimes in Article 1F(a) is limited to those offences committed during an international armed conflict is a question of law to which the standard of review of correctness applies (*Bermudez v Canada (Minister of Citizenship and Immigration)* (2000) 24 Admin LR (3d) 65 (FCTD)).

'[11] Article 1F(a) of the Refugee Convention states that

> [t]he provisions of this Convention shall not apply to any person with respect to whom there are serious reasons for considering that
> (a) he has committed a crime against peace, a war crime, or a crime against humanity, as defined in the international instruments drawn up to make provision in respect of such crimes.

'[12] The Board referred to the *Charter of the International Military Tribunal* for the definition of war crimes. In *Bermudez*, at paragraph 12, Mr Justice MacKay noted that the London Agreement of 8 August 1945, along with its annex the *Charter of the International Military Tribunal*, are the foundation documents for the concept of "war crimes." He noted that while the definition of "war crimes" in the *Charter of the International Military Tribunal* does not specifically state that it has to take place in the course of an international armed conflict, the

context in which it appears suggests this is so. He also made reference to the definition of "war crimes" in the *Criminal Code* [RSC, 1985, c C-46, s 7(3.76) (as enacted by RSC, 1985 (3rd Supp), c 30, s 1)] and concluded that "war crimes" have come to be understood internationally in the context of international conflict.

'[13] Here the Board made no reference to the interpretation of war crimes set out in *Bermudez* and simply assumed that war crimes could be committed in an internal conflict. This was an error of law. The respondent submits that the error is one of form and not substance arguing that *Bermudez* is no longer good law and that the definition of war crimes has changed so as to include acts committed during internal conflicts. The respondent bases this argument on two grounds. First, international treaty law, specifically the *Rome Statute of the International Criminal Court* (Rome Statute), recognizes that war crimes are not limited to international armed conflicts. Second, the section of the *Criminal Code* referred to by MacKay J in *Bermudez* has since been repealed [SC 2000, c 24, s 42] and has been replaced by the *Crimes Against Humanity and War Crimes Act*, SC 2000, c 24 [s 4(3)] which defines "war crimes" more broadly as "act ... committed during an armed conflict".

'[14] There is no question that the Rome Statute is an international instrument which can be used to interpret the crimes in Article 1F(a) (see *Harb v Canada (Minister of Citizenship and Immigration)* (2003) 238 FTR 194 (FCA), at paragraphs 7–8 and the UNCHR [United Nations High Commissioner for Refugees] *Guidelines on International Protection: Application of the Exclusion Clauses: Article 1F of the 1951 Convention relating to the Status of Refugees*, dated September 4, 2003) and the acts attributed to the applicant, namely the torture and murder of "prisoners of war" (Shining Path and/or Tupac Amaru guerrillas), fall within the list of acts considered war crimes in an internal conflict (article 8, paragraph 2(c)(i) of the Rome Statute).

'[15] The applicant acknowledges that the acts attributed to the applicant would be considered war crimes under the definitions set out in the Rome Statute but submits that the Rome Statute cannot be applied to the acts attributed to the applicant because it came into force on July 1, 2002 and the acts attributed to him took place between 1985 and 1992. In effect, the applicant submits that the definition of war crimes provided in the Rome Statute cannot be applied retroactively. The applicant notes that the Rome Statute contains a retroactivity clause. Moreover, the applicant relied on *Ramirez* for the proposition that a person must have the *mens rea* for an international crime in order to be found excluded from refugee protection (*Ramirez v Canada (Minister of Employment and Immigration)*, [1992] 2 FC 306 (CA)) and submits that this principle extends such that a person cannot have the *mens rea* to commit an international crime if he is not aware that the acts in question are international crimes.

'[16] I agree with the applicant that the definitions in the Rome Statute cannot be applied retroactively. The definition of "war crime" set out in the *Crimes against Humanity and War Crimes Act* supports the applicant's argument. It provides that:

4. ...

(3) ...

"war crime" means an act or omission committed during an armed conflict that, at the time and in the place of its commission, constitutes a war crime according to customary international law or conventional international law applicable to armed conflicts, whether or not it constitutes a contravention of the law in force at the time and in the place of its commission. [Emphasis added.]

'[17] Since the Rome Statute was not part of international law at the time of the commission of the acts in question reference should not be made to how it defines war crimes for the purpose of determining whether the acts attributable to the applicant constitute war crimes.

'[18] This interpretation is supported by the principle in international criminal law of non-retroactivity. This principle is described as the "second corollary of the principle of legality. It means that a person cannot be judged or punished by virtue of a law which entered into force after the occurrence of the act in question" (John R W D Jones and Steven Powles, *International Criminal Practice* (Ardsley, NY: Transnational, 2003 at 6.1.21)).

'[19] Furthermore, I conclude that the definition of war crimes provided in the Rome Statute cannot be used to determine whether the acts in question constitute war crimes because they were committed before the Rome Statute was part of international law.

'[20] Consequently, in assuming that war crimes could be committed during an internal conflict, the Board erred in law. This error was determinative given that the current definition of war crimes in international law cannot be applied retroactively. This application for judicial review will be allowed and the matter should be sent back to a different Board to be redetermined.' Ventocilla v Canada *(Minister of Citizenship and Immigration)* [2008] 1 FCR 431, 2007 FC 575, [2007] FCJ No 773 at [10]–[20], per Teitelbaum DJ

ЄВГЕН КЛОПОТЕНКО

ЗВАБЛЕННЯ ЇЖЕЮ З УКРАЇНСЬКИМ СМАКОМ

#книголав/Київ/2020

IEVGEN KLOPOTENKO

UKRAINIAN CUISINE
IN 70 DISHES

TRANSLATED FROM UKRAINIAN
BY IAROSLAVA STRIKHA

#knigolove/Kyiv/2021

УДК 641.55(=161.2)(083.12)=111
К 57

Popular edition

Klopotenko, Ievgen.

К 57   Ukrainian Cuisine in 70 Dishes / Ievgen Klopotenko; translated from Ukrainian by Iaroslava Strikha. – Kyiv: Knigolove, 2021. – 176 p.

ISBN 978–617–7820–85–6

What are the first dishes that come to mind when you hear the words "Ukrainian cuisine"? Is it borscht or dumplings? You know what else would have come to mind if you were a 19th-century Ukrainian? Shpundra, teteria, kvasha and many other dishes. What is the authentic Ukrainian cuisine, and which forgotten dishes deserve a revival? Ievgen Klopotenko is answering these questions in his new book. He has spent several years exploring Ukrainian cookbooks from different eras, travelling across Ukraine and consulting with historians to develop his own vision of the Ukrainian cuisine. This book compiles 70 recipes that could bridge the gap between the Ukrainian culinary past and the present. You will rediscover the long forgotten Ukrainian dishes with a contemporary twist and new takes on old favorites. We guarantee that you will fall in love with these dishes and will be inspired to explore Ukraine's culinary diversity with us.

УДК 641.55(=161.2)(083.12)=111

Editorial group: *Oleksii Tatianchenko, Hanna Li, Iryna Rudnievska, Yevheniia Ieskova, Olena Liubenko, Olena Parkhomets*
Food styling by *Iryna Rudnievska, Oleksii Tatianchenko*
Photography by *Yuliia Minytska, Yuliia Hamova, Mykola Borysenko*
Design by *Valeriia Likhachova*
Cover design by *Maryna Fudashkina*
Proofreading by *Dariia Puhach*
Project curator: *Oleksandra Fidkevych*

The English-language edition team:
Translator: *Iaroslava Strikha*
Consulting editor: *Oleksandra Povoroznyk*
Layout designer: *Olha Fesenko*
Executive editor: *Daryna Vazhynska*
Editor in chief: *Zhanna Kapshuk*
Responsible editor: *Sergii Kleimenov*

Signed to print 16.07.2021. Format 84×108/16. Conventional printed sheet 18,48.
Print run 1500 copies. Order. № 278/07.

Knigolove LLC, 23 Kyrylivska Str., Kyiv, 04080. Publisher's license № 5188 of 25.08.2016.
knigolove.ua • facebook.com/knygolove • instagram.com/knygolove
sayhello@knigolove.ua

Printed by Unisoft Private Enterprise, 13B Morozova Str., Kharkiv, 61036.
Publisher's license № 5747 of 06.11.2017. www.unisoft.ua

ISBN 978–617–7820–85–6

IT'S TIME TO DISCOVER UKRAINIAN CUISINE. IT'S MORE THAN WORTH THE EFFORT

CONTENTS

INTRODUCTION

Strange as it may sound, the majority of present-day Ukrainians are plagued by negative stereotypes about their own cuisine. They might know borscht and dumplings, but anything beyond that is a mystery to them. I, too, used to belong to that majority. That is all due to our history. The Soviet Union did its best to wipe out not only the Ukrainian cuisine but also the very Ukrainian worldview. The moment I realized that, I dove into research. I was stunned by the magnificence of the Ukrainian dishes that our ancestors used to cook hundreds of years ago. With each bite, you feel the connection to your history. I began to tell this to Ukrainians to help them see that the love for all things Ukrainian was alive and well in our hearts. Some keep it in the dark, chained and bound; in some, the love has just awakened, so it's still a little groggy and confused from the sleep. Some though have let their love flow freely, so it grew, blossomed and strengthened, becoming their inspiration and protection.

If you love your roots, you are never alone. You know what you live for, and you know that others just like you are always at arm's length. You know where you fit in, and you have support. Oh, and it's simply a cool thing to do: to choose to love all things Ukrainian. If you choose to love, everything you do is steeped in that feeling, empowering you to create something beautiful.

Now I'd like to share my love for all things Ukrainian with the whole wide world. One could do that through our history, or our writers and their biographies, or through the thrilling Ukrainian music. Me, I will do it through Ukrainian cuisine. The national cuisine upholds an emotional connection with the country. This is the time to ask the question: what is Ukrainian cuisine?

Everybody thinks that Ukrainian cuisine is all about borscht and dumplings... and that's about it. They couldn't be more wrong. It took me approximately four years, about a hundred cookbooks from various eras, a trip across the entire country and countless consultations with historians to form my own understanding and sense of the Ukrainian cuisine. And here's what I've got to tell you.

First, sugar beet, home-pressed sunflower oil and beetroot kvass are the three products that are a part of our very DNA. Can you imagine the rich sweet taste of a baked sugar beet? Right, it's as if God kissed you on the mouth.

Second, Ukrainian cuisine is much more versatile than you might imagine. We know barely 15% of it. It's funny, really, that we have wasted so many years without making an effort to discover it. We had a very superficial idea of it, when in reality, Ukrainian cuisine is much deeper, more serious and less stereotypical than we might believe. It may surprise you. Cook any five dishes from this book, and you will feel your heart pulse with joy and excitement. This stuff is addictive. It's like meeting a woman that you want to drown in. She's slightly older and utterly magical. Endowed with deep wisdom and electric energy, she makes you feel like a slightly better version of yourself even if she's not doing anything in particular.

Ukrainian cuisine is a great historical record of the Ukrainian past and present. Some dishes were even adopted from other cultures: you will find several such recipes on the pages of this book. They won't leave your heart cold, I promise. Not a single dish here will leave your heart cold.

This is Ukrainian cuisine for you. It's delicious, but that's not the only reason why it's important. Ukrainian cuisine will help you understand Ukrainians as a nation. It's like taking a trip, only without getting on a plane or buying museum tickets. Cook it and try it, and you'll see it for yourself. Each country's cuisine embodies its culture and values, essentially presenting the nation's culinary portrait. This book is not just a collection of 70 recipes: these are 70 histories of the nation that has suffered centuries of persecution. Despite all that, my nation managed to preserve its identity and independence, but it's only just now learning to be proud of itself. To be proud of its language, its history, and its cuisine.

Read, listen, cook, feel Ukrainian. This is why I created this book: to teach everybody to love Ukraine through food.

**With Ukraine in my heart and on my tongue,
Ievgen Klopotenko**

DISCOVER UKRAINIAN INGREDIENTS

Ukrainian ingredients are cool, even if Ukrainians themselves don't necessarily realize how lucky they are. They take it all for granted. Yes, other countries may have similar ingredients, but their Ukrainian version is quite unique. I'm now teaching my compatriots to recognize their vibrant and rich taste. How? This is what I've been telling them:

"When you are buying carrots, don't think that it's just a boring and humble thing that you chuck into a broth and then discard without a second thought. No, no, no. No product deserves that. When you are at the market, pick up that carrot. Say hello to it (silently). Say, 'Hello, carrot. Aren't you gorgeous?' Imagine that this is the best carrot you've seen in your life. While the carrot probably won't answer you, that thought process creates the right mindset. Imagine its taste. Sweet, crunchy, juicy. Imagine how you'd like to cook it. With an orange? With rosemary? Would you like it caramelized? Show an interest in it. Imagine how much effort went into growing that carrot: not just human effort either, but of nature as a whole. Isn't it a miracle? You sow seeds, and then the sun, the rain and the soil all contribute to growing something delicious beyond all imagination.

This is true not only of carrots but of any product at all. A beetroot? Enough with boiling it, I'm begging you. Roast it. Eat it raw, savoring its honey sweetness. Or take earth apples, for example. At a farmer's market, you wouldn't touch this weird alien with a ten-foot pole. Pause. Buy it, bring it home, slice it, roast it and eat it with parsley, lemon and mustard. Try fragrant home-pressed oils and learn to love their mouth-watering aroma."

I want Ukrainians to respect the fruit of their soil. Me, I'm bubbling with excitement whenever I hit the farmer's market. It's like falling in love. Everything is so fragrant, so fresh, so precious. My heart feels ready to burst out of my chest. I feel dizzy. I love this feeling. I love imagining how I'd wash these vegetables, slice them, cook them, eat them...

I feel grateful because Ukrainian vegetables, fruit and other foods are some of the most delicious in the world. Ukrainians are beyond lucky to have them within easy reach.

MEAT

Historically, meat was a rare treat for Ukrainians. First, observant Orthodox Christians in Ukraine used to spend approximately six months out of twelve fasting. Second, only the wealthiest were rich enough to regularly feast on meat. All the others had their share of meat only on major holidays. Therefore, it is assumed that up until the mid-20th century, Ukrainians had a predominantly plant-based diet. That said, they loved meat a lot and jumped at every opportunity to savor some.

What do we see now? Finally having meat aplenty, Ukrainians became ardent meat-eaters. We have it for breakfast, lunch and dinner, and get anxious whenever our meat level drops critically. As if making up for past centuries, we can even devour several meat dishes during one meal. To be perfectly blunt, we aren't content unless we have some sort of meat in the fridge. It's usually the meat of domesticated animals: poultry, beef and pork are our favorites, hands down.

We usually roast meat. Note that we have inherited this technology from our ancestors, who cooked everything in the oven. Wow, I got chills just from thinking about this connection that transcends the boundaries of time and space.

By the way, ground meat is not a typical or traditional method of processing meat for Ukrainians. We used to finely dice or chop meat into the kind of small pieces you'd see in meat rolls or homemade sausages.

That might surprise you, but the idea that Ukrainians traditionally preferred very fatty meat dishes is wrong. In reality, we always used to take good care of our bodies, and never overdid it with the fat. This changed in Soviet times, when fat was the only available source of lasting energy, given that people couldn't afford much food.

So let us leave our stereotypes behind, open the chapter with meat dishes, and enjoy the delicious authentic tastes.

HRECHANYKY (BUCKWHEAT PATTIES) WITH TOMATO SAUCE

45 MINUTES | **SERVES 6**

INGREDIENTS:

· 300 G / 10 OZ. GROUND CHICKEN

· 125 G / 1 CUP BUCKWHEAT GRITS

· 50 G / 1¾ OZ. PORK FAT / FATTY BACON

· 250 ML / 1 CUP WATER

· 2 EGGS

· ½ TSP. SALT

· ⅓ TSP. GROUND BLACK PEPPER

· 3-4 TBSP. SEMOLINA FOR COATING

· 3-4 TBSP. VEGETABLE OIL

FOR THE SAUCE:

· 2-3 TBSP. TOMATO PASTE

· 200 ML / ¾ CUP PLUS 2 TBSP. WATER

· 3-4 GARLIC CLOVES

· ½ CHILI PEPPER

· 1 APPLE

· 1 TSP. INSTANT COFFEE

· A PINCH OF SUGAR

· A PINCH OF SALT

1. Preheat oven to 180°C / 350°F degrees.

2. Cover the buckwheat grits with water, add a pinch of salt, and cook for 15 minutes until ready. Leave them to cool.

3. Add ground chicken, finely diced pork fat or fatty bacon, salt and pepper. Mix the ingredients well, and form patties.

4. Coat the patties with semolina and place them on an oiled roasting pan. Roast for 15–20 minutes.

5. **For the sauce**, mix tomato paste with water and a coarsely grated apple. Add slices of chili pepper, salt and sugar, and sauté for 2–3 minutes. Just before removing the sauce from heat, add instant coffee.

6. Serve the buckwheat patties with hot tomato sauce.

#2 ROASTED PORK FAT IN CHAMOMILE

45 MINUTES | **SERVES 4**

INGREDIENTS:

· 0.5 KG / 1 LB. PORK FAT

· 1 TBSP. DRIED CHAMOMILE
  FLOWERS

· SALT

1. Preheat oven to 180°C / 350°F degrees.

2. Rub pork fat with a generous amount of salt (if unsalted) and dried chamomile flowers.

3. Roast on a baking paper-lined tray for 35–40 minutes.

4. Cool to room temperature and serve thinly sliced.

#3 SHPUNDRY (BEETROOT AND PORK STEW)

2 HOURS | **SERVES 4**

INGREDIENTS:

- 500 G / 1 LB. PORK NECK OR RIBS
- 1-2 BEETROOTS
- 1 TBSP. VINEGAR
- 2 ONIONS
- 1 TSP. SWEET MUSTARD
- 3 CLOVES GARLIC
- 1 TBSP. VEGETABLE OIL
- 40 G / 2½ TBSP. UNSALTED BUTTER
- 2 TBSP. ALL-PURPOSE FLOUR
- 1-2 TBSP. HORSERADISH
- 2-4 TBSP. SOUR CREAM
- 3-5 SPRIGS OF THYME (OPTIONAL)
- SALT, PEPPER

1. Preheat oven to 180°C / 350°F degrees.

2. Cut the meat, season with salt and pepper to taste. Rub it with sweet mustard and sprinkle with oil. Place it on a tray with one onion sliced into thin half circles. Roast for 40 minutes.

3. When cooked, separate the meat from the ribs, or slice the pork neck into bite-sized pieces.

4. Wash the beetroot well and place it in the oven. It's best to choose smaller beets and roast the meat and the beetroots simultaneously.

5. Slice the cooked beetroot into half circles, add vinegar and water until the beets are completely covered. Leave to marinate for 40 minutes.

6. Fry a finely chopped onion in butter in a large pan, add the meat and marinated beetroots. Add half a cup of water, and let it stew for 5 minutes.

7. Add flour, salt and pepper to taste.

8. Serve *shpundry* with grated white horseradish and sour cream. You can also add fresh thyme leaves.

#4 POLTAVA HALUSHKY (DUMPLINGS) WITH SOUR CHERRIES AND MEAT

45 MINUTES | **SERVES 6**

INGREDIENTS:

- 400 G / 3½ CUPS ALL-PURPOSE FLOUR
- 250 ML / 1 CUP KEFIR (FERMENTED MILK DRINK, CAN BE SUBSTITUTED WITH THIN PLAIN YOGHURT)
- 1 EGG
- ½ TSP. SALT
- ½ TSP. BAKING SODA
- 500 G / 1 LB. GROUND-MEAT MIX
- 1 TBSP. SUGAR

FOR THE SAUCE:

- 400 G / 1 LB. FROZEN SOUR CHERRIES
- ½ TSP. GROUND CORIANDER SEEDS
- GROUND BLACK PEPPER
- ½ CUP SOUR CREAM
- 2-3 TBSP. VEGETABLE OIL

1. Prepare the dough for *halushky*. Mix flour, kefir, eggs, salt and baking soda in a bowl. Knead the dough until it is soft and not sticky.

2. Pinch off small pieces of dough and toss them into boiling salted water. Cook for 2 minutes, then remove *halushky* with a skimmer. Sprinkle the cooked *halushky* with oil so that they won't stick together. Cover with a towel and leave in a warm place to ensure that they don't cool before serving.

3. **Prepare the sauce.** Fry minced meat in a pan with a small sprinkling of oil. Season with salt, ground coriander and pepper to taste.

4. 5 minutes before the meat is ready, add defrosted, pitted sour cherries with juice.

5. Mix *halushky* with fried meat and cherries in a large bowl. Serve hot with sour cream.

#5

KRUCHENYKY (MEAT ROLLS)

 |

45 MINUTES **SERVES 2**

INGREDIENTS:

· 250 G / 0.5 LB. PORK LOIN

· 100 G / 3½ OZ. PORK FAT OR

FATTY BACON

· 1 CLOVE GARLIC

· A PINCH OF THYME

· 10-12 SPRIGS OF FRESH DILL

· 50 G / ⅓ CUP FLOUR

· 50 G / ¼ CUP SEMOLINA

· 2-3 TBSP. VEGETABLE OIL

· 1 EGG

· SALT, PEPPER

1. Preheat oven to 180°C / 350°F degrees.

2. Cut the pork loin into portion-sized pieces. Cover with plastic wrap and pound each piece until tender. Rub it with salt and pepper.

3. Mix small pieces of pork fat or fatty bacon with finely chopped garlic and dill. Add thyme and blend in a food processor until smooth.

4. Form the fat-and-herbs mass into logs, place each in the center of a pork loin piece, leaving room on the sides, then roll up. Secure each roll with a toothpick.

5. On to the two-step coating process. Coat each meat roll in flour, then dip into egg wash, and then sprinkle with semolina.

6. Place the rolls on a hot oiled pan and fry for several minutes until golden brown on all sides.

7. Move the rolls to a roasting tray lined with baking paper and roast for 15 minutes.

#6 DUCK WITH BANOSH (CORNMEAL PORRIDGE)

4 HOURS | **SERVES 4-6**

INGREDIENTS:

- 1 DUCK
- 100 G / ¾ CUP CORNMEAL
- 100 ML / 7 TBSP. HEAVY CREAM
- 100 ML / 7 TBSP. MILK
- 100 ML / 7 TBSP. WATER
- 1 ONION
- 1 CARROT
- 1 BELL PEPPER
- 2-3 CLOVES GARLIC
- 5 SPRIGS OF THYME
- ⅓ CHILI PEPPER
- 2-3 TBSP. VEGETABLE OIL
- JUICE AND ZEST OF 1 LEMON
- SALT, PEPPER

1. Preheat oven to 180°C / 350°F degrees.

2. **Prepare the banosh.** Mix cream, milk and water in a heavy saucepan, bring to a boil and cook for 3-5 minutes, whisking constantly.

3. **Vegetables.** Dice an onion, a carrot and a bell pepper. Fry them in an oiled pan until golden brown.

4. Add the vegetables to the cornmeal and mix well.

5. Rub the **duck** with salt and pepper (inside and out), sprinkle with lemon zest and juice and oil. Stuff crushed garlic cloves, sprigs of thyme and thin slices of a hot chili pepper inside the duck. Leave it to marinate for 1.5-2 hours.

6. Fill the duck with vegetable banosh and close the skin with toothpicks or kitchen twine.

7. Bake for 1.5 hours. Now and again baste the duck with its juices from the tray.

8. Serve the duck with banosh stuffing while still hot.

#7

DRAHLI (ASPIC)

3 HOURS | **SERVES 4**

INGREDIENTS:

- 500 G / 1 LB. LEAN PORK
- 2 LITERS / 8 CUPS WATER
- 30 G / 1 OZ. UNFLAVORED GELATIN POWDER
- 2-3 CLOVES GARLIC
- 3-4 ALLSPICE BERRIES
- 2-3 BAY LEAVES

FOR THE SAUCE:
- 2 CLOVES GARLIC
- ¼ TSP. BLACK PEPPER
- 2 TSP. WHITE HORSERADISH

1. Cut lean pork into bite-sized chunks, put into a saucepan, cover with water and bring to a boil. After cooking for 2–3 minutes, drain the water and wash the meat well.

2. Add new clean water, combine with crushed garlic, allspice and bay leaf, and cook over low heat for 1 hour. Add salt to taste.

3. Remove the meat, shred and place into portion-sized bowls.

4. Dissolve the previously soaked gelatin in the hot broth and pour into the bowls over the meat. After the broth cools, put the bowls in the fridge and leave for 2–3 hours for the aspic to set.

5. For the sauce, mix crushed garlic with black pepper and white horseradish. Serve the aspic with the hot sauce.

#8

ZINKIV SAUSAGE

 |

4 HOURS | **SERVES 6-8**

INGREDIENTS:

· 2 KG / 4½ LB. LEAN PORK
SHOULDER

· 1 TBSP. SALT

· 1 TBSP. FRESHLY GROUND
BLACK PEPPER OR MIXED
PEPPERS

· 3 METERS PORK INTESTINES

· 3 HEADS GARLIC

· 250 ML / 1 CUP ICE-COLD
WATER

· 500 ML / 2 CUPS FRESH PIG'S
BLOOD (YOU CAN PROBABLY
GET IT FROM YOUR BUTCHER
OR ASK AROUND AT A MEAT
MARKET)

1. Preheat oven to 160°C / 325°F degrees.

2. Cut the meat into approximately 0.5 to 1-inch (1–2 cm) cubes and put in a bowl.

3. Season with salt, freshly ground pepper and crushed garlic. Carefully mix the ingredients for 10–15 minutes until the sausage mixture becomes denser.

4. Add ice-cold water and mix thoroughly once again until the meat absorbs all liquid.

5. Soak and rinse pork intestines. You can also get artificial sausage casings, but I prefer the natural hog casing (you can order intestines from a reputable butcher or at the farmer's market).

6. Cut the intestines into 40-60 cm / 15-25 inch segments and fill them with the sausage blend using a sausage stuffer. Make sure you fill the casing as tightly as possible and close the ends with kitchen twine.

7. Rub the sausages with blood roast for 3 hours. In the early stages, remove the sausage from the oven every 20 minutes and rub with blood on both sides with a pastry brush. To make sure that the sausage turns the nice dark shade and doesn't dry out, you'll need to repeat this process 5–6 times.

8. Towards the end of the cooking time, you can place a beech or alder wood chip in a bowl, light it and put it in the oven to give the sausage a nice smoke-cured taste.

9. Serve the sausage fully cooled.

#9

VERESHCHAKA (KVASS-COOKED RIBS)

1 HOUR 20 MINUTES   **SERVES 4**

INGREDIENTS:

- 600-800 G / 1.3-1.7 LB. PORK RIBS
- 200 ML / SCANT 1 CUP BEETROOT KVASS (SEE THE RECIPE ON P. 165)
- 200 ML / SCANT 1 CUP WHEAT KVASS (YOU CAN FIND KVASS IN EASTERN EUROPEAN GROCERY STORES OR ONLINE)
- 2 SPRIGS THYME
- 1/2 TBSP. SUGAR
- 2-3 CLOVES GARLIC
- 50 G / 3½ TBSP. UNSALTED BUTTER
- 1 TBSP. FLOUR
- 2-3 TBSP. VEGETABLE OIL
- SALT, PEPPER

1. Preheat oven to 180°C / 350°F degrees.

2. Remove membranes and extra fat from the ribs. Cut into servings of 1-2 segments.

3. Rub the ribs with salt, pepper and crushed garlic.

4. Fry on a frying pan with a small dollop of vegetable oil until a golden brown crust forms on all sides.

5. Move the ribs to a deep roasting tray and add two kinds of kvass: beetroot and wheat. Roast for 45-50 minutes.

6. Once ready, remove the ribs from the tray and serve hot.

7. Meanwhile, prepare the sauce: pour the leftover juices from the roasting pan into a saucepan and reduce for 20 minutes.

8. Mix softened butter with flour until smooth. Add the mixture to the saucepan, season with sugar, salt and pepper to taste to make sure that the sauce caramelizes and glazes. Keep whisking until the sauce thickens smoothly.

9. Serve with a generous helping of the sauce.

#10 CHEBUREKY (CRIMEAN TATAR TURNOVER)

1 HOUR | SERVES 4-6

INGREDIENTS:

- 600 G / 5 SCANT CUPS ALL-PURPOSE FLOUR
- 250 ML / 1 CUP WATER
- 1 TSP. SALT
- 1 TSP. SUGAR
- 1 TSP. VINEGAR
- 1 TSP. VEGETABLE OIL

FOR THE FILLING:

- 800 G / 1.7 LB. GROUND BEEF
- 1 LARGE ONION
- 4-5 CLOVES GARLIC
- 1 TBSP. CUMIN
- 200 ML / ¾ CUP PLUS 2 TBSP. COLD WATER
- SALT, PEPPER
- FRYING OIL

1. **For the dough,** add salt, sugar, vinegar, and warm water (50°C / 120°F) to sifted flour. Knead the dough until stretchy and elastic, then cover with plastic wrap. Leave it to rest for 30 minutes in the fridge.

2. **For the filling,** finely dice the onion with a sharp knife and mix with ground beef and crushed garlic. Season with salt, pepper and cumin to taste. Add very cold water and stir very well to make the filling juicier.

3. Separate the dough into 12-15 equal portions and roll out each until thin. Brush the edges with a little bit of water to make them stickier. Place the filling over one half of the dough, then fold the other half to cover the filling and press down the edge with a fork to give it the desired wavy texture.

4. Fry *chebureky* in oil on a hot frying pan until both sides are golden brown.

5. Serve hot right from the pan.

PORK STEW

2 HOURS   **SERVES 4-6**

INGREDIENTS:

- 800 G / 1.7 LB. FATTY PORK (NECK)
- ¼ CELERY ROOT
- 6-8 POTATOES
- 3-4 TBSP. VEGETABLE OIL
- 150 G / 5 OZ. PORK FAT
- 1-2 ONIONS
- 1 CARROT
- 1 GARLIC
- 100 ML / 7 TBSP. DRY RED WINE
- 1-2 TBSP. TOMATO PASTE
- 3-5 SPRIGS OF PARSLEY FOR DECORATION
- SALT, PEPPER

1. Preheat oven to 180°C / 350°F degrees.

2. Fry pieces of meat in a hot oiled skillet until golden brown.

3. In a frying pan, render the pork fat and fry the finely chopped onions, carrot and celery with the fat. Add crushed cloves of garlic. Cook everything together until soft, then add to the skillet with the meat.

4. Peel potatoes and chop them into small pieces. Add to the skillet with salt, pepper and ½ liter / 2 cups water. Bake for 40 minutes.

5. Dissolve the tomato paste in wine and pour it into the skillet. Put it back into the oven and cook for 30–40 more minutes until ready.

6. Serve the pork stew hot. Optionally, you can garnish the stew with finely chopped green parsley.

FISH

A nation is formed by its language and cuisine. That's 2/3 of the formula for success. Whenever we travel abroad, we try to learn a couple of words in a local language and find out what the locals eat. Our introduction to a new culture usually begins with these two factors. Therefore, it comes as no surprise that I only started to feel fully Ukrainian after I began to study the national cuisine. I grew up in Ukraine and I love my country, but I always felt like something was missing, as if our relationship wasn't deep enough. After I found out that, say, our ancestors in Ukraine used to stew pork ribs in kvass, my eyes opened. I realized that, up to that day, the list of authentic Ukrainian dishes that I had tried was limited to borscht and banosh. I knew more about Italian cuisine than about my own culture.

That realization had changed everything. I began to seek out, cook and eat Ukrainian dishes. Each new flavor made my connection with Ukraine grow stronger. A couple dozen dishes, and we are no longer strangers. My knowledge about the national cuisine has unblocked our connection.

That knowledge gave me an instinctual understanding of Ukraine. I dug deeper and formed my own understanding of what it means to be Ukrainian. In my search for Ukrainian national cuisine, I ended up finding myself. It was as if a chest with a portal to a different time opened in front of me. That chest stores history and love for my country and people. That crucial chest had been hidden from me for so long that, having finally found it, I wanted to show its contents to other Ukrainians. I wanted to develop, protect and promote Ukrainian cuisine. I loved the Ukrainian part of my identity more than ever, and that has changed how I viewed others. I realized that they didn't care about certain things only because they didn't have the information that I've found. They didn't understand who they were, and they didn't have the knowledge of history that could unite them.

Food, it seems, has brought me to the authentic Ukrainian world. Not only is it a land of many wonders; most crucially, it has a future. In that future, Ukrainians are a united, strong, independent and developed nation. Every Ukrainian can access that world. All you need is an entrance ticket: a connection to your roots, an understanding of and emotional investment in your history. Can a person not of Ukrainian heritage understand that world? Sure, through Ukrainian history and cuisine, which can bring one as close to Ukrainian culture as is humanly possible without actually delving into the depths of Ukrainian national character. That understanding will be partly rational, and partly emotional because food touches the soul.

#12 SILVER CARP SALAMUR (MARINADE)

30 MINUTES   **SERVES 6**

INGREDIENTS:

· 1 SILVER CARP (700 G / 1½ LB.)

· 1 CARROT

· 1 ONION

· 1.5 TSP. SALT

· 70 ML / 4.5 TBSP. VINEGAR

  FOR THE SALAMUR

  (MARINADE):

· 40 ML / 2½ TBSP. VINEGAR

· 3 CLOVES GARLIC

· 5-7 SPRIGS DILL

· 150 ML / ⅔ CUP VEGETABLE OIL

· 1 TSP. SALT

1. Scale the fish, remove intestines and fins. Chop off the tail and the head (they will make for a delicious fish broth). Slice the fish into 2 cm / ¾ inch-thick steaks.

2. Prepare the vegetables for the broth. Slice the onion into half-circles, and the carrot into chunks of whatever size you like. Cover the vegetables with 1½ liters / 1½ quarts of water, add salt and vinegar. Mix well and heat up. Add fish steaks, bring to a boil and cook for 10 minutes.

3. For the marinade, mix oil and vinegar in a glass bowl. Add salt, finely diced green dill, and crushed garlic. Mix well.

4. Remove fish steaks from the broth and cover with marinade. Leave to rest in the fridge for 20 minutes and serve.

#13

FRIED CARP

2 HOURS 40 MINUTES   **SERVES 4**

INGREDIENTS:

- 5-8 FRESH CARPS WITH HEADS ON (DEPENDING ON THE SIZE)
- 20 G / 1½ TBSP. ALL-PURPOSE FLOUR
- ½ LEEK
- 5 SPRIGS DILL
- 2 CLOVES GARLIC
- 300 G / 10 OZ. SOUR CREAM (15% FAT)
- 200 ML / ¾ CUP PLUS 2 TBSP. WHIPPING CREAM (33%)
- VEGETABLE OIL (FOR FRYING)
- SALT TO TASTE

1. Preheat oven to 160°C / 325°F degrees.

2. Wash and scale the carps, remove gills. Pat dry with a paper towel, sprinkle with a generous amount of salt, and leave in the fridge for 1–2 hours.

3. Roll salted carps in flour and fry in a skillet with a small glug of oil for 1 minute on each side.

4. Move the carps to an oiled roasting tray lined with slices of leeks. Pour a mixture of sour cream and cream over the fish, sprinkle with diced garlic and green dill, and bake for 20–30 minutes. Serve hot.

#14

HERB-BAKED CATFISH

40 MINUTES   **SERVES 2**

INGREDIENTS:

· 1 CATFISH (300-500 G / 0.6-1.1 LB.)

· 4 TBSP. HOME-PRESSED

   VEGETABLE OIL

· 1 TSP. OREGANO

· 1 CLOVE GARLIC

· 2 TBSP. SWEET MUSTARD

· ½ TSP. DRIED ELDERBERRIES

· 3 JUNIPER BERRIES

· SALT

1. Preheat oven to 180°C / 350°F degrees.

2. Wash the catfish well, remove entrails and gills. Wash it well once again, and pat dry with a paper towel.

3. Give the catfish a generous rub of salt, then brush it with a mixture of mustard, oil, finely diced garlic, and oregano. Put crushed juniper berries into it and sprinkle it with dried elderberries.

4. Place the catfish on a baking paper-lined roasting tray and bake for 15–25 minutes, depending on the fish's size. Serve hot.

#15

BAKED CARP

1 HOUR   **SERVES 4-6**

INGREDIENTS:

· 1 CARP (APPROXIMATELY 1½ KG

  OR 3 LB.)

· 1 FENNEL ROOT

· 1 TSP. FENNEL SEEDS

· 1 LEMON

· 1 STICK CINNAMON

· 1 TBSP. SWEET MUSTARD

· 1-2 TBSP. TOMATO PASTE

  (OPTIONAL)

· 5-6 POTATOES

· VEGETABLE OIL

· SALT, PEPPER

1. Preheat oven to 180°C / 350°F degrees.

2. Wash the carp well, remove the scales, entrails and gills.

3. Pat the fish dry with a paper towel and rub it with salt and pepper. Brush it inside and out with oil. Sprinkle it with fennel seeds. Place a cinnamon stick and a fennel root, thinly sliced into half-circles, inside the fish.

4. Wash potatoes well with a sponge and cut them into large pieces. Sprinkle with salt and pepper, drizzle with oil.

5. Place the fish on an oiled roasting tray, rub with mustard and tomato paste, and sprinkle with freshly squeezed lemon juice. Put potatoes and slices of lemon around it and cook for 40–50 minutes, depending on the fish's size. Serve hot.

#16

FISH PATTIES

45 MINUTES | **SERVES 4**

INGREDIENTS:

· 600-700 G / 1⅓-1½ LB. CATFISH

  FILLETS (1 SMALL CATFISH)

· 100 ML / 6½ TBSP. VINEGAR

· 1 ONION

· 1 CARROT

· 1 EGG

· 1 TBSP. FLOUR

· 3-4 TBSP. BREADCRUMBS

· SALT, PEPPER

1. Preheat oven to 180°C / 350°F degrees.

2. Wash the catfish well, remove entrails and gills, and cut into large steaks. Put into a saucepan, add 1 liter water, vinegar, oil and carrots cut into pieces of any size. Bring to a boil and cook for 2–3 minutes, then leave to cool in the broth.

3. Remove all bones and mince the fillet with a sharp knife. Combine with an egg and flour. Season with salt and pepper to taste. Carefully knead minced fish until all the ingredients are well-blended.

4. Form small patties of approximately 50 g / 1¾ oz, and coat them with breadcrumbs.

5. Put them on a baking paper-lined roasting tray and cook for 7–10 minutes.

6. Serve with your favorite sauce.

#17

FRIED SPRAT PATTIES

25 MINUTES | **SERVES 4**

INGREDIENTS:

- 400 G / 14 OZ. SPRATS
- 1 TBSP. VINEGAR
- 200 G / 2½ CUPS ALL-PURPOSE FLOUR
- 2 EGGS
- 200 ML / SCANT 1 CUP MILK
- PINCH OF SALT
- VEGETABLE OIL FOR FRYING
- ½ LEMON
- 3-4 GREEN ONION SHOOTS FOR SERVING

1. Remove heads and backbones of sprats, leaving just the fillets. To make the taste more intense, add salt and vinegar.

2. Prepare the batter for the patties. Mix milk, eggs and a pinch of salt with flour until it reaches the consistency of dense sour cream.

3. Place 5-6 sprat fillets on a hot oiled skillet, and pour 2-3 tbsp. of batter over it, as if you were cooking a pancake.

4. Fry the patties for 2-3 minutes on either side over low heat until golden brown.

5. Serve garnished with finely diced green or red onions and freshly pressed lemon juice.

#18

SARDINE AND VEAL STEW

1 HOUR   **SERVES 2**

INGREDIENTS:

· 300 G / 10 OZ. VEAL

· 2 HEADS GARLIC

· 1 ONION

· 1 CARROT

· ¼ CELERY ROOT

· 2 CM / 1 INCH GINGER ROOT

· 5-6 SALTED SARDINES

· 2-3 CLOVES

· VEGETABLE OIL

· SALT, BLACK PEPPER

1. Preheat oven to 180°C / 350°F degrees.

2. Remove membranes from the veal. Cut into portion-sized slices.

3. Fry the meat, half-circular slices of onions, thick half-circles of carrots, and slices of celery of any size in a frying pan with a small dollop of oil. Add finely grated ginger to increase the flavor and taste.

4. Optionally, you can add potatoes at this stage. I decided not to add it just this time to preserve the intense vegetable flavor!

5. If your pan is oven-proof, add salt and pepper to taste, cloves and garlic heads sliced in half horizontally. Then cover with tinfoil and cook for 15–20 minutes. If the pan isn't oven-proof, move the dish to a roasting tray.

6. Prepare the sardines in advance: cut off the heads, remove the intestines and backbones. I would like to stress that the fish freshness is of the essence! It will have a huge impact on the taste of your dish.

7. Remove the tray from the oven, take off the foil and add the sardines.

8. Cover with foil again and cook for 15 more minutes.

9. Serve hot.

VEGETABLES AND MUSHROOMS

ON PARSNIP

In primary school, we used to sing a Ukrainian folk song, "A fish danced with a crayfish, and parsley danced with parsnip." The funniest thing about the song is not the total absence of logic but the fact that Ukrainians know the word "parsnip" since their earliest childhood, more or less, but don't have the foggiest idea what it actually is. If you ask a random person on the street, the majority won't be able to tell you what a parsnip looks or tastes like, and that's a shame. Have you ever tried parsnip? I did. And it's one hell of a dish.

Bittersweet and self-sufficient, it fits the Ukrainian culinary profile to a tee. Do you know what I mean? Take seafood, for example: it fits the culinary profile of Sicily. Tomatoes with mozzarella spell Italy. Thick chocolate smacks of Belgium. The corny, sweet and spicy taste is 100% Mexico. Meanwhile, parsnip epitomizes the Ukrainian flavor.

After I discovered and fell in love with this root, my odyssey began: I have been trying out new ways to draw Ukrainian meanings out of parsnip and increase its flavor with various cooking techniques. I baked it for 24 hours, played around with its texture, boiled it with flavorful ingredients. It all came out wrong. Instead of laying bare its Ukrainian soul, I did it all wrong. And then I finally got it. Parsnip should be baked in the oven to increase its sweetness, but not for too long. Bake it for a little while to make it easier to chew; any other actions are a step too far.

That's how cool parsnip is. Anybody who grasps its uniqueness can also grasp the essence of Ukrainian taste.

ON SUGAR BEETS

I want to kneel and thank the universe for giving Ukrainians sugar beets. The stony surface of this root hides perfection. Rude and boorish on the outside, it has a kind soul. It is sweet. It is juicy. It has a cool history. This overlooked hero is 100% Ukrainian.

It took me quite a while to find sugar beets. You can't just buy them in any old shop, but find it I did. Discovering the sugar beet's potential was the next step. I wanted to lay bare its beautiful essence and show it to the world, to improve but not to undermine its taste. That was the hardest.

I found a way. I baked it for 8 hours in a traditional Ukrainian oven, then added salted raspberries, pickled plums, mushroom broth and soft farmer's cheese. This is how it features on the menu of my restaurant, 100 Years Ago Ahead (*100 Rokiv Tomu Vpered* in Ukrainian).

You should eat it slowly, savoring every bite. Take your time to get properly acquainted. Say to it, "Hello, the little sugar beet. You might be strange, but I will try to understand you." Sugar beets are no strangers to Ukrainians; they are a part of our cultural code. They deserve to be more of a presence in the lives of Ukrainians and other nations. I will make every effort to promote them because it helps me to promote Ukraine.

Sugar beet is a bridge between Ukrainian past and future.

#19

ROASTED
VEGETABLE PÂTÉ

50 MINUTES | **SERVES 4**

INGREDIENTS:

· 1 ZUCCHINI

· 1 CARROT

· 1 RED BELL PEPPER

· ½ ONION

· 2 CLOVES GARLIC

· 3-4 TBSP. HOME-PRESSED
  SUNFLOWER OIL (CAN BE
  SUBSTITUTED WITH ANY
  VEGETABLE OIL YOU PREFER)

· ½ LEMON

· SALT, PEPPER

1. Preheat oven to 180°C / 350°F degrees.

2. Wash a zucchini, a carrot and a bell pepper well, and pat them dry with a paper towel. Poke the vegetables with a toothpick several times, drizzle with oil and sprinkle with salt. Wrap in foil and bake for 40 minutes.

3. Let the vegetables cool before peeling them. Cut the zucchini, carrot and pepper into slices of any size you like and put them into a blender.

4. Add diced garlic and onion, and blend until smooth. Add oil, salt, pepper and freshly squeezed lemon juice to taste.

5. Serve the vegetable pâté cool.

#20   VEGETABLE SALAD

15 MINUTES | **SERVES 4**

INGREDIENTS:

· 1 ZUCCHINI

· 10 SPRIGS DILL

· 1 TSP. CHILI PEPPER FLAKES

· 1 LEMON

· 10 SPRIGS MINT

· 2 CELERY STALKS

· 2-3 CLOVES GARLIC

· 5 TBSP. VEGETABLE OIL

· SALT, PEPPER

1. Cut the zucchini into thin slices with a peeler.

2. Cut celery stalks into thin slices.

3. Shred green dill manually, and pick leaves off mint sprigs.

4. Carefully mix all ingredients in a bowl.

5. Prepare the dressing. Mix salt, pepper, finely diced garlic and lemon juice with the oil. Add the dressing to the salad and mix carefully.

6. Sprinkle with red chili pepper flakes and serve.

#21

BATTER-FRIED
OYSTER MUSHROOMS

30 MINUTES | SERVES 4

INGREDIENTS:

· 400 G / 14 OZ. OYSTER

   MUSHROOMS

· 100 ML / 6½ TBSP.

   VEGETABLE OIL (FOR FRYING)

FOR THE BATTER:

· 240 G / 1½ CUP ALL-PURPOSE

   FLOUR

· 2 EGGS

· 200 ML / SCANT 1 CUP PALE

   ALE OR WHEAT KVASS

FOR THE SAUCE:

· 200 G / SCANT 1 CUP SOUR

   CREAM

· 2-3 CLOVES GARLIC

· FRESH HERBS TO TASTE

   (PARSLEY, DILL)

· SALT, PEPPER

1. Wash oyster mushrooms and split them into smaller segments. Lay them out on an absorbent paper towel to dry.

2. **Prepare the batter.** Season the eggs with salt and pepper to taste and whisk with a fork. Add ale or kvass, then mix again. Add flour and mix until you get the kind of batter you'd use in pancakes.

3. Dip oyster mushrooms into the batter and place on a hot oiled frying pan. Fry until golden brown on all sides.

4. Remove the mushrooms from the pan with a skimmer and place them on a paper towel to remove excess oil.

5. **Prepare the sour cream sauce.** Add finely chopped green dill, parsley and pressed garlic to sour cream. Season with salt and pepper to taste.

6. Serve batter-fried oyster mushrooms with the sour cream sauce.

#22

BAKED PARSNIP

 |

60 MINUTES   **SERVES 2**

INGREDIENTS:

· 4 PARSNIP ROOTS

· SALT

 FOR THE SAUCE:

· 4 TBSP. SOUR CREAM

· 4 PRUNES

1. Preheat oven to 180°C / 350°F degrees.

2. Wash parsnip roots with a brush and peel with a peeler.

3. Give them a generous rub of salt and wrap in foil. Bake for 45–50 minutes.

4. **Prepare the flavorful sour cream sauce.** Add finely diced prunes to sour cream. Mix well.

5. Serve baked parsnips with the sour cream sauce.

#23 TOVCHANKA (POTATO AND BEAN MASH)

60 MINUTES | **SERVES 6**

INGREDIENTS:

- 5-6 POTATOES
- ½ CUP DRIED PEAS
- ½ CUP BEANS
- 3 TBSP. POPPY SEEDS
- 50 G / 3½ TBSP. UNSALTED BUTTER
- SALT AND PEPPER TO TASTE

1. Soak the peas and beans overnight for faster cooking.

2. Cook potatoes, beans and peas in separate pans until ready.

3. Mash potatoes, beans and peas with a potato masher.

4. Season with salt and pepper, add poppy seeds soaked in boiling water, and unsalted butter. Regulate the desired consistency with potato cooking water.

#24

WHITE (OR BLACK) RADISH SALAD WITH SOUR CREAM SAUCE

10 MINUTES | **SERVES 2**

INGREDIENTS:

- · 2-3 RADISHES
- · 1 TSP. SWEET MUSTARD
- · 2-3 TBSP. SOUR CREAM
- · 2 TBSP. HOME-PRESSED
  SUNFLOWER OIL (CAN BE
  SUBSTITUTED WITH ANY
  VEGETABLE OIL YOU PREFER)
- · 1 TBSP. LEMON JUICE
- · 2-3 SPRIGS DILL
- · SALT, PEPPER

1. Wash the radishes well and peel them. Grate on the coarse side of the grater or slice into long thin pieces.

2. Add the dressing: home-pressed sunflower oil with mustard, sour cream and lemon juice.

3. Add finely minced dill, mix and season with salt and pepper.

#25

QUICK PICKLED CUCUMBERS IN A PUMPKIN

 |

**3 HOURS
(AND 2 DAYS
FOR PICKLING)**

SERVES 4-6

INGREDIENTS:

· 1 LARGE PUMPKIN

· 1 KG / 2¼ LB. SMALL

  CUCUMBERS

· 3 TBSP. SALT

· 1 LITER / 4 CUPS WATER

· 5 BLACK PEPPERS

· 5 ALLSPICE BERRIES

· 3-5 BAY LEAVES

· 5-8 CURRANT LEAVES

· 5 CLOVES GARLIC

· 10 SPRIGS DILL

1. Scrub the cucumbers well and soak them in very cold water with ice for 2–3 hours to make them crunchier. Cut off ends and poke with a toothpick to ensure that the cucumbers are pickled all the way through.

2. Wash a large pumpkin well and cut off the top. Remove the seeds and flesh with a spoon to make room for pickles.

3. Fill the pumpkin with cucumbers, dill and currant leaves in layers, add allspice and black pepper, bay leaves and crushed garlic.

4. Dissolve salt in water and pour the brine into the pumpkin so that it covers the cucumbers. Place the cut-off top back in place to cover the pumpkin, and leave it in a cold place for 1–2 days. After the waiting is over, enjoy!

#26

POTATO SAUSAGE

60 MINUTES | **SERVES 4**

INGREDIENTS:

· 6-8 POTATOES

· 150 G / 5 OZ. PORK FAT

· 2-3 ONIONS

· A PINCH OF CRUSHED BAY LEAF

· 3-4 CLOVES GARLIC

· SAUSAGE CASING

· SOUR CREAM FOR SERVING

· SALT, PEPPER

1. Preheat oven to 180°C / 350°F degrees.

2. Boil unpeeled potatoes until ready. Leave them to cool, then peel.

3. Cut pork fat into small cubes and melt on the skillet until soft. In the lard, fry finely diced onions and garlic.

4. Mash or blend the potatoes, add fried pork fat, onions and garlic, season with salt and pepper to taste, add crushed bay leaves and mix well.

5. Fill sausage casings with mashed potatoes to make 12–15 cm / 5–6-inch-long sausages. Poke them with a toothpick several times to make sure that the casings won't break during roasting.

6. Place the sausages on an oiled roasting tray, and cook for 15–20 minutes until golden brown.

7. Serve potato sausages hot with sour cream.

#27 HASH BROWNS BAKED WITH MINCED MEAT

1 HOUR   **SERVES 4**

INGREDIENTS:

- 6-8 POTATOES
- 150 G / 5 OZ. PORK FAT OR FATTY BACON
- 200 G / 1 SCANT CUP SOUR CREAM (AND 1 TBSP. FOR THE DOUGH)
- 2 ONIONS
- 2 EGGS
- 4-5 TBSP. FLOUR
- 350 G / 12 OZ. HOMEMADE MINCED MEAT
- 2 TBSP. TOMATO PASTE
- 5-6 TBSP. VEGETABLE OIL
- SALT, PEPPER

1. Preheat oven to 180°C / 350°F degrees.

2. Grate peeled potatoes on the coarse side of the grater. Add 1 tbsp. sour cream, 1 finely grated onion, eggs, salt, pepper and flour. Mix well and fry hash browns on a hot oiled frying pan until either side is golden brown.

3. On the second frying pan, sweat the cubed pork fat and fry the onion cut into small cubes. Add minced meat and fry it until half-cooked. Add tomato paste, a little bit of water, salt and pepper. Cook for 5 minutes until extra liquid evaporates.

4. Put hash browns and minced meat into a pot in alternating layers. Add 2 tbsp. sour cream to each pot.

5. Bake for 15–20 minutes. Serve with sour cream.

#28

BORENCHYK (POTATO PIE)

1 HOUR | **SERVES 6**

INGREDIENTS:

- 1 KG / 2¼ LB. POTATOES
- 4 TBSP. CORN FLOUR
- 4 TBSP. WHEAT FLOUR
- 3 EGGS
- 150 ML / ⅔ CUP WHIPPING CREAM (33%)
- 5 SPRIGS THYME
- 200 G / 1 CUP UNSALTED BUTTER

FOR THE SAUCE:

- 3-5 CLOVES GARLIC
- ½ TSP. RED PEPPER
- 1 TSP. SMOKED PAPRIKA
- 1 TSP. PAPRIKA FLAKES
- 1 LEMON
- 1 TBSP. SUGAR
- 2-3 TBSP. TOMATO PASTE
- SALT, PEPPER

1. Preheat oven to 180°C / 350°F degrees.

2. Grate peeled potatoes on the coarse side of the grater. Season with salt and pepper. Add cream, eggs, corn and wheat flour.

3. Grease a ceramic baking tray with butter and dust with corn flour. Fill with potato mass, put 100 g / ½ cup worth of small butter slices on top, and sprinkle with thyme leaves.

4. Bake for 35–40 minutes.

5. Tomato paste. Mix garlic, tomato paste, three types of pepper and a bit of water in a saucepan. Bring to a boil and cook for several minutes, season with salt, sugar, pepper, lemon juice and lemon zest to taste. Blend until smooth.

6. Cut the pie into portion-sized slices. Serve with tomato sauce and melted butter.

APPETIZERS

ABOUT POLTAVA

I have travelled all over Ukraine before reaching Poltava at the very end of my trip. I saved the best for last, so to speak, and it turned that I was hella right. Poltava is a concentrated dose of all things Ukrainian, and a very logical last step for my exploration of the national cuisine. It's not just a regular town: it's the culinary hub of Ukrainian cuisine. During the whole period when Ukrainian identity was under systematic attack, Poltava seemed to have lingered under a protective dome. There was this Ukrainian writer by the name of Ivan Kotliarevsky. A Poltava native and resident, he created the modern Ukrainian literature and encoded dozens of Ukrainian dishes in his 18th-century work *The Aeneid*. He did that so elegantly that the Soviets missed the hint and didn't destroy it the way they used to destroy all things Ukrainian. I wouldn't be too surprised to learn that, since the 1800s to the present, Poltava residents had been reading Kotliarevskyi's *Aeneid* instead of their evening prayers, and cooking traditional Ukrainian dishes first thing in the morning: *shpundra* (meat baked with pickled beets), *halushky* (dumplings without filling), *putria* (a dish of ground barley) and more, all in order to keep the Ukrainian cuisine alive both in their memory and in their lived reality. They were so successful in preserving their Ukrainian identity because they cherished the traditions and the atmosphere that others only knew from books. Yes, Poltava cuisine might not be the most refined; it might be a tad too fatty; their *halushky* are probably not to everyone's taste. Ukrainian cuisine definitely could evolve further, but Poltava has the most important thing: the foundations. And their foundations are a hundred percent Ukrainian. They have even retained the authentic recipes for sugar beet and beetroot kvass, which is quite an achievement. Most importantly, Poltava managed to preserve unique Ukrainian cooking techniques. All you need to do is to take it up and develop it a step further. (Spoilers: this is exactly what I did. I took the basics and developed them to perfection.)

Globally speaking, Poltava residents are foodies as much as the French. They have even installed a monument to *halushky* smack in the town center to admire their culinary heritage 24/7. With a little effort, the amazing Poltava cuisine could beat just about any competitor, hands down. It just needs a little bit of refining and adaptation to contemporary demands, which, it goes without saying, wouldn't change their cuisine's national essence. This mission is wholly possible because Poltava residents have just the right mentality. They cherish, love and cook Ukrainian food. Back in the day, they have even inspired Gogol to write highly evocative descriptions of the national cuisine. Therefore, if you are really serious about reconstructing the Ukrainian national cuisine, you could do worse than to start with Poltava and its take on the matter.

ABOUT ODESA

My relationship with Odesa wasn't love at first sight. Not even at tenth sight. I didn't get what all the fuss was about, I didn't get its jokes, and I didn't like its food; in other words, I didn't understand the first thing about it. I didn't get it until I stumbled into a small courtyard, met an amazing Ukrainian Jewish family, wandered the Pryvoz Market with them, and cooked their borscht. As we sat outside, with the whole courtyard slurping borscht in unison, I finally felt the unique Odesa magic. It didn't matter *what* you were eating, but rather *who* you shared the meal with. Above all else, Odesa residents treasure strong family connections, community spirit and a sense of unity. They aren't quick to welcome strangers into their network of connections, which they take very seriously. At the same time, they also know how to laugh at life, which makes them so charming. Relying on their community, they have created a separate world to which strangers aren't privy. The insouciance with which they flirt with fate had helped them to survive the dark times. Due to all these factors, Odesa, much like Poltava, has kept its traditions and cuisine intact through the ages.

29

PALIUSHKY (POTATO FINGERS)

60 MINUTES   **SERVES 6**

INGREDIENTS:

· 1 KG / 2¼ LB. POTATOES

· 3 CLOVES GARLIC

· 1 BAY LEAF

· 3 EGG YOLKS

· 160-200 G / 1 CUP ALL-
  PURPOSE FLOUR

· 1 BUNCH PARSLEY

· 50 G / 3½ TBSP. UNSALTED
  BUTTER

· SALT, PEPPER TO TASTE

FOR THE SAUCE:

· 5 SPRIGS PARSLEY

· 5 SPRIGS DILL

· 100 ML / 6½ TBSP. WATER

· 100 ML / 6½ TBSP.
  VEGETABLE OIL

· 50 G / 1¾ OZ. HARD CHEESE

· JUICE OF HALF A LEMON

· 2 CLOVES GARLIC

· SALT, PEPPER

1. Preheat oven to 180°C / 350°F degrees.

2. Cut peeled potatoes into slices of any size. Cover with water and cook with salt, bay leaf and 3 cloves garlic for 15–20 minutes until ready.

3. Drain the cooked potatoes, discard garlic and bay leaf: you'll no longer need them. Mash potatoes until smooth. If you have leftover cooked unpeeled potatoes from the night before, you can also put them through a blender.

4. Add 2 egg yolks, salt, pepper and flour. Mix the dough.

5. Form potato fingers/batons with a spoon or a pastry bag and place them on a baking paper-lined roasting tray.

6. Wash in egg yolk with a silicone brush and bake for 15 minutes until golden brown.

7. **Green sauce.** Put diced green parsley and dill, water, oil, grated hard cheese, lemon juice, garlic and salt in a blender, and blend until smooth.

8. Serve with the green sauce, either hot or cold.

#30

LIVER PÂTÉ

 |

50 MINUTES   **SERVES 4-6**

INGREDIENTS:

- 500 G / 1 LB. CHICKEN LIVER
- 150 ML / ⅔ CUP WHIPPING
  CREAM (33%)
- 70 ML / 5 TBSP. BRANDY
- 100 G / 6½ TBSP. UNSALTED
  BUTTER
- 1 ONION
- 1-2 CLOVES GARLIC
- 2-3 SPRIGS OF THYME
- 2 TBSP. VEGETABLE OIL
- SALT, PEPPER

FOR THE SAUCE:

- 500 G / 1 LB. BLACK CURRANTS
- 250 G / 1¼ CUP SUGAR
- A PINCH OF GROUND BLACK
  PEPPER
- A PINCH OF SALT

1. Fry diced onions and garlic on a mixture of butter and oil. The onion should turn soft and transparent. Afterwards add a sprig of thyme and a pinch of salt.

2. Remove fat and membranes from chicken liver. Put it on the skillet with the onions and fry until ready.

3. Pour in the brandy and give it a couple minutes to evaporate. Turn off the heat and leave the liver to cool.

4. Remove sprigs of thyme and put liver into a blender. Add heavy cream, the rest of butter, pepper and another pinch of salt. Blend until smooth.

5. **Prepare the sauce.** Mix black currants and sugar in a saucepan. Add a little bit of water and boil for 10 minutes. Add a pinch of ground black pepper and salt. Blend until smooth. Serve cool with the currant sauce.

#31   KVASHA (FRUIT-AND-KVASS DESSERT)

 |

25 MINUTES   **SERVES 2-4**

INGREDIENTS:

· 300 ML / 1¼ CUP KVASS

· 100 G / 3½ OZ. SUN-DRIED
  OR SMOKED PEARS, PRUNES,
  APRICOTS AND APPLES

· 5 SLICES OF RYE BREAD
  (ADDITIONAL 150 G / 5 OZ.
  BREAD FOR THE CHIPS)

· 50 G / ½ CUP WALNUTS

· A PINCH OF GROUND RED
  PEPPER

· A PINCH OF SALT

· JUICE OF ½ LEMON

1. Preheat oven to 180°C / 350°F degrees.

2. Soak 5 slices of rye bread in kvass for 10 minutes. Add sun-dried or smoked pears and apples (similar to what is used in *uzvar*) to the bread-and-kvass mixture.

3. Bring the mixture to a boil the mixture and leave it to cool fully. Once cooled, remove boiled pears and apples.

4. Either pass the soft rye bread mass through a sieve or pulse in a blender until creamy. Add lemon juice, ground black pepper and salt to taste.

5. Cook rye bread chips. Cut the bread into thin slices and dry in the oven for 3 minutes.

6. Serve *kvasha* sprinkled with finely chopped walnuts. Decorate with rye bread chips.

#32

CHICKEN PUTRIA (GROUND BARLEY PORRIDGE)

1 HOUR | SERVES 2

INGREDIENTS:

- 100 G / ½ CUP GROUND BARLEY
- 200 ML / A SCANT CUP HOME-MADE WHEAT KVASS
- 1 CHICKEN BREAST
- 1 CARROT
- 1 ZUCCHINI
- 1 TSP. PAPRIKA
- 1 TBSP. LEMON JUICE
- 1 TBSP. VEGETABLE OIL
- SALT, PEPPER

HOMEMADE MAYONNAISE:

- 1 EGG YOLK
- ½ TSP. SWEET MUSTARD
- 100-150 ML / 6½ TBSP. TO ⅔ CUP VEGETABLE OIL
- 1 TBSP. LEMON JUICE
- SALT, PEPPER

1. Preheat oven to 180°C / 350°F degrees.

2. Soak fine-ground barley in homemade kvass for at least 6–8 hours, preferably overnight.

3. Marinate chicken breast for 10 minutes in salt, pepper, ground paprika, lemon juice and oil.

4. Place chicken breast on a baking paper-lined roasting tray, and cook for 25–30 minutes. It has to be well done.

5. Cut the carrot and the zucchini into very thin slices with a peeler.

6. For the **homemade mayonnaise**, mix egg yolk, mustard, salt and pepper in a bowl, add lemon juice and start whisking. Slowly add the oil at a dribble and mix well until the mayonnaise is smooth and thick.

7. Dress the vegetables with home-made mayonnaise, and put them into individual plates.

8. Put thin slices of the chicken breast and soaked ground barley over the vegetables and serve immediately.

33

PICKLED MUSHROOMS, APPLES AND ONIONS

15 MINUTES   **SERVES 6**

INGREDIENTS:

BUTTON MUSHROOMS:

· 400 G / 14 OZ. BUTTON
  MUSHROOMS

· 500 ML / 2 CUPS WATER

· 4 TBSP. VINEGAR

· 1 TSP. SUGAR

· 2 BAY LEAVES

· 5 BLACK PEPPERCORNS

· 3 ALLSPICE BERRIES

· 3 SPRIGS DILL

· ½ TSP. CORIANDER SEEDS

· 2-3 CLOVES GARLIC

· ½ ONIONS

· 3 TSP. SALT

APPLES:

· 4 APPLES

· 5 TBSP. SUGAR

· 4 TSP. SALT

· 3 SPRIGS DILL

· 8 BLACK PEPPERCORNS

RED ONIONS:

· 3 RED ONIONS

· 1 TSP. CORIANDER SEEDS

· 2 TSP. SALT

· 8 TBSP. SUGAR

· 500 ML / 2 CUPS WATER

· 5 BLACK PEPPERCORNS

Pickled mushrooms. Wash the mushrooms well and pat dry with a paper towel. Prepare the marinade. Add the following ingredients to 500 ml / 2 cups water: vinegar, sugar, bay leaf, black pepper and allspice berries, finely diced dill, coriander seeds, pressed garlic, salt and onions cut into thin half-circles. Warm the water to help salt and sugar dissolve, and to make sure that the spices release their flavors. Cover the mushrooms with the marinade and leave for at least 1–2 hours.

Pickled apples. Wash apples well and slice into thin slices horizontally. Sprinkle with sugar and salt. Add finely diced dill and pepper berries. Add a little bit of water and leave to marinate for 1 hour.

Pickled red onions. Mix room temperature water with sugar and spice until sugar dissolves fully. Peel the onions and slice into thin circles or semicircles. Cover the sliced onions with the marinade in a small bowl and leave for 1–2 hours.

SOUPS AND BROTHS

ABOUT BORSCHT

Borscht is the first dish I've ever cooked. My father taught me when I was eight. I came back from school one day, and without a word of warning, dad shoved a cabbage at me and solemnly told me that it was time. None too happy with this turn of events, I obediently hacked at the cabbage, and at some point began to enjoy it. My dad and I cooked borscht according to the recipe that is handed down in our family from father to son. That borscht was special. I was brimming with joy and pride, and that's what I have always felt when cooking ever since then.

This is how my cooking history began. For a while, I thought I was the odd one out: nobody in my family is that big on cooking. Most of my relatives treat it like a chore, but eventually I found out that my grandpa was crazy about cooking. Therefore, it wasn't that I was odd: borscht and the love for bringing out various tastes were in my DNA.

By the way, whenever I need a pick-me-up, I think about borscht. You have to take your time and savor borscht, slurp it, and make your enjoyment last. You can eat it with a slice of bacon on a piece of rye bread, or you can chase it with a shot of cold vodka. You can also eat it with onion and garlic, to add a pleasantly sharp tang.

I know that borscht is not just my history. I decided to travel across Ukraine, meet people from every region, and cook borscht with them according to their local recipes. That trip has changed my life. My faith in borscht has grown ever stronger. From a dish that every Ukrainian cooks, borscht has become for me a symbol of the nation's unity. Consider this. We might have different lifestyles, personalities, preferences or views, but one thing unites us all, and that is our love for borscht. If you tell me that the liquid that runs in Ukrainians' veins is blood, I'll just shake my head. Dear friends, it's red borscht that has been coursing in the veins of Ukrainians for ages.

I've tried goose borscht with prunes, cooked from a recipe shared by my artist friends. In Poltava, I tried black borscht with smoked pears and borscht with *halushky*. In the village of Topilche (Ivano-Frankivsk region in the west of the country), I tried the kind of borscht popular with the Hutsul ethnic group: without tomatoes but with *huslianka*, a very cool local fermented milk product. Having tried fish borscht in the village of Vylkove, I finally realized why Shevchenko loved carp borscht. In case you didn't know, Taras Shevchenko wasn't just a Ukrainian poet. He was also a passionate foodie. Give him his oysters, give him his

sparkling wine. Contrary to the popular belief, his life wasn't all woe, and those who had been promulgating this idea had bowdlerized the writer's bio. The life of every party, he was fun to be around. After he was released from serfdom, he led a rich life filled with interesting events, people and tastes. It is really no wonder that his menu included carp borscht. In Odesa, a Jewish family shared their recipe of chicken borscht with me. In Uzhhorod, I cooked *bohrach* borscht, with hot peppers and homemade sausages, over an open fire. High up in the mountains, I met Yanko, who treated me to borscht with mushrooms and local herbs, and poured me a shot of his homemade infused vodka (let's skip over the details of the latter). On the border with Belarus, I found a lone house. Its master, the 80-year-old Mykola Pylypovych, preserves the ancient recipe of borscht with sauerkraut and honey. Each of these types of borscht was so delicious it made my hairs stand on end. I've lost count of the times I wept with joy. Incredible taste. Incredible people. Incredible borscht. And it's all ours, Ukrainian.

#34 CHICKEN SOUP WITH HOMEMADE NOODLES

60 MINUTES | **SERVES 6**

INGREDIENTS:

· ½ CHICKEN

· ⅓ CELERY ROOT

· 1 ONION

· 1 HEAD GARLIC

· 1 CARROT

· 2 RED ONIONS

· 2 TBSP. VINEGAR

· 1 TBSP. SUGAR

· 2-3 SPRIGS DILL

· 1 TBSP. VEGETABLE OIL

· SALT, PEPPER TO SEASON THE CHICKEN

  FOR THE DOUGH:

· 200 G / 1¼ CUP ALL-PURPOSE FLOUR

· 2 EGGS

· 1 TBSP. VEGETABLE OIL

· 1 TSP. SALT

1. Preheat oven to 220°C / 425°F degrees.

2. Rub chicken with salt, pepper and 1 tbsp. oil. Put it on a roasting tray lined with parchment paper and roast for 20 minutes.

3. Put the roasted chicken in a saucepan, cover with water (2½ liter), and make a broth. Add large chunks of celery, onions, pressed garlic and carrot cut into pieces of any size. Cook for 40 minutes. Add salt to taste.

4. **Dough for homemade noodles.** Combine flour, salt and 1 tbsp. oil. Knead the dough until firm. Leave it to rest in the fridge for 20 minutes.

5. Cut red onions into thin rings and marinate in vinegar with sugar, salt and finely chopped dill. Add a dollop of water.

6. Roll dough thinly and slice into long noodles with a knife. When the soup is almost ready, add the noodles and cook for 1–2 more minutes. The soup is ready.

7. Serve with marinated onions.

#35

VEGAN BORSCHT WITH DUMPLINGS AND BEETROOT KVASS

50 MINUTES | **SERVES 6**

INGREDIENTS:

· ¼ CELERY ROOT

· 1 ONION

· 1 CARROT

· 1 BEETROOT

· 2 BAY LEAVES

· 3 ALLSPICE BERRIES

· 2-3 CLOVES GARLIC

· 2 LITER / 8 CUPS WATER

· ½ WHITE CABBAGE

· 3-4 POTATOES

· 3-4 TBSP. VEGETABLE OIL

· ½ RED BELL PEPPER

· 1 CUP TOMATO JUICE

· SALT, PEPPER

FOR THE BEETROOT KVASS:

· 0.5 KG / 2.2 LB. BEETROOTS

· 200 G / 1 CUP SUGAR

THE DOUGH FOR DUMPLINGS:

· 150 G / 1 CUP ALL-PURPOSE FLOUR

· 75 G / ⅓ CUP WATER

· 1 TBSP. VEGETABLE OIL

· A PINCH OF SALT

1. Prepare beetroot kvass in advance (see the recipe on p. 165).

2. Make the dough for dumplings. Combine all-purpose flour with water, a pinch of salt and 1 tbsp. oil. Knead dough until elastic and no longer sticky. Leave it to rest under a cloth towel or a plastic wrap in a fridge for 20 minutes.

3. Cook vegetable broth. You'll need large chunks of celery root, carrots, garlic and onion, bay leaf, allspice and salt.

4. Cut potatoes into medium-sized cubes and add to the broth. Cook for 10 minutes.

5. Cut the cabbage finely and add to the boiling borscht.

6. Fry the red bell pepper on a skillet for a bit before adding tomato juice. Sautee until it reaches mash consistency, then add to borscht.

7. Form small pieces of dough into dumpling shapes and add to the saucepan with the boiling borscht.

8. After the dumplings begin to float to the surface, pour in beetroot kvass, and add salt and pepper to taste.

VYLKOVE FISH SOUP WITH SALAMUR (MARINADE)

30 MINUTES   **SERVES 6**

INGREDIENTS:

· 1½-2 KG / 3¼-4½ LB. CARP

  (SILVER CARP)

· 1 RED BELL PEPPER

· 4-5 POTATOES

· 3 LITER WATER

· 2-3 TOMATOES

· 1 PARSLEY ROOT

· 3-5 CLOVES GARLIC

· 2 BAY LEAVES

· 2-3 TBSP. VEGETABLE OIL

· 5 SPRIGS DILL

· 2-3 TBSP. VINEGAR

· 1 SLICE BREAD

· SALT, PEPPER TO TASTE

FOR SALAMUR:

· 1 CUP FISH BROTH

· 5 SPRIGS DILL

· 2 CLOVES GARLIC

· 2-3 TBSP. VINEGAR

1. Scale the fish, remove guts and gills. Wash well and cut into large pieces.

2. Put the fish in a saucepan, cover with water and cook for 10 minutes with parsley root (chopped into large chunks), 2 cloves garlic, bay leaves, and bell pepper cut into small cubes. Season with salt and pepper.

3. Remove 1 cup broth for *salamur* and cool it in a glass jar.

4. Add potatoes diced into medium-sized cubes to the broth. Cook until potatoes are tender.

5. At the very end, add peeled and grated tomatoes. Bring the soup to a boil, cook for 4–5 minutes and switch off the heat. The fish soup is ready.

6. **Salamur.** Add finely chopped dill, pressed garlic and vinegar to the glass jar with cold fish broth.

7. Serve the fish soup hot with *salamur* and a slice of flavorful bread.

#37 BOHRACH (HUNGARIAN STYLE STEW)

90 MINUTES | SERVES 6

INGREDIENTS:

· 100 G / 3½ OZ. PORK FAT OR

 FATTY BACON

· 600 G / 1⅓ LB. BEEF

· 4-5 POTATOES

· 2 BELL PEPPERS

· 2 TOMATOES

· 1-2 TBSP. TOMATO PASTE

· 1-2 ONIONS

· ½ HOT CHILI PEPPER

· 1-2 TBSP. SMOKED PAPRIKA

· 1-2 TBSP. PAPRIKA

· SALT, PEPPER

1. Cut pork fat into small cubes and render in a deep skillet.

2. Cut beef into bite-sized pieces and fry in the skillet until golden brown on all sides in the pork fat.

3. Cut the onions into 4–8 segments and add to the skillet.

4. Add potatoes cut into pieces of any size to the skillet.

5. Cut tomatoes and bell peppers and add to the skillet.

6. Pour in enough water to cover all ingredients, add tomato paste and stew for 30–40 minutes.

7. Add slices of hot pepper, smoked and regular paprika, salt and pepper to taste.

8. Once cooked, leave bohrach for 20–30 minutes to make it more flavorful. Serve hot.

KHOLODNYK (COLD SOUP)

90 MINUTES | **SERVES 4**

INGREDIENTS:

· 2 BEETROOTS

· 300 ML / 1¼ CUPS WATER

· ½ ONION

· 2 TSP. VINEGAR

· 3 SPRIGS PARSLEY

· 3-4 BLACK PEPPERCORNS

· 2 EGGS

FOR MUSHROOM JUICE:

· 150 G / 5 OZ. BUTTON OR

  OYSTER MUSHROOMS

· 500 ML / 2 CUPS COLD WATER

· JUICE OF ½ LEMON

· SALT

1. Preheat oven to 180°C / 350°F degrees.

2. **Button mushroom or oyster mushroom juice.** Cover finely chopped button mushrooms or oyster mushrooms with water, add salt and lemon juice. Blend until smooth and leave for 1–2 hours for more intense flavor and taste. Put the mash through a sieve to get the juice.

3. Wash one beetroot well. Without peeling, bake it for 1 hour.

4. Peel the second beet and grate it on the coarse side of the grater. Cover it with cold water and vinegar, add onion and black pepper, and boil for 15–20 minutes. Before removing from heat, season with salt. Leave the broth to cool fully, then strain.

5. Cook the eggs for 3–4 minutes, then instantly dip into cold water.

6. Peel the baked beetroot and cut it into thin slices.

7. Put the beetroot into a deep bowl, add mushroom juice and beetroot broth. Cut the cooked and peeled eggs in halves and add them to *kholodnyk*. The yolks have to be runny and leak into the soup.

8. Serve garnished with finely diced parsley.

#39

TARATUTA (COLD BEETROOT SOUP)

90 MINUTES | SERVES 4

INGREDIENTS:

· 2 FRESH BEETROOTS

· 1-2 GREEN SOUR APPLES

· 1 SMALL ONION

· 500 ML / 2 CUPS BEETROOT
  KVASS

· JUICE OF ½ LEMON FOR THE
  DRESSING (OPTIONAL)

· 2 PICKLED CUCUMBERS WITH
  BRINE

· 1 TBSP. HORSERADISH

· SALT, PEPPER

1. Preheat oven to 180°C / 350°F degrees.

2. Wash the beetroots, pat them dry, wrap them in cooking foil and bake until ready (approximately 1 hour 15 minutes).

3. Peel boiled and cooled beetroots and cut into thin slices.

4. Cut apples and pickled cucumbers into sticks.

5. Cut the onion into thin circles.

6. Mix beetroots with cucumbers and apples, add horseradish and lemon juice, cover with beetroot kvass (for the recipe, see p. 165) and brine from the pickles. Stir well.

7. Season with salt and pepper.

8. Leave it to steep for about an hour in a cool place. Serve cooled.

#40 DUCK NECK SOUP

4 HOURS | **SERVES 4**

INGREDIENTS:

· ½ KG / 1 LB. DUCK NECKS

· 1 DUCK CARCASS OR 300 G /
  10½ OZ. BEEF BONES

· 2.5 LITER WATER

· 100 G / 1 SCANT CUP
  BUCKWHEAT

· 1 ONION

· 1 CARROT

· ¼ CELERY ROOT

· 2-3 CLOVES GARLIC

· 2 BAY LEAVES

· 5 ALLSPICE BERRIES

· 150 ML / ⅔ CUP TOMATO JUICE

· 2 APPLES

· SALT

1. Wash buckwheat well several times under running water and cover with tomato juice and water at the ratio of 1:1. Leave it to soak for 2 hours.

2. In the meantime, cook the duck neck and duck carcass/ beef bone broth. Remove the skin from the necks and cut them into 1.5–2-inch-long pieces. Add the rest of the water, onion, garlic, carrot and celery cut into big chunks of any size.

3. Add 1 apple, cut into quarters, allspice and bay leaves. Cook the broth for 90 minutes. Discard the vegetables (they have already given their flavor to the broth). Add salt to taste. Add soaked buckwheat and cook for 5 more minutes.

4. Cut the second apple into thin slices and fry on a frying pan for 1–2 minutes on each side until soft.

5. You can remove the bones from duck necks, but I like to serve them in portion-sized pieces.

6. Before serving, put several slices of fried apple into each dish.

#41

GREEN BORSCHT

1 HOUR   **SERVES 6-8**

INGREDIENTS:

· 2 CHICKEN LEG QUARTERS

· 3 LITER WATER

· 2 ONIONS

· 1 CARROT

· ¼ CELERY ROOT

· 2-3 BAY LEAVES

· 3-4 ALLSPICE BERRIES

· 3-4 POTATOES

· 1 BUNCH SORREL

· 1 BUNCH NETTLE

· 3-4 EGGS

· 3 TBSP. VEGETABLE OIL

· 10 SPRIGS PARSLEY

· SALT

1. Wash the chicken well and pat dry with a paper towel. Cover with water, add a whole onion. Cut half a carrot and a celery root into large chunks, add bay leaf and allspice. Cook over low heat for 30 minutes. Discard the vegetables (they have already released their flavor into the broth, and you won't need them anymore).

2. Cut the second onion into small cubes and fry on a lightly oiled frying pan until soft. Add half of a carrot grated on the coarse side of the grater. Fry everything together for 5 minutes.

3. Cut potatoes into cubes of any size and add to the soup. Cook for 15 minutes.

4. Put eggs in a pan with salted water, bring to a boil and cook for 5 more minutes, then drain and douse with cold water to make peeling easier.

5. A minute before borscht is ready, add chopped greens: half a bunch of sorrel and the nettles.

6. **Green mix.** Cover the remaining sorrel and parsley with 150 ml water (⅔ cup) and blend until smooth. Put it through a sieve and add to the borscht together with the greens. Bring the borscht to a boil, and turn off the heat.

7. Serve hot, adding half a boiled egg to each plate.

#42 KALATUSHA (VEGETABLE AND FISH SOUP)

1 HOUR 20 MINUTES

SERVES 4-6

INGREDIENTS:

FOR THE BROTH:

· 1 CARP OR OTHER SMALL FISH

· 30-40 G / 1-1½ OZ. DRIED PORCINI MUSHROOMS

· 10 SPRIGS PARSLEY

· 5-6 SPRIGS DILL

· 5-6 BLACK PEPPERCORNS

· 2 BAY LEAVES

· 1 CARROT

· 1 ONION

· VEGETABLE OIL

FOR THE SOUP:

· 2 TBSP. ALL-PURPOSE FLOUR

· 2 TBSP. UNSALTED BUTTER

· 3-4 CARROTS

· 1 CELERY ROOT

· SALT, PEPPER

1. Preheat oven to 180°C / 350°F degrees.

2. For the broth, fry carrots and onions cut into pieces of any size on a dry frying pan until they become flavorful and burnt patches begin to appear on the sides.

3. Transfer the vegetables to the saucepan where you'll cook the soup. Pour a little bit of oil onto the frying pan and fry the cleaned fish. Transfer the fish to the saucepan with the vegetables, and cover with 1½ liter / 6 cups water.

4. Add black peppercorns, bay leaf, salt, green parsley and dill. Cook for 40 minutes for intense taste.

5. Strain the broth and put it back in the saucepan. Now add dried porcini mushrooms, and cook for 30 more minutes.

6. In the meantime, prepare **vegetables for the soup**. Peel a celery root and a carrot. Cut them up, sprinkle with salt and oil, and bake for 25–30 minutes until soft. Puree the baked vegetables in a blender.

7. Strain the cooked broth one more time. Put it back in the saucepan, bring to a boil, condense by gradually adding a smooth mixture of 2 tbsp. flour with 2 tbsp. unsalted butter, and carefully stirring with a whisk.

8. To serve, put 1 tbsp. of carrot-and-celery puree into each plate, and carefully cover with the broth. You can decorate it with porcini mushrooms and pieces of boiled fish, removing all bones before serving.

9. Serve hot.

PORRIDGES

ON ROLLED PORRIDGE

I first discovered rolled porridge in the village of Opishnia. You take millet and roll it around in eggs and wheat flour for several hours until each grain of millet gets coated in dough, triples in size and becomes perfectly round.

I'm crazy about this technique. It's so real, so authentic and so Ukrainian that it leaves me speechless. It's the same feeling you get when you see an old friend from a completely new perspective. I picked up a dough-coated grain of millet, took a good look at it, and thought, "That's almost the same technique that Italians use with pasta, but it's ours: our very own and very unique trick."

At the same time, I looked back to my childhood and remembered trying corn sago. I loved that chewy, smooth, round texture in my mouth. And here I am, years later, discovering that we have rolled porridge with the same abso-freaking-lutely amazing texture. Since that trip to Opishnia, I learned even more about Ukrainian cuisine and reached the conclusion that rolled porridge is not exclusive to Poltava region. It's known across eastern Ukraine, Dnipro, Donetsk and Luhansk regions. For me though, it will always be associated with Poltava, because I had discovered it thanks to an ethnographer from Opishnia.

#43 OYSTER MUSHROOM BANOSH

20 MINUTES | **SERVES 2**

INGREDIENTS:

· 100 G / 3½ OZ CORNMEAL

· 210 ML / 1 SCANT CUP MILK

· 85 G / ⅓ CUP SOUR CREAM

· 20 G / ⅔ OZ. HARD BRYNDZA

CHEESE (CAN BE SUBSTITUTED

WITH SHARP CHEDDAR OR

FETA)

· 300 G / 10 OZ. MOZZARELLA

· 1 RED ONION

· 150 G / 5 OZ. OYSTER

  MUSHROOMS

· 2 TBSP. VEGETABLE OIL

· SALT, PEPPER

1. Fry the cornmeal on a hot dry skillet for 2 minutes.

2. Add milk and cook, stirring constantly, for 2 more minutes. Add sour cream and cook for 1–2 more minutes until ready, seasoning with salt and pepper to taste.

3. Pour a glug of oil onto the second skillet and fry the onion for 2–3 minutes until golden. Add oyster mushrooms, having previously torn them into smaller segments. Fry until all liquid evaporates and mushrooms begin to brown.

4. To serve, sprinkle one layer of hot banosh with grated bryndza (can be substituted with sharp cheddar or feta) and small pieces of mozzarella, and cover with a second layer of banosh and fried oyster mushrooms. Serve hot.

SEMOLINA WITH HEMP OIL

5 MINUTES   **SERVES 2**

INGREDIENTS:

· 100 G / ½ CUP + 1 TBSP.

  SEMOLINA

· 500 ML / 2 CUPS MILK

· 2 TBSP. HEMP OIL

· 2 TSP. HEMP SEEDS

· SALT, PEPPER

1. Fry semolina on a hot dry skillet until golden and flavorful. Pour in the milk and cook, stirring constantly, for 2–3 minutes until ready and of the desired consistency. Add salt and pepper to taste.

2. Serve for breakfast with a sprinkling of hemp oil and hemp seeds.

#45 KULISH (SAVORY MILLET PORRIDGE) WITH SOUR PICKLED TOMATO AND MOZZARELLA

 |

45 MINUTES   **SERVES 6**

INGREDIENTS:

- 100 G / 3½ OZ. PORK FAT
- 150 G / ¾ CUP MILLET
- 2 AVERAGE-SIZED MOZZARELLA BALLS
- 1 LITER / 4½ CUPS MILK
- 3 PICKLED TOMATOES
- 3-4 AVERAGE-SIZED POTATOES
- 1-2 ONIONS
- 1-2 BAY LEAVES
- 3-5 ALLSPICE BERRIES
- ¼ CELERY ROOT
- 1 CARROT
- 1 PARSLEY ROOT
- 2-3 CLOVES GARLIC
- 1 LITER / 4½ CUPS WATER
- 3-4 TBSP. VEGETABLE OIL
- GREEN PARSLEY AND DILL TO TASTE
- SALT, PEPPER

1. Cut the pork fat into small cubes of about half an inch (1–1.5 cm). Render it in a cast-iron skillet.

2. Dice the onions, crush the garlic cloves with the flat side of a knife. Add to the skillet with pork fat and fry until translucent.

3. Add carrot, celery root and parsley cut into pieces of any size. Cover with water and milk. Cook the soup for 15 minutes.

4. Add bay leaf and allspice.

5. Peel the potatoes, cut them into pieces of any size, and add to the skillet.

6. Wash and soak the millet in boiling-hot water to make sure that it isn't bitter. Drain the water and add millet to the skillet. Stew everything until ready on low heat for 30 minutes.

7. Season with salt and pepper to taste. Let the skillet rest for several minutes to make *kulish* even more flavorful.

8. To serve, add a sour tomato and a ball of mozzarella to each plate.

9. Serve hot with finely diced parsley and dill (optional).

#46 PUMPKIN PORRIDGE

1 HOUR   **SERVES 4**

INGREDIENTS:

- 500 G / 1 LB. PUMPKIN
- 200 G / 1 CUP MILLET
- 1 LITER / 4½ CUPS MILK
- 1 PINCH OF SALT
- 4 TBSP. SUGAR
- 1 CINNAMON STICK
- 100 G / 7 TBSP. UNSALTED
  BUTTER
- MARIGOLDS (OPTIONAL)

1. Preheat oven to 180°C / 350°F degrees.

2. Peel the pumpkin and cut it into small cubes. Rinse the millet well a couple of times and cover with milk. Add sugar and a pinch of salt.

3. Add pumpkin cubes, half the butter and a cinnamon stick to your millet-and-milk mixture. Cook for 20 minutes over low heat, stirring occasionally.

4. Pour the pumpkin porridge into a cast-iron skillet and add the rest of the butter. Cook in the oven until ready (about 30 minutes).

5. Serve warm. Optionally, you can garnish it with marigold (calendula) flowers to add their unique flavor to the porridge.

#47

TETERIA (MILLET RISOTTO)

30 MINUTES | **SERVES 2-4**

INGREDIENTS:

- 200 G / 1 CUP MILLET
- 100 G / 7 TBSP. UNSALTED BUTTER
- 1 SMALL ONION
- 1 CELERY STALK
- 1 CARROT
- 60 ML / ¼ CUP DRY WHITE WINE
- ½ HOT PEPPER
- 2-3 CLOVES GARLIC
- 30 G / 1 OZ. PARMESAN CHEESE
- 50 G ROLLED BUCKWHEAT
- VEGETABLE OIL

1. Finely dice the onion, celery stalk and carrot.

2. Fry on a skillet with unsalted butter for 2–3 minutes until the onion is translucent.

3. Add millet and pour in dry white wine. Evaporate for 5 minutes.

4. Add slices of hot pepper and minced garlic. Stew with 150-200 ml / ⅔ cup to a scant cup of water for 5–7 minutes. Add the next portion of water and repeat the procedure in 5–7 minutes, the way you would with a risotto. You can replace the water with vegetable or chicken stock (whichever one you like best).

5. To serve, I usually decorate the plate with rolled buckwheat and grated parmesan cheese to balance the textures.

#48

CORNMEAL GRANOLA

45 MINUTES | **SERVES 2-4**

INGREDIENTS:

· 150 G / 1 CUP CORNMEAL
  (POLENTA)

· 60 G / 5 TBSP. SUGAR

· 120 ML / ½ CUP WHIPPING
  CREAM (33%)

· 60 ML / ¼ CUP WATER

· 1-2 TBSP. HONEY FOR SERVING

· 50 G / ½ CUP WALNUTS

· 400 ML / 1⅔ CUPS PLAIN
  YOGHURT

· PINCH OF SALT

1. Preheat oven to 180°C / 350°F degrees.

2. Fry cornmeal on a dry, hot frying pan for 2–3 minutes until it turns golden. Add a pinch of salt to bring out its taste.

3. Add sugar and stir constantly to ensure that the caramel doesn't burn and doesn't melt in large chunks.

4. Wait until cornmeal begins to form caramelized lumps.

5. Add cream and water and keep stirring until you get a uniform mix.

6. Put the mixture on a baking paper-lined baking tray and press down into a layer about an inch thick.

7. Bake in a pre-heated oven for 20–25 minutes until golden brown. Cool thoroughly.

8. Crumble the granola into pieces of any size. Store into a dry glass jar; if hermetically sealed, it can store for up to 1 month.

9. Serve with yoghurt in a bowl.

10. Add your favorite berries, honey and walnuts, and enjoy the splendid taste of a quick breakfast meal while replenishing your vitamins and minerals.

BAKED GOODS

ABOUT BREAD

You should bake your own bread. I'll teach you if you don't know how. If you do, you'll find some new, extra-cool recipes in this chapter. Learning to bake bread is like becoming a magician who can transform water into wine and rocks into gold with a single touch of his fingertips. To learn to bake bread is to get that divine power.

Your relationship with food will reach a new level, more sensual and authentic. You'll love food and know that it loves you back. Bread won't come out delicious unless you love it truly. Baking bread is a highly ritualistic and meditative process: it's all about being in the moment. When you bake, the world disappears in the background, leaving nothing but yourself, your dough and your energy on the center stage. That might sound pompous, but trust me: baking straddles the line between magic and philosophy.

You take the ingredients, mix them and watch the dough come to life and begin to breathe. It plumps up and tries to escape the bowl to be closer to you. You pet it, push it down and soothe it, admiring its perfection. Then you send it into the oven. At this stage, the dough matures and metamorphoses into lovely bread, hot, soft, with a crunchy crust. Making you happy is the meaning of its existence. Making sure that whenever you have a slice, you feel boundless love. The slice of bread you hold in your hands is a fruit of your efforts, brought into the world by your spiritual energy. This is what real bread is all about: it's not about the ingredients and proportions but about love, friendship and authenticity. You can never ever compare it to the bread you can buy in stores.

Bake your own bread. Be empowered. Enjoy.

#49

HAMULA (APPLE COOKIES)

90 MINUTES | **SERVES 4**

INGREDIENTS:

FOR THE DOUGH:
· 2 APPLES
· 2 TBSP. SUGAR
· 50 G / 3½ TBSP. UNSALTED BUTTER
· 1 EGG
· 75 G / ¾ CUP OAT FLOUR
· 170 G / 1 CUP + 2 TBSP. ALL-PURPOSE FLOUR
· PINCH OF SALT

FOR THE APPLE MOUSSE:
· 2-3 APPLES
· 3 EGG YOLKS
· 100 ML MILK
· 2 TBSP. SUGAR

1. Wash the apples well. Cut each apple in half and slice out the core. Preheat the oven to 200°C / 400°F. Arrange the apple halves face-down on the foil and bake for approximately 40 minutes or until soft.

2. Remove the skins from the soft cooked apples. The puree will be used both in the dough and in the mousse.

3. **Cookies.** Mix oat and wheat flour, add a pinch of salt and sugar, and mix well. Add unsalted butter and rub ingredients together by hand until you get buttery lumps.

4. Add an egg and 100 g / 3½ oz. of apple puree. Knead dense shortbread dough. Cover it with plastic wrap and leave it in the fridge to rest for 20–30 minutes.

5. Roll out the dough between two sheets of baking paper into a layer 0.5 cm / 0.2 inch thick. Cut out cookie shapes with a glass or a cookie cutter, and place them on a baking paper-lined tray.

6. Bake for 7–10 minutes. Leave the cookies to cool.

7. **Apple mousse.** Mix egg yolks with 225 g / 8 oz. apple puree, milk and sugar in a heatproof bowl. Stirring carefully, heat the bowl with apple mousse for 10 minutes over a pan with simmering water until it thickens slightly.

8. Serve the cookies with cooled apple mousse.

SEMOLINA CAKE

50 MINUTES | **SERVES 6**

INGREDIENTS:

· 400 G / 2½ CUP SEMOLINA

· 200 ML / ¾ CUP PLUS 2 TBSP. MILK

· 160 G / 5½ OZ. UNSALTED BUTTER

· 10 G / 1 TSP. BAKING POWDER

· 250 G / 1¼ CUP SUGAR

· 8 EGGS

· POWDERED SUGAR, FOR DECORATION

1. Preheat oven to 180°C / 350°F degrees.

2. Separate egg yolks from egg whites. Add half the sugar to egg yolks and mix well with a whisk.

3. Mix semolina with baking powder, add the yolk mass. Mix well.

4. Dissolve butter in warm milk, add the milk mix to the dough. Mix again until smooth and uniform.

5. Beat egg whites with the rest of the sugar until you get soft peaks. Carefully knead it into the dough.

6. Grease the baking form (22–24 cm / 8–10 inches in diameter) with unsalted butter and carefully transfer the dough to it.

7. Bake for 30–40 minutes or until ready.

8. Cool the cooked semolina cake in the baking form to room temperature. Decorate with powdered sugar and serve.

#51

COOKIES WITH POPPY SAUCE

45 MINUTES   **SERVES 6**

INGREDIENTS:

- 200-250 G / 1¼ CUP PLUS 1 TBSP. TO 2 CUPS FLOUR
- 75 G / 5 TBSP. UNSALTED BUTTER
- 100 G / ½ CUP SUGAR
- 1 EGG
- 2 TBSP. SOUR CREAM
- 1 TBSP. POPPY SEEDS
- ½ TSP. BAKING POWDER
- A PINCH OF CUMIN
- A PINCH OF SALT

FOR THE POPPY SEED SAUCE:
- 100 G / 3½ OZ. POPPY SEEDS
- 250 ML / 1 CUP MILK
- 1 TSP. CINNAMON POWDER
- 2 TBSP. HONEY

1. Preheat oven to 185°C / 365°F degrees.

2. Make the dough. Whisk together the flour, baking powder, a pinch of salt, cumin, poppy seeds and sugar.

3. Add unsalted butter and rub ingredients together by hand until you get buttery lumps.

4. Add egg and sour cream. Knead dough until firm.

5. Roll it out between two sheets of baking parchment into a layer 3 mm / 0.1 inch thick. Poke it with a fork multiple times and bake for 15 minutes until golden.

6. **Prepare the poppy seed sauce.** Mix poppy seeds, milk, cinnamon powder and honey in a saucepan, and simmer for 5–10 minutes.

7. Crumble the cooked flat cake into small pieces and serve in bowls with poppy seed sauce.

8. Serve with hot milk.

52

BEETROOT BREAD

4 HOURS   **SERVES 4–6**

INGREDIENTS:

· 500 G / 4 CUPS ALL-PURPOSE
  FLOUR

· 300 ML / 1¼ CUPS WATER

· 10 G / ⅓ OZ. ACTIVE DRY YEAST

· 1 TSP. SUGAR

· ½ TSP. SALT

· 150 G / 5 OZ. BEETROOT

· 100 G / 3½ OZ. BACON

· VEGETABLE OIL (TO GREASE
  THE BOWL)

1. Wash the beetroot, wrap it in foil and bake at 185°C / 365°F for 60–90 minutes (depending on size). Leave it to cool, then peel and cut into small cubes.

2. Dice the bacon and fry until golden brown.

3. Put flour through a sieve and mix with salt. Dissolve the yeast in warm water, add sugar. Leave it for 15 minutes to give the yeast time to wake up and become active.

4. Add yeast to the mixture of flour with salt, and knead the dough until soft and elastic. Knead in the fried bacon and beetroot cubes. Form a dough ball and carefully move it to an oiled bowl. Leave it in a warm place for 40 minutes until bread rises and doubles or triples in volume.

5. Press down the dough and form a round shape. Place it on a baking paper-lined tray and sprinkle it with flour. Leave for 30 more minutes to rise some more.

6. Bake at 220°C / 425°F for 5 minutes. Then turn the temperature down to 180°C / 350°F and cook for 30 more minutes.

#53

PAMPUSHKY (BUNS) WITH MUSHROOM SAUCE

 |

2 HOURS | **SERVES 4-6**

INGREDIENTS:

FOR PAMPUSHKY (BUNS):

- 500 G / 4 CUPS ALL-PURPOSE FLOUR
- 25 G / 1 OZ. ACTIVE DRY YEAST
- 125 ML / ½ CUP MILK
- 125 ML / ½ CUP WATER
- 1 EGG + 1 EGG YOLK
- 1 TSP. SALT
- 1 TBSP. SUGAR
- 3 TBSP. VEGETABLE OIL

FOR THE SAUCE:

- 400 G / 14 OZ. BUTTON MUSHROOMS
- 1 ONION
- 2-3 TBSP. VEGETABLE OIL
- 200 ML / ¾ CUP PLUS 2 TBSP. HEAVY CREAM (20-30%)
- SALT, PEPPER

1. **Make yeast dough.** Dissolve the yeast in warm water, add sugar. Put flour through a sieve and mix with salt, egg, oil, yeast mixture and water. Knead soft dough. Form a dough ball and leave it in an oiled bowl for 40 minutes.

2. Press down the dough and form small bun shapes. Oil the baking tray and place the buns at a small distance from one another.

3. Leave the buns for 20 minutes for the dough to rise, then brush with egg yolk. Bake at 180°C / 350°F for 20–25 minutes until a shiny golden brown crust forms.

4. **In the meantime, make the mushroom sauce.** Fry finely diced onion on an oiled frying pan for 3–5 minutes, then add sliced button mushrooms and cook until all liquid evaporates. Add heavy cream and simmer for 3 more minutes. Season with salt and pepper to taste. Serve *pampushky* with the sauce.

#54

LEMISHKA (CRISPY FLATBREAD)

45 MINUTES | **SERVES 4-6**

INGREDIENTS:

· 120 G / 1 CUP RYE FLOUR

· 30 ML / 3 TBSP. WATER

· 2 CLOVES GARLIC

· 1 TSP. FLAXSEED

· A PINCH OF SALT

1. Preheat oven to 160°C / 325°F degrees.

2. Thoroughly mix the flour with boiling hot water.

3. Add flaxseed, salt and crushed garlic. Mix well. Use a silicone brush to spread the mass across the baking paper in a layer 2–3 mm / approximately 0.1 inch thick.

4. Bake for 25–30 minutes.

5. Leave *lemishka* to cool fully before crumbling it into small pieces. Serve with any dish as a bread substitute.

#55

KUCHERIAVTSI (CRUMBLE CAKE)

50 MINUTES | **SERVES 4-6**

INGREDIENTS:

· 400 G / 2½ CUPS ALL-PURPOSE FLOUR

· 200 G / 7 OZ. UNSALTED BUTTER

· 2 EGG WHITES

· 4 COOKED EGG YOLKS

· 70 ML / SCANT 5 TBSP. WATER

· 100 G / ½ CUP SUGAR

· 100 G / 1 CUP CHOPPED WALNUTS

· 1 TSP. VANILLA SUGAR

· PINCH OF SALT

1. Preheat oven to 200°C / 400°F degrees.

2. Knead the dough. Mix flour with sugar, softened unsalted butter and vanilla sugar. Add cooked egg yolks put through a sieve, finely chopped walnuts, a pinch of salt and water.

3. Roll out ⅔ of the dough on baking paper into a square layer 3–4 mm / approximately 0.1–0.15 inch thick.

4. Beat egg whites to soft peaks and rub the dough with them.

5. Grate the rest of the dough on the coarse side of the grater and evenly sprinkle the egg whites-covered dough with it.

6. Cut into portion-sized squares of 5×5 cm / 2×2 inch with a sharp knife and bake for 20–25 minutes until it turns brown.

7. Optionally, you can sprinkle cooked *kucheriavtsi* with powdered sugar.

56

APPLE VERTUTA

1 HOUR | **SERVES 4**

INGREDIENTS:

FOR THE DOUGH:

· 300 G / 2 SCANT CUPS ALL-PURPOSE FLOUR

· 100 G / 7 TBSP. VEGETABLE OIL

· 100 ML / 6½ TBSP. WATER

· 1 EGG + 1 EGG YOLK FOR BRUSHING

· ½ TSP. SUGAR

· PINCH OF SALT

FILLING:

· 2 APPLES

· 50-75 G / ⅓ TO ½ CUP RAISINS

· 1 TBSP. CINNAMON POWDER

· 2 TBSP. SUGAR

· 1 LEMON

CREAM GLAZING:

· 200 G / 1¾ CUP POWDERED SUGAR

· 200 G / 7 OZ. CREAM CHEESE

· JUICE ½ LEMON

· 2 TBSP. MILK

1. Sift the flour. Make a well in the flour and add the egg, salt, warm water, oil, and sugar. Knead the dough until soft and elastic.

2. Cover with a linen towel and leave to rest for 40 minutes.

3. In the meantime, prepare the filling. Peel the apples and grate on the coarse side of the grater. Add raisins, lemon juice, cinnamon powder and sugar. Mix well.

4. Roll out the dough in a very thin layer. Cover evenly with the filling and twist into a roll.

5. Put the rolls on the parchment paper-lined baking tray, brush them with egg yolks and bake at 180°C / 350°F for 20 minutes until a shiny golden brown crust forms

6. Once cooked, brush the rolls with the glazing. Whisk cream cheese together with sugar powder, lemon juice and milk until the ingredients are thoroughly blended.

#57 KIFLYKY (ROLLS)

1 HOUR 40 MINUTES

SERVES 6-8

INGREDIENTS:

DOUGH:

- 320 G / 2½ CUPS WHEAT FLOUR
- 260 G / 2 CUPS CORN FLOUR
- 200 G / ¾ CUP PLUS 2 TBSP. UNSALTED BUTTER
- 1 EGG
- 350 G / 1½ CUP SOUR CREAM
- 10 G / ⅓ OZ. ACTIVE DRY YEAST
- 3 TBSP. SUGAR
- PINCH OF SALT
- 1 EGG YOLK, BROWN SUGAR (OPTIONAL)

FILLING:

- 200 ML APRICOT PRESERVE
- 3 TBSP. POPPY SEEDS
- POWDERED SUGAR FOR SERVING

1. Mix flour of both types with cold unsalted butter grated on the coarse side of the grater. Rub the mixture with your hands until buttery crumbles form. Add sugar, salt and eggs.

2. Dissolve the yeast in sour cream and add to the dough. Knead the dough until elastic. Regulate the consistency by adding more sour cream or flour.

3. Wrap the dough in cling film and leave it to rest in the fridge for 1 hour.

4. Take the dough out of the fridge and divide it into two halves. Roll each one out into a layer approximately 20 cm / 8 inches in diameter. Divide it into 6–8 triangular segments. Put the filling (a mixture of apricot preserve with poppy seeds) on the wider side of each segment. Twist into crescent-shaped rolls and put on a baking paper-lined tray at the distance of at least 2 cm / 0.8 inch from one another.

5. Optionally, brush the rolls with egg yolk and sprinkle them with brown sugar. Bake at 400°F / 200°C for 15–20 minutes.

6. Give the baked *kiflyky* a generous sprinkling of powdered sugar.

DESSERTS

THE TASTE OF CHILDHOOD

Love needs no reason. It just is. A combination of various factors provokes a chemical reaction in our bodies, causing an addiction with no objective explanation. The same is true of food, especially if that love stems from childhood.

That's the story of my relationship with cherry dumplings. Nobody cooked them better than my grandma. Even at the Dumpling World Championship with experienced grandma contenders, I would still publicly declare that those dumplings that I ate as a child were the best. I used to think that grandma knew some special trick or added a secret ingredient. Once I was old enough to learn that secret, I walked into the kitchen, closed the door firmly

and asked grandma for a recipe for her addictive dumplings. To make sure that nobody overheard our conversation, I even asked her to write the recipe down. Then I cooked the dumplings myself, following the recipe down to a tee, and they still came out wrong. Because it's never about the recipe, you see.

Your memories, the atmosphere, associations, sounds, visuals, emotions, the people around you or, vice versa, your solitude — it all affects your sense of taste. If even one element is missing, love won't happen.

It all happens subconsciously and cannot be explained. If you can pinpoint the reason why you love something, it's no longer love.

#58 LVIV CHEESECAKE

75 MINUTES | **SERVES 6**

INGREDIENTS:

- 0.5 KG / 1 LB. COTTAGE CHEESE
- 2 BOILED POTATOES
- 50 G / 3½ TBSP. UNSALTED BUTTER
- 150 G / ½ CUP SUGAR
- 3 EGGS
- ZEST OF 1 LEMON
- ZEST OF 1 ORANGE
- 50 G / ½ CUP CHOPPED WALNUTS
- 10 G / 2 TSP. VANILLA SUGAR
- 50 G / ⅓ CUP RAISINS
- 1 TBSP. FLOUR
- A PINCH OF SALT

FOR THE CHOCOLATE GLAZE:

- 100 G / 3½ OZ. DARK CHOCOLATE WITH AT LEAST 80% COCOA CONTENT
- 30 G / 2 TBSP. UNSALTED BUTTER
- 80 ML / ⅓ CUP WHIPPING CREAM (33%)

1. Preheat oven to 180°C / 350°F degrees.

2. Make the batter. Mash salt, sugar and vanilla sugar into unsalted butter. Add lemon and orange zest.

3. Separate egg whites from egg yolks.

4. Add egg yolks to the butter mix one at a time, mixing with a whisk after each one until well-blended.

5. Grate boiled potatoes with a fine grater and add to the egg-and-butter mix.

6. Put the cheese through a sieve and add to the mix. Add raisins and knead well.

7. Beat egg whites until stiff and gently fold into the batter.

8. Grease the baking tray with unsalted butter and sprinkle with flour. Gently move the batter into the tray and smooth the surface.

9. Sprinkle the cheesecake with chopped walnuts. Bake for 1 hour.

10. **Make the chocolate glaze.** Mix chopped chocolate with unsalted butter and heavy cream in a heat-resistant bowl. Melt the mixture over boiling water, stirring constantly, until it is well-blended.

11. Pour the chocolate glaze over the cooled cooked cheesecake.

#59

CHEESE KLUSKY (BITES)

20 MINUTES   **SERVES 6**

INGREDIENTS:

- 200 G / 7 OZ. BUCKWHEAT FLOUR
- 720 G / 3 CUPS COTTAGE CHEESE (5% FAT)
- 6 EGGS
- 1 TSP. SALT
- 3 TBSP. SUGAR
- 50 G / 3½ TBSP. UNSALTED BUTTER
- 3 TBSP. HONEY

1. **To make dough for *klusky***, put cottage cheese through a sieve, add salt and sugar. Blend in the eggs one at a time, mixing them in carefully. Add the buckwheat flour and knead the dough. The exact amount of flour may vary depending on how moist the cheese is.

2. Roll out the dough into a long sausage shape, approximately 1.5 cm / 0.6 inch in diameter. Cut into pieces approximately 3 cm / 1 inch long.

3. Cook *klusky* in salted water for 2 minutes after they float to the top.

4. Serve with melted unsalted butter and honey.

#60 CREPES WITH NUTS AND SWEETENED CONDENSED MILK

 |

60 MINUTES | **SERVES 6**

INGREDIENTS:

- 520 G / 4 CUPS ALL-PURPOSE FLOUR
- 6 EGGS
- 900 ML / 4 SCANT CUPS MILK
- 2 TBSP. VEGETABLE OIL
- 2 TBSP. SUGAR
- 1 TSP. SALT

FOR THE TOPPING:
- 100 G / 1 CUP CHOPPED WALNUTS
- 1 TIN OF CARAMELIZED SWEETENED CONDENSED MILK

1. Combine eggs, sugar, salt and flour in a bowl. Mix thoroughly until all ingredients are well-blended. Add the milk and mix well once again until smooth, then add the oil and leave the batter to rest for 20 minutes.

2. Fry the crepes on a dry frying pan on both sides until golden brown.

3. Brush each crepe with caramelized sweetened condensed milk and sprinkle with chopped walnuts. Roll the crepes up the way you like them, and serve immediately.

#61

SOUR CHERRY DUMPLINGS

 |

45 MINUTES   **SERVES 4**

INGREDIENTS:

DOUGH:

· 250 ML / 1 CUP KEFIR OR THIN PLAIN YOGHURT

· 450 G / 3 CUPS ALL-PURPOSE FLOUR

· 0.5 TSP. SALT

· 0.5 TSP. SUGAR

· 0.5 TSP. BAKING SODA

· 1 EGG

· 100 ML / 0.4 CUP SOUR CREAM (FOR SERVING)

FILLING:

· 400 G / 1 LB. SOUR CHERRIES

· 1 TBSP. SEMOLINA

· 2-3 TBSP. SUGAR

· 50 G / 3½ TBSP. UNSALTED BUTTER

1. **Make the dough for the dumplings.** Mix flour with eggs, salt, sugar, kefir or thin plain yoghurt and baking soda. The dough has to be soft, elastic and not sticky. Form a dough ball, move gently to an oiled bowl, and cover with a towel. Leave it to rest for 15–20 minutes.

2. **In the meantime, make the filling.** Pit the cherries (if you are cooking the dumplings out of season, defrost the cherries first). Add 1 tbsp. sugar and semolina.

3. Fold the dumplings by wrapping about a tablespoonful of cherries in a rolled out piece of dough. You can add decorative pleats to the edge when folding the dumpling together.

4. Cook in salted water until the dumplings float to the top. Remove them from boiling water and sprinkle them with sugar to make sure that they don't stick. Drizzle with melted unsalted butter.

5. Serve with sour cream or cherry sauce (*kysil*).

#62 COLD APRICOT SOUP

20 MINUTES | **SERVES 2**

INGREDIENTS:

· 250 G / 9 OZ. APRICOTS

· 100 ML / 6½ TBSP. WATER

· 70 G / ⅓ CUP SUGAR

FOR THE MILK SAUCE:

· 400 ML / 1⅔ CUPS MILK

· 1 TBSP. SUGAR

· 3 EGG YOLKS

OPTIONAL:

· MINT, HOT PEPPER, DRIED

  NUTS, CINNAMON POWDER,

  VANILLA SUGAR

1. Pit the apricots. Dissolve sugar in water and add pitted apricots. Bring to a boil over medium heat, then puree in a blender until smooth.

2. Whisk or blend the milk, egg yolks and sugar until they are well blended together.

3. Add the milk mixture to the apricot mixture and stir carefully until they are well blended together. Simmer over low heat for 10 minutes, stirring constantly, until the mass begins to thicken.

4. Optionally, you may add cinnamon powder, vanilla sugar, mint, hot pepper or dried nuts.

5. Leave the soup to chill in the fridge for 2–3 hours. It tastes best cold.

LEKVAR (TRANSCARPATHIAN PLUM PRESERVE)

3 HOURS | **SERVES 4-6**

INGREDIENTS:

· 500 G / 1 LB. PLUMS

· 250 G / 1 CUP SUGAR

· 50 G / 1¾ OZ. PRUNES

1. Wash the plums well and pat them dry with a paper towel. Pit the plums and transfer to the saucepan where you will cook the preserve.

2. Add sugar to the pitted plums and leave them for 1-2 hours to let out the juice.

3. Cook for 5 minutes over high heat. Then reduce the heat to medium and cook for 45–50 more minutes until the mixture condenses to the consistency of caramel.

4. Add prunes and puree with a blender until smooth. Put the mass back in the saucepan, bring to a boil again and cook for 5–10 minutes.

5. Pour into sterilized jars and seal. Leave the jars to chill, then store in a cool place.

#64 HOMBOVTSI (PLUM AND CHEESE DESSERT)

45 MINUTES | **SERVES 2**

INGREDIENTS:

- 300 G / 10 OZ. COTTAGE CHEESE
- 1 EGG
- 200 G / 1¼ CUPS ALL-PURPOSE FLOUR
- 50 G / 4 TBSP. SUGAR
- PINCH OF SALT

FOR THE FILLING:

- 100 G / ½ CUP SUGAR
- 100 ML / 6½ TBSP. WATER
- 6-8 PLUMS

FOR THE DUSTING:

- 100 G / 1 SCANT CUP CORNMEAL
- 50 / 4 TBSP. SUGAR

1. **Cheese dough.** Put cheese through a sieve, add an egg, flour, salt and sugar, and knead the dough. If the cheese is very moist, you might need slightly more flour. The dough has to be dense enough to form cheese balls.

2. **The filling.** Pit the plums and dice them finely. Add sugar and water, then cook for 7–8 minutes until soft. Drain excess syrup: for the filling, you will need only cooked plums without excess liquid.

3. Roll out the cheese dough and put the filling on top. Seal the edges the way you would with a dumpling or pierogi, and form the dough into a round shape.

4. Cook in salted water until *hombovtsi* float. Transfer to a bowl with a strainer and add unsalted butter to make sure they don't stick.

5. **For serving**, I recommend making caramelized cornmeal. Heat the cornmeal on a dry frying pan. Add sugar and fry until the sugar begins to melt and caramelize. Keep stirring until cornmeal begins to stick in lumps, then break them up into small crumbs. Transfer to baking paper and leave to cool.

6. Before serving, sprinkle *hombovtsi* with caramelized cornmeal crumbs.

DRINKS

ABOUT BEETROOT KVASS

Imagine the world in which Ukraine developed with no obstacles. Imagine the world in which nobody tried to erase Ukrainian national identity. Imagine Ukrainians preserving their traditions and enriching them with new knowledge. In this world, every family would have had their own recipe of beetroot kvass: another unique Ukrainian product, another page in our history that was almost wiped out. Ukrainians managed to preserve it though. Beetroot kvass is a fermented drink with a sour, somewhat earthy taste. It breathes new life into things.

Beetroot kvass should run in the veins of Ukrainians instead of blood. My research even helped me to formulate my own theory about the origins of this drink. I think it all started with the Rurik dynasty, the Scandinavians that came to the Ukrainian territories and founded the princely dynasty. It is likely that, at the time, both Scandinavians and Ukrainians knew beetroot. The Ruriks saw a familiar product and decided to make it a smash hit. There was one problem though: the climate. Used to cooler climes, Scandinavians could keep beetroots fresh for months and months. This wasn't an option in our hot summers, so Ukrainians began to ferment beetroots. Therefore, we have been making beetroot kvass since the late 9th century CE, give or take. Imagine the extent of damage to our national memory if our generation, by and large, has never even heard of beetroot kvass.

I want to unlock the memory of beetroot kvass in our cultural code. Make it, drink it, add it to other dishes, and feel centuries of Ukrainian history course through your veins.

#65

VARIANKA (FRUIT VODKA)

5 HOURS | SERVES 6-8

INGREDIENTS:

- 200 G / 7 OZ. SUN-DRIED OR SMOKED PEARS, PRUNES, APRICOTS AND APPLES
- 1 LITER VODKA
- 500 G / 4 CUPS ALL-PURPOSE FLOUR
- 300 ML / 1¼ CUPS WARM WATER
- SALT
- 1 ROUND BREAD OR ROLL

1. Wash dried fruit under running water and put it into a heatproof ceramic pot. Cover the mixture with vodka and leave the fruit to soak for 30 minutes.

2. Make the dough, mixing flour and warm water with a pinch of salt. Divide it into 2 halves.

3. Seal the pot with the first half of the dough. Cover it with a bread crust or several bread slices before sealing it again with the second half of the dough to ensure that the pot is sealed tight.

4. Put it in the oven at 210°F / 100°C and leave to simmer for 4 hours.

5. Wait for *varianka* to cool and then chill it well.

6. Serve the drink with soaked dry fruit.

SPOTYKACH (MULLED VODKA)

30 MINUTES (AND ADDITIONAL 10 DAYS TO INFUSE) | **SERVES 6-8**

INGREDIENTS:

· 500 ML VODKA

· 6 CLOVES

· A PINCH OF NUTMEG

· 1 TBSP. VANILLA SUGAR

· 100 G / ½ CUP SUGAR

· 100 ML / 6½ TBSP. WATER

· 1 LEMON

1. Put cloves, nutmeg and vanilla sugar into the bottle with vodka. Stir well and leave in a dark place for 7–10 days. Don't forget to stir the mixture every day to make it more flavorful.

2. Make a simple syrup, combining an equal volume of sugar and water. When it's still warm, mix it with the infusion and stir well. Squeeze the juice of half a lemon into the drink, and stir once again.

3. Serve cooled.

#67 MULLED UZVAR (DRIED FRUIT DRINK)

40 MINUTES | SERVES 6-8

INGREDIENTS:

· 350 G / 12 OZ. SUN-DRIED OR
  SMOKED PEARS, PRUNES,
  APRICOTS AND APPLES
· 3 L / 12 CUPS WATER
· 7-8 TBSP. HONEY
· 3 CLOVES
· 1 TBSP. POPPY SEEDS

1. Wash dried fruit well in a skimmer under running water. Cover with water and simmer over low heat for 30 minutes with the lid on to make the taste more intense.

2. Turn off the heat, add cloves and poppy seeds. Mix well and leave to cool.

3. While *uzvar* is still warm, add honey to taste.

4. Cool well and serve.

BEETROOT KVASS

**15 MINUTES
(AND 4 DAYS
TO FERMENT)**

SERVES 6

INGREDIENTS:

· 1 KG / 2¼ LB. BEETROOT

· 400 G / 2 CUPS SUGAR

· WATER

1. Wash the beets well and peel them. Dice them finely and put into a 3-liter / 3 quart glass jar. Beetroots will take up approximately 2/3 of its volume.

2. Add sugar and cooled distilled water to a level 3–5 cm / 1–2 inches above the beetroots.

3. The jug has to have room for kvass to ferment. When bubbles appear on the surface, it's a sign that the fermentation process is underway.

4. Cover the jar with a cheesecloth folded in 4 layers, and leave it in a warm place for 3–4 days.

5. Once the kvass is ready, store it in the fridge.

#69

HONEY KVASS

10 MINUTES
(AND 5 DAYS
TO FERMENT)

SERVES 4

INGREDIENTS:

· 300 G / 10 OZ. HONEY

· 1 L / 4 CUPS WATER

1. Dissolve the honey in warm distilled water. Pour into a glass jar and cover with a cheesecloth folded in 4 layers. Leave in a warm dark place for 5–6 days to ferment.

2. By the end of that period, the fermentation process should be completed. You can seal the jar tightly with a lid and store it in the fridge.

3. Serve this non-alcoholic beverage cooled. Optionally, you can add sparkling water and enjoy the taste.

BERRY KYSIL (STARCH DRINK)

20 MINUTES   **SERVES 6-8**

INGREDIENTS:

· 400 G / 14 OZ. OF

  BLACKCURRANTS,

  REDCURRANTS, CHERRIES AND

  STRAWBERRIES

· 10 TBSP. SUGAR

· 2½-3 LITER / 2½-3 QUART

  WATER

· 5 TBSP. STARCH

1. Bring water to a boil in a saucepan and add sugar (it has to dissolve fully). Add a mixture of your favorite fruit and berries. Cook for 5–10 minutes to infuse the water with their taste.

2. Dissolve starch in a glass of cold water and gradually add to the fruit mixture, stirring constantly to avoid the formation of starch clots.

3. Cook for several more minutes until the *kysil* thickens.

4. Serve *kysil* well cooled.

HOW THE SOVIET CUISINE CAME TO REPLACE
AND DISPLACE THE UKRAINIAN CUISINE

When I was pursuing a degree in international finance, I did a lot of travelling abroad and researched how different countries interacted and influenced one another. When I switched to culinary arts and began working with various national cuisines, I already had a basic map of global relations in my head. Whenever I encountered a new product or dish, I automatically mapped its relations to various countries: how Chinese cuisine came to Italy and the UK, changing in the process; how and where forks first appeared, etc., etc. Much like a language, cuisine is always in flux as it migrates from one region to the next. We are enriched with new products and cooking techniques adopted from other traditions, much like our language is enriched with loan words.

As a child, I was suspicious of the dishes that everybody used to cook. The traditional holiday food for the New Year season was especially unappetizing. As a young boy, I expressed my opinion of this festive cuisine as "ew, yuck." Once I grew up, I tried to make sense of my feelings. I went to a culinary school in Paris and finally figured out why I had distrusted Soviet cuisine. The French had similar dishes, but with a different meaning and different cooking principles. For example, let's take aspic, which we eat as a meat jelly. The French cook aspic too, not as a standalone dish, but as a sauce thickener. When I told French chefs that we eat meat jelly as a standalone dish, they thought I was crazy. I became the butt of all jokes. Later

I found out that vinaigrette, a beloved salad in all former USSR countries, is one of the five basic French sauces, its name deriving from the French word for vinegar. I have no idea why we use the word to describe a salad of beetroot, potatoes, carrots, pickles and sauerkraut. Mayonnaise? Yup, that's a basic French sauce too. The French have a fairly elegant approach to eating it, whereas in the Soviet Union, people used to smother all salads with mayo. Mix boiled potatoes and carrots with sausage or canned and/or salted fish, add mayo, and you have all salads in the Soviet Union: oodles of mayonnaise over boiled vegetables. Never mind the difference in taste between the French mayonnaise and what was known under this name in the USSR. The famous Soviet salad "Mimosa" (boiled potatoes, carrots, eggs, fresh onion, canned fish and the inevitable mayo) is a bastardized version of the eponymous French dish. The French "Mimosa" is a kind of devilled eggs. The French have sautés too, but they use ingredients like celery roots, whereas in the Soviet Union it was a different story altogether. Not a single interesting taste: just oil, carrots and onions.

To sum up, the Soviets took the French cuisine, stripped it of its taste and meanings, and based the Soviet meal plan on these bastardized foundations. Food for the working class: let them stuff their faces and not think about it too much. Sounds plausible? Absolutely. The Russian Empire was friends with France. French chefs lived and worked on the territory that later became the Soviet Union. The new regime took their culinary know-how, simplified it, cheapened it to make it more accessible to the poor controllable population, and handed it down to the people. These bastardized dishes were first cooked in factory canteens; having tried them, the workers brought that meal plan back home with them. The food for the masses, neither nutritious nor delicious, is what we inherited from the Soviet days. For whatever reason, we keep reproducing it with loving care.

Under the circumstances, Ukrainian cuisine didn't stand a chance. Propaganda, food shortages and outright prohibitions made short work of it. Also, authoritarianism, dictatorship and fear. Our language, literature, traditions and church were all banned, and so was our cuisine. Our books were being destroyed, our material heritage was being shipped abroad. The oppressor's logic was simple: if you want to conquer and remake a nation, take away its food. It's nothing short of a miracle that Ukrainians managed to save several cookbooks and the genetic knowledge of their identity through centuries of oppression. This is evidence that Ukrainians have a strong backbone. If not for it, I wouldn't have found the forgotten recipes, wouldn't have revived them and showed these discoveries to Ukrainians and the world. We have *The Aeneid* by Ivan Kotliarevskyi, an epic poem with long lists of Ukrainian dishes. The names of national dishes hidden in last names and place names by our ancestors had helped us to keep an unbroken connection to our past. Our ears are still familiar with the words *putria*, *shpundra* and *vereshchaka*. The Soviet regime had tried to rob us of our traditions, but we have proven that authentic and integral symbols inscribed in the heart of the nation can never be destroyed.

INDEX:

WE BELIEVE THAT
LOVE IS THE BEST GIFT.

To love yourself is to make time just for yourself. To love your children is to want them to grow up in a world without borders and boundaries, believing in miracles and knowing that they the sky's the limit. To love your near and dear is to want to share not just a few experiences but the whole world with them.

We are committed to publishing the books worthy of love: the books that tell spellbinding stories, inspiring the readers to dream and learn; the books that reveal the vibrant world, sweeping perspectives and endless opportunities; the books that become an expression of love when you share them.

We are happy that you are holding this book. We know that #knigolove is the best gift because #knigolove is love, and love begets love.

#knigolove